Additional Praise for
The Transformative Church

"Not unlike my journey and many other Evangelical theologians sojourning in a post-Christian world, Oden's yearning to find and feast on the 'words of life' eventually became a quest to abide in Christ's vision and mission for the church. My pursuit led me to focus on Dallas Willard. Oden's path led him to Jürgen Moltmann. Both seek to understand, reimagine, and articulate the means and ends of Jesus' gospel in and through holistic covenantal communities. Patrick has given us a wonderful gift. He helps us to develop eyes to see more clearly and ears to hear more distinctly how our lives, and our churches, can better manifest the transformative power of God's love, hope, freedom, and grace *in* our world, without falling prey to the systems *of* our world."

Gary Black Jr.
Azusa Pacific University

"This is the book that we have needed. The explosion of emergent and missional churches is a global phenomenon, and it is exhilarating to watch. But too often these efforts lack serious theological and biblical foundation. This is just what Oden provides. In a dialogue with the thought of Jürgen Moltmann and many of the emergent leaders, he offers a Trinitarian framework for understanding these emerging forms as transformative sites where God's kingdom purposes are exhibited and extended. Highly recommended."

William A. Dyrness
Fuller Theological Seminary

The Transformative Church

The Transformative Church

Church

New Ecclesial Models and the Theology of Jürgen Moltmann

Patrick Oden

Fortress Press
Minneapolis

THE TRANSFORMATIVE CHURCH

New Ecclesial Models and the Theology of Jürgen Moltmann

Cover design: Alisha Lofgren

Library of Congress Cataloging-in-Publication Data

Print ISBN: 978-1-4514-7470-1

eBook ISBN: 978-1-4514-7992-8

The paper used in this publication meets the minimum requirements of American National Standard for Information Sciences — Permanence of Paper for Printed Library Materials, ANSI Z329.48-1984.

Manufactured in the U.S.A.

This book was produced using PressBooks.com, and PDF rendering was done by PrinceXML.

For Vianne and Oliver

Contents

Acknowledgements

At the beginning is the end. The end of a long process of reading, writing, talking formally and informally with so many others. Along this way, I have had so many people who have influenced me in my thinking, in my faith, in my perseverance, pointing me toward a way of hope. Many of those I am not in regular contact with anymore and yet I would not be at this point if not for their influence. Thank you, dear friends who have walked a long or a little ways with me along the road. I value your friendship likely more than I ever expressed.

Others have had a more direct involvement in this process. Dr. Veli-Matti Kärkkäinen stands out in this regard. He was a significant influence during my MDiv studies and years later, when I was at another crossroads of vocation, he invited me to apply to study with him at Fuller for a PhD. His graciousness throughout has been inestimable, and more than this, it is a graciousness mixed with a sharp eye toward stretching, training, and sharpening me. In many ways, his mentoring took the shape of what follows; he spurred me on and gave space for my participation, always encouraging and with a sincere excitement about my progress. His sense of humor, mixed with a depth of insight and mastery of so many topics, serves as a continuing example of the kind of scholar I seek to be. While I do not quote his own works extensively throughout this present work, his stamp of influence is profound throughout, in both major and minor ways. He is my Doktorvater and my friend.

Jürgen Moltmann also deserves personal appreciation. He was gracious in responding to notes and in encouraging my theological studies. He continued to be gracious in opening up his home for a few sessions of conversations in 2011. His openness to me was a great encouragement and is a great model. He truly lives out what he writes.

My parents supported me through the ups and the downs, believing in me when I was confident about God's work in my life, and believing in me when I wandered a while through a wilderness. They taught me to follow Jesus from my earliest days and have continued to be not only my family, but my also my friends and a key part of my spiritual community. They are my mentors in life, in pressing onward, in seeking after God in the good times and in the struggles, able to talk over the deep things of Scripture or theology, laugh together in considering the absurdities of life, and celebrate together in the triumphs. I owe them much more than I can possibly say.

I want to thank all those at Fortress Press. I have appreciated their insights and have learned from them, helping me to sharpen my text as it goes from dissertation to publication. Michael Gibson was especially involved in this process, with a particular gift at providing pointed critique and guidance in a constructive way. His experience in both theology and publishing is a great boon to the authors he works with. I also want to thank Lisa Gruenisen and those involved in the later stages of editing and marketing. The writing of a book can often be an isolating task, but the publishing of a book is the work of a team, and the team at Fortress has been a great pleasure to work with from beginning to the end.

My wife Amy has been my dearest friend, my constant encourager, the love of my life. She is a faithful follower of Christ, and I love being a team with her in this journey. I treasure her wisdom, her passion, her heart, the way she radiates the fullness of Christ, the way she hopes with me and for me, constantly pointing me toward God's work. She is also much better at grammar than I am and helped me sort out many issues in what follows, fixing all manner of punctuation and being willing to tell me when something just plain didn't make sense, as well as encouraging me when she read something that she loved. In big and small ways, her assistance is invaluable, and more than this, enjoyable. Thank you for helping life be fun even in the seriousness!

This work is about the church. And while it may be wonderful to see transformative ecclesiology taking shape sooner rather than later, the reality is that any transformation of the church is like turning a cargo ship. It doesn't happen quickly. With that in mind, I realize that what follows is an expression of hope for future generations. Along the way of writing this, one particular member of this future came into my life, my daughter Vianne, who was born very early in the morning on Easter, 2012. Along the way of publishing this, another particular member of this future came into my life, my son Oliver, who was born at the end of July, 2014. I continue to see the task of theology in all its forms as a way of helping provide for them a way forward in their faith and hope and participation with Christ. She is a constant delight and a wonderful gift from God. He is a joy and a blessing. I dedicate this book to them, with hope that they will see the wonders and promises of Christ become ever more present during the course of their lives, and that they will participate in this with a deep sense of joy.

Patrick Oden
San Dimas, Labor Day, 2014

Abbreviations

In the notes, the following abbreviations are used for Moltmann's works.

CG   *The Crucified God*

CoG   *The Coming of God*

CPS   *The Church in the Power of the Spirit*

GC   *God in Creation*

SL   *The Spirit of Life*

TH   *Theology of Hope*

TK   *Trinity and the Kingdom*

WJC   *The Way of Jesus Christ*

Full bibliographic details will be found in the bibliography.

1

Defining Transformative Churches

In early 2003, just when the so-called emerging church was growing in publishing popularity, I burned out with church. Not burned out with ministry in particular, but with the politics and dysfunctions that I had experienced while working in churches. I was not alone. Indeed, such burnout in others helped spark the initial turn toward emerging church models and helped these models attract so much attention. What was curious about my situation is that, just as the emerging church was gaining in attention, I burned out in particular with the emerging church.[1]

I had become involved in new approaches to church in 1991, during my last year in high school. I began to attend what was then the most dynamic church in the area: NewSong, founded by Dieter Zander.[2] It grew out of a college-aged Bible study, beginning in an apartment and then moving to a succession of theaters and gyms as

---

1. For works expressing this new popularity see, for example, Dan Kimball, *The Emerging Church: Vintage Christianity for New Generations* (Grand Rapids: Zondervan, 2003) and Doug Pagitt, *Church Re-Imagined: The Spiritual Formation of People in Communities of Faith* (Grand Rapids: Zondervan, 2005).

it grew in numbers. The mission was to reach out to "Generation X," which was seen as a generation alienated from church in general and standard models of Christianity in particular.[3] It was, in some ways, the epitome of the church growth models initiated by Willow Creek, updated for a new generation, seeking to reach out to the unchurched through a shared language and a Sunday service that had appealing elements.

Indeed, the music on Sunday mornings was quite engaging, and the preaching was superb. There was more than this, however. It was not a professional-led community. It was an involved community where college-aged young people were both the target audience and made up the bulk of the voluntary leadership. The people were empowered to engage in ministry as small group leaders, in service to the broader community, and in other ways. I became part of real community of friends, seeking depth together and with God, seeking to reflect this in our whole lives. Other friends became part of two separate church plants, both in nearby cities, where the goals of these new church communities were taking on even more elements of what would later be characterized as the emerging church.[4]

While in seminary, I moved from being a voluntary participant to becoming an intern at NewSong, working with other leaders in small group communities and in developing expressions of participatory worship.[5] This later led to leading a young adult community where

2. See Eddie Gibbs and Ryan Bolger, *Emerging Churches: Creating Christian Community in Postmodern Cultures* (Grand Rapids: Baker Academic, 2005), 323–38.

3. See Dieter Zander, "The Gospel for Generation X," Christianitytoday.com, April 1, 1995, http://www.christianitytoday.com/global/printer.html?/le/1995/spring/5l2036.html for an article by Zander on this topic written a few years after I started attending his church. Cf. Tom Beaudoin, *Virtual Faith: The Irreverent Spiritual Quest of Generation X* (San Francisco: Jossey-Bass, 1998).

4. See Michael Frost and Alan Hirsch, *The Shaping of Things to Come: Innovation and Mission for the 21st-Century Church* (Peabody, MA: Hendrickson, 2003), 28–30 for a description of one of the church plants initiated by friends at NewSong Church.

5. For example, see Patrick Oden, "Art and the Contemporary Church," http://www.dualravens.com/fullerlife/artandthecontemporarychurch.htm.

the teaching style took on the kind of shared conversation that has later become popular in emerging church circles.[6] All of these experiences were indeed initially very motivating and invigorating, both for my creative interest in ministry and my growth in community with God and with others. Yet the frustrations abounded as well. There were issues in both my own experiences and in the experiences of those I knew who were involved in these protoexpressions of emerging church models.

When Brian McLaren's *A New Kind of Christian*, and then Dan Kimball's book *Emerging Churches*, popularized for a new audience that which I had been involved with for a number of years, I reacted not with excitement about the new possibilities but with curious ambivalence.[7] These models and insights were not all they claimed to be. They offered a fresh expression but could not seem to sustain themselves without running into their own particular problems, as well as the problems that plague churches in general. With such texts pointing toward a new wave of church renewal, a renewal that I had engaged in and found wanting, I became disillusioned with both the emerging church movement and with church ministry in general. Where was I to turn? The prophet Jeremiah seemed to have words for me: "Thus says the Lord: Stand at the crossroads, and look, and ask for the ancient paths, where the good way lies; and walk in it, and find rest for your souls."[8]

I left NewSong, and left ministry in general, moving to the mountains for an extended time, where I read Scripture anew, the early church fathers, as well as monastic writings such as the four volume *Philokalia* and John Cassian.[9] After a while, I began turning

---

6. See Tim Conder and Daniel Rhodes, *Free for All: Rediscovering the Bible in Community* (Grand Rapids: Baker, 2009).

7. Brian McClaren, *A New Kind of Christian: A Tale of Two Friends on a Spiritual Journey* (San Francisco: Jossey-Bass, 2001).

8. Jeremiah 6:16. All Scripture quotations will be from the NRSV unless otherwise noted.

to more contemporary theologians whom I discovered while in seminary. I dove into Pannenberg's *Systematic Theology* and other writers, not for philosophical information but because their studies of God were devotional for my soul. I was seeking depth and breadth in my parched faith. Fuller Seminary offered a class on Moltmann, which I audited, and with this course as a guide, I read all of his major works—having only read a couple texts prior to this. Early on in such reading, I was struck by a very curious insight. What Moltmann was discussing in his systematic theology was very similar to the kinds of discussions I had heard in emerging church circles. Moltmann was certainly more robust, yet the discussion was oriented in the same basic direction. With this realization, Moltmann revived my interest in the emerging church conversation, a conversation he had never heard about, yet he seemed to be sharing many similar themes and priorities.[10] How so? The answer to that question is the basis of this study.

Purpose and Thesis

The purpose of this present work is to develop in writing that which more instinctively occurred to me while reading—namely, that there

9. *The Philokalia: The Complete Text*, trans. G. E. H. Palmer, Philip Sherrard, and Kallistos Ware, 4 vols. (London: Faber and Faber, 1979–95); John Cassian, *The Conferences*, trans. Boniface Ramsey (New York: Paulist, 1997).

10. As far as I know, I was the first to bring the emerging church to his attention when I wrote an introductory study relating Moltmann and the emerging church in 2007, which I mailed to him. He responded, welcoming the study and noting he had not heard of this movement. I subsequently sent him a copy of *Emerging Churches* by Gibbs and Bolger. In 2009, he participated in an emerging church conference in the Chicago area hosted by Tony Jones and Doug Pagitt. It should be noted that while Moltmann had not heard about the more recent expression of the emerging church, he had been involved with forms of Christian community that presaged the emerging church movement, most notably the Open Door community in Atlanta, Georgia. See Peter R. Gathje, *Sharing the Bread of Life: Hospitality and Resistance at the Open Door Community* (Atlanta: Open Door Community, 2006) and Eduard N. Loring, *The Cry of the Poor: Cracking White Male Supremacy—An Incendiary and Militant Proposal* (Atlanta: Open Door Community, 2010).

is a vital connection between the practices of these new model churches and the theology of Jürgen Moltmann. Over the last few years, this connection has become even clearer. Indeed, even as Moltmann revived my interest in emerging church possibilities, the emerging church itself has continued to develop, honing and expanding the discussion, bringing together other similar ecclesial streams into a more cohesive expression—one to which I will, for the sake of simplicity, apply the term *transformative churches*. What does it mean to be a transformative church? Two elements orient my overall purpose. A church is transformative when it engages in the development of people to better reflect the life of Christ in their lives, and when this transformation then extends itself beyond the boundaries of a church community, as such people live their lives in new ways wherever they are.

It is this, then, that forms the basis of my thesis throughout the present work: we become in the church who we are to be in the world. This understanding of a transformative mission of the kingdom is, I assert, at the heart of both Moltmann's theological project and the ecclesiological project of transformative churches.

There are two possible approaches to participatory and communal transformation, each of which we can find in both church history and contemporary theology. One is the sectarian approach, in which the religious community develops a distinct boundary between itself and the surrounding world, ideologically and often geographically. This religious community is able to develop within itself the transformative ideals that can be, then, a model *to* those outside of its boundaries. They do not necessarily exclude others, but may seek to include, indeed invite, them to participate. This then requires their full transition from one mode of being in the world and inclusion into the boundaried community. The second approach is an embedded system. Here, the religious community provides an orientation that is to be lived within the broader community. The church its own separated reality but a participant in the mission of God, which is open to all, and intended to be a transformative reality for all contexts.

Both Moltmann and the transformative churches express the second, embedded, model of church community. Indeed, Moltmann is especially wary about any division whatsoever between the church and the world. He argues that the world is in the church and good things are found in the world.[11] Yet, in general, there are still two contradictory forms of identity expressed in the world: that of God and that of not-God. This means that the church has a formative function even in the nonsectarian approach, which becomes about orienting people how to live in the world rather than how to live separated from the world. We become in the church who we are to be in the world.

This is a nondivisive distinction, utilizing the terms *church* and *world* not as separated, or inherently antagonistic, "cities," but as differentiated levels of community. The church cannot be opposed to the world any more than a school of fish can be opposed to water; it is the milieu in which it expresses its reality. The church, however, is a necessary distinction as an identity-establishing system within the world that contrasts with other identity-establishing systems.[12]

---

11. Jürgen Moltmann, interview by author, Tübingen, Germany, May 17, 2011. In May 2011, I traveled to Tübingen to consult with Moltmann about this present project. Over the course of three days we had three sessions of conversations. I was able to discuss my burgeoning proposal and ask related questions, all which he graciously answered. At the beginning of the first conversation I asked permission to record the sessions, which Moltmann graciously allowed. I have since posted these discussions on my website: http://www.dualravens.com/phd/moltmann.htm. This present reference is at twenty-five minutes into the first session.

12. I continue to utilize the term *church* rather than other proposed alternatives so as to emphasize this community as consistent with the historic expression of Christian community and to affirm its identity as particularly formed with Christ. Other alternatives, such as Martin Luther King Jr.'s *Beloved Community*, may be more appropriate and less weighed down with historic and philosophical baggage; however, they also loses *church*'s reference to the particular developments of the last two thousand years and its inherent communion with both early

Such alternative identity-establishing systems create meaning and offer alternative forms of identity that are likewise both communal and participatory.[13] We can characterize these other systems by such terms as *world* or *flesh* in Scripture. However, these are used more as reductionist labels expressing the gathered multiplicity of alternatives to God's Kingdom rather than inherently opposed to the more precisely defined *flesh* and *world, both of which God made.* God's reality is the defining reality and God's reality gives meaning to the form of community, and the expression of identity, within the church. We should not take the world more seriously than the God who seeks to redeem it. We should not see the world as an inherently unclean setting. When Jesus encountered the lepers, they were made clean. He transformed the setting. The church, as the body of Christ, is not an object that can be gazed upon as the model for the world; it is a collection of participants in whom the Spirit of God is forming the expression of the fullness of Christ, as individuals with each other, in this present reality we call the world.

This means, I assert, that the church is not the subject of God's work, nor is it the object that gives formative meaning and contrast. The church exists as the church of Christ only inasmuch as the participants are being formed into the likeness of Christ, expressing this likeness in a multiplicity of ways in diverse settings. This expression is not simply about being a model for how to live, nor is it merely a particular set of ethics or moral expressions that contrast with deficient models. As a participant with Christ, in the Spirit, a person who is being formed into the likeness of Christ becomes a domain of resonance of Christ, resonating the reality of Christ in distinct practices but also in participatory presence.[14] Thus, a person

expressions of Christian community and other models of such community in the present, such as the Catholic or Orthodox churches.

13. Inasmuch as being human itself is inherently both communal and participatory.

who gathers with others likewise oriented reverberates the resonance of Christ in a community. This community can exist on many scales, from the local to the regional to the global to the cosmic. The self-similarity with Christ expands into a self-similar fractal across larger scales, beginning in Christ, and then in the one formed into a model of Christ, then into the body of Christ that is the church, then into the world, ultimately drawing all of creation into a new communion with God.[15]

This transformative integration is how Moltmann seems to understand the role of the church and this understanding is a significant part of his overall theology. Moltmann's interest in ecclesial renewal is itself longstanding, reflected in his earliest writings and deriving from both his studies and his own work as a parish minister in Germany. This means that it is not, after all, surprising that Moltmann's theology would have much to contribute to transformative churches, as we find his own proposals for such communities in almost all of his texts—from his concluding chapter in *Theology of Hope* to his most recent *Ethics of Hope*. Indeed, such theological contribution is already imbued within transformative

14. See Michael Welker, *God the Spirit*, trans. John Hoffmeyer (Minneapolis: Fortress Press, 1994), 311–15. Here, the contributions of Luhmann may be helpful, with Luhmann's suggestions of autopoietic systems providing a potential model for how a system can be embedded and multiply within a broader setting, thus lending itself to a fractal model of transformative church development that retains its identity in Christ as it is expanded across multiple scales. Welker himself was part of a Luhmann discussion group in Tübingen that sought to assess Luhmann's religious insights. See esp. Michael Welker, *Theologie Und Funktionale Systemtheorie—Luhmanns Religionssoziologie in Theologischer Diskussion* (Frankfurt am Main: Suhrkamp, 1985); Niklas Luhmann, *Introduction to Systems Theory*, trans. Peter Gilgen (Malden, MA: Polity, 2013); Niklas Luhmann, *A Systems Theory of Religion*, ed. André Kieserling (Palo Alto: Stanford University Press, 2013).
15. On the possibility of self-similarity across scales being applied to human reality, see John Lewis Gaddis, *The Landscape of History: How Historians Map the Past* (New York: Oxford University Press, 2002), ch. 5. Gaddis applies this to historiography, although it seems equally appropriate to apply it to theological studies as well. See Patrick Oden, "Spirits in History," in *Interdisciplinary and Religio-Cultural Discourses on a Spirit-Filled World: Loosing the Spirits*, ed. Kirsteen Kim, Veli-Matti Kärkkäinen, and Amos Yong (New York: Palgrave MacMillan, 2013), forthcoming.

church insights, with his writings influencing key early leaders, such as Tony Jones, in both subtle and in more explicit ways. With Moltmann's insights shaping my reading, I began seeing the missional and emerging conversations not as postmodern attempts at ecclesial readjustments but as substantive theological contributions in their own right, pointing through practices toward a holistic expression of God's work in the world and humanity's participation with this work.

By putting together the practical expressions of transformative churches and the systematic insights of Jürgen Moltmann, it is my goal to begin to construct a more adequate transformative ecclesiology.[16] More than this, however, I also seek to imbue the transformative church conversations with theological intent, seeing their practices as being much more than church growth techniques, or attributes of a narrowly defined practical theology. By bringing these writers and thinkers into conversation with Moltmann, my goal is to substantiate their practices as being themselves topics of theology. Just as hope became a topic in theology, I assert so also should other practices of the church, because they are first expressions by God to the world. All theology, in such an approach, is practical. We are to be hospitable, for instance, because God is hospitable. We are to welcome strangers, for instance, because God is the welcoming God. Our practices illuminate our expressed theology, incarnating continually Christ's identity into this world.

"To live is Christ," Paul wrote to the Philippians. While this statement may take on various elements of meaning, I argue that this is not merely an ethical exhortation or a religious orientation. This is an ontological transformation in those who are participants in Christ

16. For a brief discussion of this goal in a more general sense, see Michael Welker, "Christian Theology: What Direction at the End of the Second Millennium," in *The Future of Theology: Essays in Honor of Jürgen Moltmann,* ed. Miroslav Volf, Carmen Krieg, and Thomas Kucharz (Grand Rapids: Eerdmans, 1996).

through the Spirit with the Father. We do not lose our identity, we gain it. In becoming transformed into the likeness of Christ we become most fully who we truly are, our identity enlivened inasmuch as it is rooted in the source of all identity, that of God.[17] The process of this ontological transformation is the process of salvation and sanctification. The mode of this transformation is participatory and communal, initiated by God, oriented by God, inviting us toward responsibility in responding to this transformation.[18]

It is participatory in that we are not passively formed but formed through our contextual practices, practices that shape our response to this world, to God, to ourselves in ways that either lead us toward fulfillment in God or dissolution away from God. This is not a salvation by works. Grace continually sustains and orients us, a free space within which we can find real freedom of being. It is communal in that our participation is never isolated but always involves other people, and it is only in the context of other people that we learn what it means to be free as a person in the fullness of God's identity.

This transformative work then take shape along the lines of the Philippians 2 hymn (Phil. 2:6-11), involving both a *kenosis* and a *perichoresis*, a letting go and a drawing together, a breathing out and a breathing in. In our experiences, this transformative work of God is liberation, initially and continually. We are liberated from alternative forms of identity and liberated into the identity of Christ. What we are liberated from can take on different expressions depending on our contexts. It is this reality that forms a secondary thesis, one that relates more specifically to transformative churches as they tend to exist in the industrialized West. The transformative churches are

---

17. Cf. Jon Huckins, *Thin Places* (Kansas City: The House Studio, 2012), 94.
18. For responsibility as a theological category, see Dietrich Bonhoeffer, *Ethics*, trans. Reinhard Krauss, Charles West, and Douglas Stott, vol. 6 of Dietrich Bonhoeffer Works (Minneapolis: Fortress Press, 2005), 220–45.

expressing a liberation theology, one that emphasizes the liberation of the oppressor. As such, these churches are a particular expression of a broader conversation, sharing a similar emphasis on the need to be liberated from deficient systems of identity formation, which are different in each context.

What we are liberated into remains constant. The liberation of humanity in Christ leads to the same place together with Christ. Thus, we should talk about coordinating ecclesiologies of liberation that arise from distinct contexts. This concern is at the heart of Moltmann's ecclesial interests and, indeed, part of his own personal and theological journey, leading him to be a helpful guide in understanding the present thesis. Becoming in the church who we are to be in the world assumes the answers to two distinct questions, each of which, I believe, is best answered by one of the present conversation partners. The two questions are, "Who are we to be?" and "How are we to become?" Moltmann, with his systematic theology interest, answers the former most fully, and the latter secondarily. The transformative churches, in contrast, answer the latter more fully and the former secondarily. By putting these two interlocutors together, we can arrive at a more holistic discussion of this proposal.

Transformative Church Theology

The previous section described my thesis and related assertions. It is the task of this present work to substantiate these claims as well as develop them as themes with particular meaning and expression. Before I begin this task more fully, first it is important to describe what I mean by transformative churches, describing this movement in terms of its literature as it has developed in four streams.

Overview

Transformative church theology is written primarily by pastors both for other pastors and for those within the broader emerging and traditional church communities. The emphasis is primarily on practices, and so much of the nascent theology is indirect or found in imprecise statements and approaches.[19] In their seminal book *Emerging Churches*, Eddie Gibbs and Ryan Bolger specify nine practices that emerging churches share and that, as a framework, can help define this movement.[20] Rather than relying on their own preferences and assumptions, Gibbs and Bolger surveyed leaders in the United States and the United Kingdom to determine the common expressions found across the range of these "emerging" Christian communities.[21] They define emerging churches as "communities that practice the way of Jesus within postmodern cultures."[22] This practice begins with three primary emphases, which then lead into the next six.

They write,

> Emerging churches (1) identify with the life of Jesus, (2) transform the secular realm, and (3) live highly communal lives. Because of these three activities, they (4) welcome the stranger, (5) serve with generosity, (6) participate as producers, (7) create as created beings, (8) lead as a body, and (9) take part in spiritual activities.[23]

19. Not unlike Pentecostalism, which has now had about a century to reflect on its practices and now produces quite sophisticated contributions to academic theology. However, one distinction is that transformative church thinkers and writers are explicit about their own academic sources, relying on work by theologians and missiologists to provide academic foundations for practical development. See Gibbs and Bolger, *Emerging Churches*, 49.
20. See also Eddie Gibbs, *ChurchNext: Quantum Changes in How We Do Ministry* (Downers Grove, IL: InterVarsity, 2000) for an excellent study of the church context leading into emerging church development and significant insight into the theological and pastoral developments that emerging churches exemplify.
21. See the preface and appendixes of Gibbs and Bolger, *Emerging Churches*, for more detailed description of their research methodology and sources.
22. Ibid., 44.

This has served as the most common framework for understanding transformative church emphases and practice. It also serves as the source of fruitful study for continued theological reflection on relevant topics.[24] However, they may not be as effective for understanding the underlying theological emphases of transformative church thought. To add to these nine characteristics, I turn to another framework developed by Ryan Bolger in which he discusses the emerging church as reflecting a series of "movements of the reign of God."[25]

The first movement is "a communal movement." Bolger writes, "The main task of kingdomlike churches is to equip those within the community to serve under the reign of God. To embody this kingdom, community formation must be central and involves a practical training in the gospel: how to serve, how to forgive, how to love, and how to open up your home."[26] The next movement Bolger notes is a "movement of reconciliation" in which "the church must involve all peoples who submit to God's rule, creating a new kind of people. They are to model a different way of human interaction between unlike parties."[27] Third is "the movement of hospitality." The context of the Western church is one of consumerism, in which money and goods are expressions of personal value and success. Instead of expressing the concept that "greed is good" reflected in much of the culture, and far too often in much of the church, those

23. Ibid., 44–45.
24. For instance, see Patrick Oden, "An Emerging Pneumatology: Emerging Church and Jürgen Moltmann in Conversation," *Journal of Pentecostal Theology* 18, no. 2 (2009): 263–84, where I argue these are elements of a more holistic pneumatology, similar to that proposed in the various writings of Jürgen Moltmann.
25. Ryan Bolger, "Following Jesus into Culture: Emerging Church as Social Movement," in *An Emergent Manifesto of Hope*, ed. Doug Pagitt and Tony Jones (Grand Rapids: Baker, 2007), 134.
26. Ibid., 135.
27. Ibid., 135–36. Cf. Miroslav Volf, *Exclusion and Embrace: A Theological Exploration of Identity, Otherness, and Reconciliation* (Nashville: Abingdon, 1996), 131.

who seek to illustrate the kingdom of God will live in a way that models "the gift rather than the exchange."[28]

The fourth movement of kingdomlike churches is "a movement of freedom" in which those who participate in the church are allowed to have equal space. This is not anarchy, where there is no leadership. Rather, those who lead do so apart from the imposition of power, recognizing the contributions each person brings.[29] Instead of a hierarchy, leaders in this movement help to create and maintain contexts where others find freedom to be who they are called to be in the context of a whole community.

Finally, there is the movement of spirituality. "Kingdomlike churches," Bolger writes, "pray together, confess their sins to one another, watch over each other, and encourage one another. At times they suffer together—sometimes as a result of one another."[30] This movement explores the depth of relationship with God and with each other in ways that bring spiritual maturity and increase love toward one another and toward God. These five movements are at the core of both worship and theology for transformative churches and serve not only as a description of what transformative churches value but also as a helpful standard when corrections and adjustments are necessary either for practice or for theology. Each of these aspects is rich in theological discovery and leads to continual reflection and reexamination in light of new questions and new experiences.

Even a cursory knowledge of church history makes clear that the transformative churches are not entirely new or original in most of their methods or their emphases. The historical uniqueness of this movement is in the forms of communication that burst onto the scene

---

28. Bolger, "Following Jesus into Culture," 137–38.
29. Kester Brewin writes that the "route to change must not be through the exercise of power but through an exercise in empowerment." Kester Brewin, *Signs of Emergence* (Grand Rapids: Baker, 2007), 34.
30. Bolger, "Following Jesus into Culture," 138.

in the late twentieth and early twenty-first centuries. The rise of the Internet, and with it e-mail, blogs, chat rooms, websites, social media, and other forms of information sharing allowed the dispersed transformative churches to discover they were not alone in either their ecclesial discontent or their creative explorations. At the same time, there develops channels of sharing that provide unprecedented interaction and encouragement across geographical distance.

Because one key role of a hierarchy is the sharing, or control, of information, the ability to find even more efficient methods of communication allows for a transformation of interaction, enabling otherwise isolated groups to find solidarity and communion while at the same time entirely bypassing any centralized authority. Unlike the situation with the base communities, this also means there is no controlling authority that can effectively interfere in the development or continuation of these small communities. Occasional, dynamic expressions have arisen throughout history, but these have tended to be eradicated or controlled by a hierarchy. Such expressions can now develop and continue without the need for any outside sanction.

In each of the approaches listed above, and the many others to be found in print or online, it becomes quite clear that the authors are not seeking to provide an official statement of doctrine or a definitive model, but rather are trying to describe what is happening in small communities around the world. The general themes point to resisting any central object that would give definition to these communities, or to the people involved with them. These themes emphasize the ideal of relationship. With the person of Christ providing a primary focus for the diverse and unified subjects, the individuals gather as a community in pursuit of a transformative reality with each other, for the church and for the world.

Over the last few years, however, many have dismissed the transformative church expressions as an unreliable movement that could not sustain the weight of its own perceived importance. Declared dead and even buried, it may seem curious to focus on it in a new study.[31] Yet there are still pockets of the movement existing in most, if not all, major cities and in many smaller towns.[32] Expressions continue to take shape in a variety of contexts, both as an independent movement and as an intrachurch reform movement. There is, I can say confidently, still a movement out there, which is pushing and leading churches toward distinctive expressions of ecclesiality that differ from the standard approaches from the past. Conversations still happen and meetings still take place, now without the often-diffusing elements that come with being the trendy movement of the moment.

It is also the case that since *Emerging Churches* was published, the already loosely cohesive emerging church has seemingly separated into disparate parts. There are a number of attempts to categorize these differing emphases and priorities, all of which have weaknesses and are susceptible to becoming quickly outdated. With this in mind, I will propose my own general typology, not claiming this as in any way official, but, rather, more as a convenient way to categorize the streams of literature that I am uniting under my broad term *transformative churches*. This typology does not emphasize nuanced approaches to topics, instead focusing on distinct influences found in each category and the different ways particular communities came

31. See for example Url Scaramanga, "R.I.P. Emerging Church: An Overused and Corrupted Term Now Sleeps with the Fishes," Out of Ur, entry posted September 19, 2008, http://www.outofur.com/archives/2008/09/rip_emerging_ch.html.

32. This may be even more true in contexts other than North America. In Britain, for instance, the Fresh Expressions movement is entering into a season of popularity and even predominance as a model for new churches. Because of their distinct context, and my lack of experience in that context, my focus will be on the experiences primarily in the United States and Canada. However, there is tremendous overlap in the priorities and methods, which allows for a shared discussion. If the churches in Britain are, in fact, more advanced in their acceptance of these new model churches, it is likely due to the fact they are also more advanced in experiencing the decline of the institutional church.

into being. There are four such formative streams: *Emerging, Missional, Fresh Expression,* and *Neo-Monastic.* All of these are represented in the early Gibbs and Bolger book. Because of the great amount of writing on the emerging church, and its various expressions, found in print and online, in what follows I will briefly describe each of these four streams and provide a representative example that can serve as a general guide.

Emerging

The emerging church stream maintains the earliest name, though this name has certainly become alienated and alienating over the years. In general, this movement derived from pastors and leaders who were dissatisfied with the ecclesial approaches of their particular church or with their general movement, such as Evangelicalism. While there were some early attempts to form a "church within a church" as a response, for the most part these attempts were unsuccessful and led to new church plants with independent goals. This stream, then, tends to focus on issues related to the field of practical theology, and can be considered a church renewal stream. While there may be early leaders—some of whom have left behind this label—there is not a particular founder or even a set of founders. Rather, the impulses that led to a more cohesive conversation developed seemingly independently in different parts of the country.[33]

At this point, an important and relevant work on this topic is *The Church is Flat: The Relational Ecclesiology of the Emerging Church Movement.*[34] This is the published dissertation of Tony Jones, one

---

33. This statement is derived from my specific experiences, as well as consideration of the movement's early development as related in appendix 2 of Gibbs and Bolger, which gives brief biographical information about early leaders.
34. Tony Jones, *The Church Is Flat: The Relational Ecclesiology of the Emerging Church Movement* (Minneapolis: The JoPa Group, 2011).

of the key early and continuing leaders in the emerging church movement. In this book, Jones looks specifically at five emerging communities, with the goal of assessing their ecclesiology and then putting this in conversation with Jürgen Moltmann's relational ecclesiology. At first glance, this may seem to invalidate the originality of this present work, given the nature of both Jones's conversation partners and his main thesis about the relationality of the church. However, Jones was working within a practical theology framework, leading his work to be more descriptive and sociological in scope. While he does some focused work on Moltmann's ecclesiology, this is somewhat limited. In addition, he tends to dismiss Moltmann's rising interest in both charismatic and liberation ecclesiologies as being naïve.[35] This supposed naïveté will be important for my own proposal; thus I will offer a substantive implicit response in my own work.

This is not to dismiss Jones's work, as it is, as a whole, a very worthwhile and helpful text, especially in terms of providing an overview of the current emerging church movement, defining it as a new social movement and aligning it with Moltmann's relational ecclesiology. We agree on the fact that Moltmann offers a constructive proposal for an ecclesiological framework for emerging and other transformative churches, sharing a goal if not a method or focus. Jones's dissertation, as well as his other useful texts, will serve as significant resource.[36] Indeed, as Jones has contributed such

---

35. Ibid., 149–50. Jones, 151–52, goes on to note that this naïvetéleads to an uncritical idealism by Moltmann. And this idealism leads to problems with people putting his theology into practice. Jürgen Moltmann, interview with the author, Tübingen, Germany, May 18, 47:25 responds to such criticism. Jones, *The Church Is Flat*, 152 goes on to note that no churches have followed his ecclesiology, and "he has failed to find exemplary communities that have actually practiced his ecclesiology." Jürgen Moltmann, interview with the author, Tübingen, Germany, May 18, 51:20, asks that if I want to know his vision of the church, how it is to be worked out in practice, that I should study the Jakobuskirche in Tübingen. This is his "vision of the future of the church." He goes on to add, "Not from the past, not from the objects, but from the subjects."

significant research on the history and research on the emerging churches, his book is one of the most important texts on the literature and expression of the emerging church stream at present.[37] By emphasizing the transformative church as a charismatic, liberation community and by exploring these themes primarily from a systematic theological perspective, however, I will be taking these themes in a different direction.

Another useful text is *Listening to the Beliefs of the Emerging Churches*, edited by Robert Webber.[38] Here, Webber gives an excellent introduction to the history of emerging churches, and indeed renewal movements in general, then hands over the discussion to five emerging church leaders, or at least those who were known as such at the time. This is useful as it allows each leader to respond to key theological issues, then gives the other leaders space to respond to each other. These leaders are on a spectrum of theological belief, ranging from more conservative to more liberal. At least one, Mark Driscoll, now openly rejects the emerging church.[39]

While interesting and certainly useful, *Listening to the Beliefs of the Emerging Church* tends to see the emerging church as offering different answers to the standard ecclesial and theological questions, and so shapes the book in a way as to solicit responses to these standard questions—thus, in a way, pigeonholing them into preestablished categories. This is a deficient approach as the emerging church is not simply another mode of expression of either liberal or conservative churches but rather, at its core, is coming to the issues of church and theology with oftentimes very different questions

---

36. Of these other writings the most important is likely Tony Jones, *The New Christians: Dispatches from the Emergent Frontier* (San Francisco, CA: Jossey-Bass, 2008).

37. See Jones, *The Church Is Flat*, ch. 1 for both a substantive discussion of definitions of the emerging church and an up-to-date survey of the literature relating to the emerging church.

38. Robert Webber, ed., *Listening to the Beliefs of Emerging Churches: Five Perspectives* (Grand Rapids: Zondervan, 2007).

39. We can even see the reasons why clearly developing in his contributions here.

and thus very different answers to these questions. Topics such as the inerrancy of Scripture, which continues to be a major topic in Evangelical circles, is not really an issue with transformative churches, which tend to be more pre-modern in their use of Scripture.[40]

Many other books fit into the emerging stream, such as Danielle Shroyer's Moltmann-inspired *The Boundary Breaking God,* or any of the numerous texts by Doug Pagitt, or the more activist and practically minded text *Everyday Justice: The Global Impact of Our Daily Choices* by Julie Clawson.[41] In general, as it stands at this point, the emerging church should be understood as the more progressive theologically and more politically engaged stream, tending to be the most polarizing as it seems to reflect "progressive" positions on topics that tend to be reactionary against popular Evangelicalism.[42] As such, early leaders such as Dan Kimball have intentionally stepped away from the terminology not because they have changed their methods or goals, but because it became too much effort to defend the sometimes totalizing rhetoric of other participants in the movement.[43]

Missional

Related to the emerging church discussion in many ways, and as such included within the scope of my particular interests, is the missional

---

40. Emerging churches tend to be very comfortable with a narrative reading of Scripture in which it is accepted as it is, without requiring more closely defined definitions of its authority.

41. Danielle Shroyer, *The Boundary-Breaking God: An Unfolding Story of Hope and Promise* (San Francisco: Jossey-Bass, 2009); Julie Clawson, *Everyday Justice: The Global Impact of Our Daily Choices* (Downers Grove, IL: IVP, 2009).

42. In this way, this stream tends to be very much aligned with Moltmann's own political contributions, both his political theology and his political involvement in Germany.

43. See, for example, Dan Kimball, "Wheaton College and Positive Things About the Emerging Church," DanKimball.com, entry posted January 22, 2010, http://dankimball.com/just-got-back-from-a-really-great-time-at-wheaton-college-i-was-there-for-a-2-day-event-put-on-by-the-christian-ethics-cente/.

movement. This movement derives primarily from missiological studies, especially as such have begun to see post-Christian societies as themselves requiring missiological assessment and response. The influence of Lesslie Newbigin is particularly important here, as his teaching and writing became the substantive guide for the earliest formation.[44] It is through the book *The Missional Church*, a collection of essays from key thinkers, however, that this movement became more developed and more influential.[45] Such prolific writers as Alan Hirsch and Michael Frost can be included in this category as well, with their work being very influential across Australia, Europe, and the United States.

Likely, the most helpful key text at this point is *The Missional Church in Perspective*.[46] In many ways, this book is for the missional movement what Jones's book is for the emerging church movement, providing an overview of the literature, assessment of the movement, and pointing to substantive theological models that can help the movement further develop. Indeed, Craig Van Gelder and Dwight J. Zscheile likewise show an affinity for Moltmann's works in such theological development. This text provides more substantive interaction and insight than Jones's book does, and as it includes the emerging church, in part, as within the broader missional movement, this is likely the most important text on the broader transformative church movement at this point.

---

44. For instance, see Lesslie Newbigin, *The Gospel in a Pluralist Society* (Grand Rapids: Eerdmans, 1989).

45. Darrell L. Guder, ed. *Missional Church: A Vision for the Sending of the Church in North America* (Grand Rapids: Eerdmans,1998). I first heard of this book in 1998, when Dieter Zander told me it was one of the most important books he had read. He also mentioned George R. Hunsberger and Craig Van Gelder, eds., *The Church between Gospel and Culture: The Emerging Mission in North America* (Grand Rapids: Eerdmans 1996). See also Darrell L. Guder, *The Continuing Conversion of the Church* (Grand Rapids: Eerdmans, 2000).

46. Craig Van Gelder and Dwight J. Zscheile, *The Missional Church in Perspective: Mapping Trends and Shaping the Conversation* (Grand Rapids: Baker Academic, 2011).

The texts that derive from the missional stream tend to be the most academic in nature, often written with professional pastors, missionaries and other academics in mind, and often utilizing the specialized language common in missiological studies, including sociology, but with primarily leadership and business motifs. With this, the trend is to be less theological and pastoral, while being more interested in organizational development and methodology. This is not to say the former elements are absent—as missional texts often offer the most sophisticated theological insights—but rather to say that these texts are predominantly utilizing organizational theories and categorization as a way of developing their themes.

Fresh Expressions and Neo-Monasticism

The Fresh Expressions movement is the formal name given to the coordinated renewal impulse within the Anglican Church. As Graham Clay, the leader of this initiative, puts it, "'Fresh expressions of church' is a term coined by the Church of England report *Mission-shaped Church* and used in the Church of England and the Methodist Church for the last five years."[47] He proceeds to describe it this way:

> It is a way of describing the planting of new congregations or churches which are different in ethos and style from the church which planted them; because they are designed to reach a different group of people than those already attending the original church. There is no single model to copy but a wide variety of approaches for a wide variety of contexts and constituencies. The emphasis is on planting something which is appropriate to its context, rather than cloning something which works elsewhere.

47. Graham Clay, "An Introduction," http://www.freshexpressions.org.uk/about/introduction. See also Mission and Public Affairs Council (Church of England) and Rowan Williams, *Mission-Shaped Church: Church Planting and Fresh Expressions of Church in a Changing Context* (London: Church House, 2004).

This movement emphasizes what is very much a distinct situation in the United Kingdom and thus deserving of its own categorization, both in terms of the specific Fresh Expressions movement and in regard to the general experience of churches outside of the United States. As a more general category, I also see this stream reflecting the ways transformative models develop within established and traditional denominations. Whereas the emerging church in the United States tends to be separatist (often, though, not always of its own choosing), the same transformative impulses have been embraced within other church communities as part of the continuing tradition. This is most often because declining attendance or leadership radicalized responses in a way that the American churches have not had to face.[48]

A key text in this stream is *Ancient Faith, Future Mission: Fresh Expressions in the Sacramental Tradition*, which is a collection of essays that describe the impulse and examples of the Fresh Expressions movement, especially as it is taking place in England.[49] In general, the themes, emphases, and impulses tend to be the same, and as such so would much of the critiques. The main distinction this stream adds, however, is its expression as a renewal movement rather than as an ecclesially separatist church. This then allows other denominations an open door to discover how similar impulses might develop in their own church bodies, not unlike how the charismatic movement

48. Not only because of our more religious tendencies but also because nontraditional churches, whether nondenominational or radical reformation, have had a long standing presence and influence, so that "mainline" denominations can decline without there being, it seems, a sense that Christianity itself is in trouble in our nation. Reformers within denominations, then, are much more able to simply join another denomination or start their own independent congregation, often finding significant success in doing so. This has been the case throughout the history of America, as a country and as a colony.

49. Steven J. L. Croft, Ian Mobsby, and Stephanie Spellers, *Ancient Faith, Future Mission: Fresh Expressions in the Sacramental Traditions* (New York: Seabury, 2010). Of course, the inclusion of an essay by Brian McClaren and an essay by Karen Ward, who at the time worked in Seattle with an Episcopal congregation, are less cohesive to the overall pattern.

helped broaden the influence of the Pentecostalism impulse by arising within established churches, such as the Roman Catholic Church. Indeed, with only minor rhetorical revisionism, it is possible to suggest the base communities of liberation theology as being essentially a fresh expression movement within the Roman Catholic Church, albeit certainly one that predates the contemporary transformative church movement as a whole.[50]

Another very useful text is *Church in the Present Tense*.[51] While not itself formally representing the Fresh Expressions movement, this collection of essays represents much of the Fresh Expression stream, as it is nonseparatist and more theological in scope, representing the broader style of Fresh Expression studies in tone, and open to being useful for established traditions seeking renewal, and new congregations seeking theological orientation. While as a whole these essays are representative of the transformative church movement, two authors in particular are especially helpful for my present task, Kevin Corcoran and Jason Clark, as they provide the best theoretical connections with Moltmann's work.

A fourth stream of transformative churches has been inspired by the monastic movement, generally its Western expressions, and seeks to incorporate these practices within contemporary Christian communities, practices that, as it happens, are similar to the ideals of other transformative churches. Shane Claiborne's book *The Irresistible Revolution*, was among the more significant examples of this movement, with other examples and communities throughout the

---

50. See esp. Leonardo Boff, *Ecclesiogenesis: The Base Communities Reinvent the Church,* trans. Robert Barr (Maryknoll, NY: Orbis, 1986).

51. Jason Clark et al., *Church in the Present Tense: A Candid Look at What's Emerging* (Grand Rapids: Brazos, 2011). Scot McKnight is a major contributor to this text, and while he is certainly expressing more of the North American perspective, he also very much expresses the kind of approaches reflected in the British context. This text also comes with an accompanying DVD that included videos of the authors and other key leaders, including Rowan Williams, then Archbishop of Canterbury.

world taking up similar themes with similar motives.[52] Claiborne continues to be involved in related discussions as an author and speaker. This neo-monasticism tends to have a somewhat narrow perspective on monastic life, as it is urban and socially involved, reflecting more of an early Franciscan ideal. New expressions of contemplative monasticism do not seem to have gained similar publicity. The Fresh Expressions movement has become particularly interested in the overlapping motifs, which is not surprising given the proximity to Celtic monastic centers such as Iona and Lindisfarne.[53]

Methodology

As my goal is not to probe the nuances of missional, emerging, or related movements, nor offer a comprehensive survey of the literature—both of which have been done sufficiently by Jones and by Van Gelder and Zscheile—I will be gathering together the emerging and missional texts as speaking from a common voice with shared concerns. While they certainly may show distinct missiological approaches, and even within the categories there are substantive distinctions, these do share, I assert, a common theological milieu—both in context and in theological response. Indeed, in many cases trying to parse the distinctions of writers and leaders that work within overlapping categories becomes more of a matter of semantics, one that is increasingly garbled as many communities and leaders simply do not fit into one definition, and as such definitions become more a matter of personal preference than settled meaning.[54]

52. Shane Claiborne, *The Irresistible Revolution: Living as an Ordinary Radical* (Grand Rapids: Zondervan, 2006).

53. See Graham Cray, Ian Mobsby, and Aaron Kennedy, eds., *New Monasticism as Fresh Expression of Church* (Norwich, England: Canterbury, 2010).

54. For example, while Alan Hirsh as a writer is generally categorized as being "missional," the church he is a part of in Los Angeles called Tribe is mostly indistinguishable from churches previously and presently categorized as emerging churches.

That all these streams, in general, tend to gravitate toward a critical appreciation of Moltmann lends credence to using these together and for pursuing my project as a whole. Indeed, I can say this present work is itself motivated by seeing how three distinct starting points—missiology, ministry and church planting, systematic theology—have coalesced into a shared trajectory. This shared trajectory is one of liberation—liberation out of insufficient forms of ecclesiality and sociality, and liberation into the anticipating and experiencing life of the Kingdom of God.[55]

Having briefly examined the four streams that make up the transformative churches, it is now possible to propose a theological method that ties these together in a more comprehensive theology. Following this, I return to the other partner in this conversation, Moltmann. Because discussions of his method and theology are already quite numerous, many of which are indeed accurate reflections of his work, my focus will consist of supplementary comments to these more comprehensive discussions. I will focus on methodological elements of his theology that have become guides for my own reading and that are pertinent for my interpretation of Moltmann and for this present study. Finally, I will present the method that will shape this present work.

Emerging Method

A study of transformative church writings suggest three areas that pursue the same approach to theology as a whole: transformative church theology is holistic, it is contextual, and it is vernacular. The idea of a holistic theology means there is a movement away from the division between sacred and secular, as well as between reason

---

55. See Jürgen Moltmann, *Jesus Christ for Today's World*, trans. Margaret Kohl (Minneapolis: Fortress Press, 1994), ch. 1.

and experience. Theological insight is applied to all areas of life, within the church and outside of it, assuming that the kingdom of God affects all reality, rather than purely spiritual topics. Doug Pagitt writes, "Our efforts are built upon the assumption that we are able to imagine and create something of greater beauty and usefulness if we move away from speaking of spiritual life in dualistic tones, as if the spiritual part of a person is a separate component that can be worked on and developed in isolation from the rest of the person."[56]

Transformative church theology expresses this in the practice of "transforming secular space," which is about understanding that all parts of life—those termed secular and those termed sacred—are arenas of participation with God.[57] This emphasis arises due to a perceived compartmentalization of life in much of modern society, where church is often a Sunday event unrelated to "real life."[58] Theology and spirituality, however, are inseparable from the needs and experiences of actual lives as lived throughout the week. This means all areas of life must discover the hope of God that leads toward transformation. This hope spurs men and women to action as God seeks Christ-oriented participation in this world in worship, service, and liberation.[59]

Second, transformative church theology is contextual, meaning it derives its specific emphases and expressions from the particular contexts in which particular communities are developed. Robert Webber notes, "While the Christian faith has a fixed framework of creation, fall, incarnation, death, resurrection, church, and new heaven and new earth, this framework and the story of God it reveals

---

56. Pagitt, *Church Re-Imagined*, 19.
57. See Gibbs and Bolger, *Emerging Churches*, ch. 4.
58. Frost and Hirsch, *The Shaping of Things to Come*, 19.
59. "Liberation is an all-embracing process that leaves no dimension of human life untouched, because when all is said and done it expresses the saving action of God in history." Gustavo Gutiérrez, *We Drink from Our Own Wells: The Spiritual Journey of a People*, trans. Matthew J. O'Connell, 20th anniversary ed. (Maryknoll, NY: Orbis, 2006), 2.

is always *contextualized* into this or that culture."[60] While this may always be the case, it is not always the case that Christianity acknowledges or emphasizes this contextualization. Webber writes, "Now the church must engage with the emergence of a postmodern, post-Christian, neo-Pagan world."[61] Theology is not merely adapted to fit the context, the context itself helps to shape and determine theology. Contexts reach back into theology and provoke reflection. Dan Kimball writes, "The more I engaged in the emerging culture, it just didn't allow me to give the packaged and somewhat simplistic answers you could get away with within the church subculture. People outside the church were asking deeper theological questions than were people inside the church."[62] This contextualization does not imply or encourage theological isolation resulting in small pockets of separated communities, each with a wholly unique theological perspective. Rather, it is out of the contexts that one experiences God so that, then, one can interact with and compare other experiences from other contexts so as to find greater wisdom.

Finally, transformative church theology is primarily, using the terminology of William Dyrness, "vernacular theology," which he defines as "that theological framework constructed, often intuitively, by Christians seeking to respond faithfully to the challenges their lives present to them."[63] This vernacular theology has three aspects. The

---

60. Robert Webber, introduction to *Listening to the Beliefs of Emerging Churches*, 9.

61. Ibid., 9.

62. Dan Kimball, "The Emerging Church and Missional Theology," in Webber, *Listening to the Beliefs of Emerging Churches*, 90–91. Cf. Brewin, *Signs of Emergence*, 96.

63. William A. Dyrness, *Invitation to Cross-Cultural Theology: Case Studies in Vernacular Theologies* (Grand Rapids: Zondervan, 1992), 16. This idea arose as Dyrness was confronted with people who were expressing a clear theology, even as they were not theologians. He was unsure how to properly relate this to academic theology. He writes, "My understanding of theology was limited almost entirely to reading and explicating published texts, and to helping my students write commentaries on these texts (i.e., produce more texts). What about the vast majority of Christian communities for whom texts are marginal and whose reflection is largely informal—what kind of 'theological reflection' do people like this do?" William Dyrness, "Vernacular Theology," in Hunsberger and Van Gelder, *The Church between Gospel and Culture*,

first is that vernacular theology is "a communal rather than individual project."[64] Harvey Cox notes that base communities—which can be considered transformative churches—are "congregations of those attempting through their collective action not just to rise individually but to change the system which perpetuates top and bottom patterns."[65] Those who seek to develop theology from transformative communities will likewise be communal in both thought and practice. This communal element is not limited to a fixed location, as participants have significant access to the technology that allows them more public, and farther reaching, expressions of their experiences and considerations. Ryan Bolger has frequently noted that blogs remain the best way to get an understanding of insights as they develop—blogs not only by leaders but also by those who are participants and even by those who are outside a church community but spiritually interested.[66]

The second aspect of a vernacular theology is the following: "The theological framework will be thought of as embodied and expressed in beliefs and attitudes, as well as practices, as all of these grow out of the specific social and cultural situation."[67] Contextual theology that is holistic theology is not a one-way street, but rather continually reflects upon, changes, adapts, and assesses both thought and practice, learning from and analyzing at the same time so that theology and practice mature together. Webber notes that transformative churches attempt to "construct theology out of God's story as it dynamically connects with our own story. This theology is a life lived in harmony

260–61. To be sure, not all theology being written from the perspectives of liberation or emerging church theology should be considered vernacular. Rather, the idea of vernacular theology emphasizes the primary source for the theologies without limiting who can discuss them.

64. Dyrness, "Vernacular Theology," 266.

65. Harvey Cox, *Religion in the Secular City: Toward a Postmodern Theology* (New York: Simon and Schuster, 1984), 157.

66. Cf. Pagitt, *Church Re-Imagined*, 11.

67. Dyrness, "Vernacular Theology," 266.

with God and with God's agenda for the world."[68] This harmony attempts to answer "new challenges that can only be answered out of a theology that lives in an embodied community of interpretation."[69]

The third aspect involves this application of action and belief becoming itself another source of reflection. The theologian "will want to know what the 'consumer' of this framework means by it. This attitude will help us discover ways in which Scripture or parts of the tradition are used in ways suited to the people's needs."[70] An implication of this is the reality that any given theologian or group of theologians never fully expresses these particular theologies, nor can any given minister or theologian necessarily be seen as the sole judge of what is acceptable. These theologies come out of the community and speak for the community, with theologians contributing only a certain part of a much larger project.

This last point raises a particular question that has different answers given the context. What are the people's needs? This is not a question directed to any individual's own assessment of existential inadequacy or expression. The word *need* is often overused and underconsidered. Rather, the idea of the needs of the people is itself a formulation that comes from theological consideration on Scripture as well as personal and historical experience. It is also important to note that in most cases transformative church theologians are not seeking answers to their own individual needs, but rather have broader interests in mind.[71]

---

68. Webber, *Listening to the Beliefs of Emerging Churches*, 17.

69. Ibid., 18.

70. Dyrness, "Vernacular Theology," 268.

71. This might be the best way of distinguishing transformative church theology from other forms of "seeker-sensitive" and "postmodern" minded ecclesiastical reforms that adapt in order to be "attractional," that is try to lure new participants by indulging their assumed interests and tastes (rather than actual needs). So while "experience" is a key aspect of emerging and liberation theologies it is not implying a continuation of the stream of theology that derives from Schleiermacher. "Thinkers of this tradition all locate ultimately significant contact with whatever is finally important to religion in the prereflective experiential depths of the self

Transformative church theologies have come under a great deal of scrutiny and critique, especially from the theological communities from which they derive. The charge primarily laid against transformative church theology is that it is uncritically postmodern, embracing deconstruction and truth-denying relativism. Indeed, it is postmodern, moving past the foundationalism that characterized modern forms of theology.[72] Because many critics are themselves writing from a modern, foundationalist perspective, they interpret the development of these theologies from preestablished categories.[73] The idea of experience acting as an essential contribution to a theological system seems, in their understanding, to reflect clear liberal epistemology.[74] Because of preestablished categories and an inability for flexibility within this foundational approach, there is a reductionist tendency that mischaracterizes precisely how both transformative church thinkers are in fact understanding and communicating truth. The key question for analysis is, then, what kind of postmodernism these theologies represent.

Because a significant amount of attention focuses on the continental forms of postmodernism, for many this is the only form of postmodernism. However, as postmodernism is not itself a defining category but rather emphasizes something other than

and regard the public or outer features of religion as expression and evocative objectifications (i.e., nondiscursive symbols) of internal experience." George Lindbeck, *The Nature of Doctrine: Religion and Theology in a Postliberal Age* (Philadelphia: Westminster, 1984), 21.

72. See F. LeRon Shults, *The Postfoundationalist Task of Theology: Wolfhart Pannenberg and the New Theological Rationality* (Grand Rapids: Eerdmans, 1999) and Stanley J. Grenz and John R. Franke, *Beyond Foundationalism: Shaping Theology in a Postmodern Context* (Louisville: Westminster John Knox, 2001).

73. For instance, see D. A. Carson, *Becoming Conversant with the Emerging Church* (Grand Rapids: Zondervan, 2005). Carson, 29, writes, "For almost everyone within the movement, this works out in an emphasis on feelings and affections over against linear thought and rationality; on experience over against truth; on inclusion over against exclusion; on participation over against individualism and the heroic loner." His emphasis on "over against" suggests he views these as alternate approaches to knowledge.

74. See Nancey Murphy, *Anglo-American Postmodernity: Philosophical Perspectives on Science, Religion, and Ethics* (Boulder, CO: Westview, 1997), 113–14.

modernity, there are in fact various postmodern approaches, some of which have a quite sophisticated understanding of truth. While transformative church theology could in fact develop in terms of continental postmodernity, this approach does not into account the full body of writings that derive from these ecclesial movements. Instead, such attempts tend to begin with continental postmodernism and try to fit transformative church theologies within the developed models.[75] Indeed, such philosophy also tends to be quite esoteric, and thus removed from the communal conversation, so that attempts to utilize this philosophy are, as such, inadequate for communicating a vernacular theology.[76]

Instead of depending on continental postmodernism, it would be more effective to see transformative church theology as expressing an Anglo-American postmodern thought, one that replaces the model of foundationalism with Quine's "web of belief."[77] In order to adapt this model to the particulars of Christian theology, Alasdair MacIntyre expands this web of belief to include three dimensions.[78] From this model, and MacIntyre's own account of truth, Murphy develops an understanding of truth that allows for asserting truth while avoiding an absolute judgment that is outside our present capability, due to our

75. Peter Rollins, *How (Not) to Speak of God* (Brewster, MA: Paraclete, 2006) attempts an emerging church theology with strong regard for continental postmodernism that, while quite interesting, and, indeed, invigorating is, in my estimation, of limited reach and not entirely adequate as theology itself must be stretched and weakened to fit into the increasingly outmoded twentieth-century continental postmodernisms.

76. A discussion of the inappropriateness of continental postmodernism as *the* model for understanding transformative church theology is itself worth a significant study, far outside both the present goals of this paper and my own expertise. While ultimately not himself contributing a cogent expression of Christian theology after modernity, David Bentley Hart, *The Beauty of the Infinite: The Aesthetics of Christian Truth* (Grand Rapids: Eerdmans, 2003) offers a strong critique of continental postmodernism as it relates to Christian theology. His main critique is that such philosophy is, ultimately, a rhetoric of violence and domination, that it is less actually postmodern and more a continuation of modernism as pursued by Nietzsche.

77. See Nancey Murphy, *Beyond Liberalism and Fundamentalism: How Modern and Postmodern Philosophy Set the Theological Agenda* (Valley Forge, PA: Trinity International, 1996), 94–96. and Murphy, *Anglo-American Postmodernity*, 27–28.

78. See Figure 6.2 and 6.3 in Murphy, *Anglo-American Postmodernity*, 121.

limited perspective.[79] Rather than two entirely independent models, each built on separate foundations of Scripture *or* experience, this model of truth no longer depends on truth being either absolute *or* relative, but rather as a spectrum that can exist between the decidability of truth on various issues. [80] Key to this model as well is the idea of a particular assertion of truth gauged by its "unsurpassability."[81] This involves a particular understanding being able to explain its own intellectual crises while its rival cannot, as well as being able to solve outside problems its rival cannot.[82]

In their use of Scripture and tradition, transformative church theologies reflect the web of belief rather than foundationalism, a fact that confuses those who cannot understand truth apart from the older foundationalist model.[83] However, these add what is, I think, a distinctive to the idea of the web of belief in how they go about their particular development and goals of theology. For the most part, theological method has been interested in the idea of coherence, which is the fitting together of beliefs, built either upon a set foundation or as fitting together within a broad web. "Rather than remaining a collection or aggregate of disjointed, discrete members that have nothing whatsoever to do with one another, the set of beliefs must form an integrated whole, and this whole must carry 'explanatory power.'"[84] Thus, systematic theology has concerned itself with how the various aspects of theology fit together with one

---

79. Ibid., 128.

80. Ibid., 129.

81. Ibid., 125.

82. These are called synchronic and diachronic justification. Ibid., 124. Another aspect of diachronic justification is being able to explain why a rival or preceding model could not solve the crisis.

83. Dyrness, *Invitation*, 26 writes, "Symbols, rituals, confessions of faith, and religious behavior must all be understood in a single web of meaning that makes up religion." When religion is not a separate category but encompasses all of life, this web of meaning includes far more than particularly liturgical categories.

84. Grenz and Franke, *Beyond Foundationalism*, 39.

another, insistent that a "good" theology is one that is the most coherent in understanding and expressing its constitutive parts. Because of the influence of foundationalist models of truth, this idea of coherence remains the primary goal of most theologies, a goal that has often kept theology distant from the lives of those who are poor, who are oppressed, alienated, or oversatiated: in general, all those who are in need of liberation.[85] A theological system can be entirely coherent while at the same time not speaking into the lives of those involved within Christian communities.

In a way, this pursuit of coherence is a little like performing scientific experiments in a vacuum. To be sure, the results might describe truth and offer an accurate model of reality. However, results developed in a vacuum cannot often apply outside of the sterile conditions of a lab. While they are intellectually interesting and contribute to knowledge, this cannot be the sole goal of either science or theological inquiry. This distinction is vital for transformative church theology. For this theology is not as much concerned about coherence as is about integrity, integrity with the full revelation of God and integrity with the contexts in which such a theology is declared.

As a vernacular theology deriving from particular contexts and interested in holistic application and understanding of theology, transformative church theology is willing to forego the rigorous pursuit of making sure each particular aspect of theology fits nicely together.[86] Instead, it is concerned with theology expressed in action

85. An extreme example of this disconnection is the quite disparate realities of the Nazi regime in World War II and the otherwise very sophisticated German theology at the time. German theology was, one might argue, extremely coherent and yet almost entirely unhelpful in providing substantive guidance for the nation, until it was too late. The Confessing Church, of course, was an expression of this realization, and an attempt to offer alternatives, which has continued in many streams of German theological, philosophical, and sociological thought after World War II.

86. It is not *uninterested* in this task, rather this is seen as a secondary, or even tertiary, task rather than a primary task of theology.

and understood in experiences. Theology has real consequences in real lives and participants are willing to adapt theology in order to maintain integrity with what they expect to discover. Beliefs constantly rub up against the experiences of men and women in all kinds of circumstances, as experiences do not match expected outcomes or as experiences defy established suppositions.[87] While this maintains Quine's assertion that beliefs and experiences are not "connected," it asserts that there is contact, continual and active contact, that rubs the edges of the belief web, and as such results in friction.[88]

To MacIntyre's three-dimensional image of the web moving forward through time, we can add another aspect that helps illustrate this idea of friction. As it moves through time, the web of belief is also rotating, thus rubbing up against a constant variety of both historic and contemporary experience, an image shown in Figure 1.1.[89] With this model, not only is experience and practice the context to interpret and apply the various beliefs, these experiences themselves have the ability to critique and induce a change in the beliefs. Friction works both ways.

---

87. The book of Job serves as a fundamental example of this process, and its allowance in Jewish and Christian theology. See Gustavo Gutiérrez, *On Job: God-Talk and the Suffering of the Innocent*, trans. Matthew J. O'Connell (Maryknoll, NY: Orbis, 1987).
88. See Murphy, *Anglo-American Postmodernity*, 51.
89. Adapted from Figure 6.3 in Murphy, *Anglo-American Postmodernity*, 121.

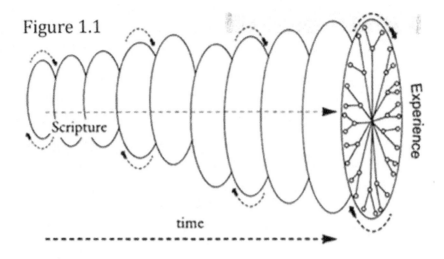

Figure 1.1

Scripture

time

Experience

Traditionally, the pursuit of developing theology through conflicting positions is called dialectic theology. Lonergan writes,

> Dialectical distinctions involve mutual repudiation. Each considers repudiation of its opposites the one and only intelligent, reasonable, and responsible stand, and when sufficient sophistication is attained, each seeks a philosophy or a method that will buttress what are considered appropriate views on the intelligent, the reasonable, the responsible.[90]

Indeed, transformative church theologians do often engage in a form of dialectic theology, particularly as it relates to issues of justice. However, as Lonergan notes, dialectic theology emphasizes what are inherently conflicting issues, and attempts to find resolution in the light of these two, seemingly contradictory, realities. In the case of transformative church theologies, the conflict is not only with what is clearly opposed to Christian theology. This theology has discovered that beliefs and experiences that should, in all expectation, fit smoothly together can also be in conflict. The web of beliefs *should* rotate smoothly in the lives of those who experience the effects of this theology. The church should have unity in its theology and in

90. Bernard Lonergan, *Method in Theology* (New York: Herder and Herder, 1972), 248.

its influence. Far too often, this does not happen. Poorly developed theology can induce unchristian experiences. When this happens, there is friction that requires either an adjustment of practice or the adjustment of the theology itself.[91]

Instead of conflict being between Christian theology and the unfortunate realities of a sin-drenched world, this conflict is oftentimes with the Christian influences themselves. Christian beliefs and experiences do not match up, and in doing this cause significant damage.[92] As experiences rub up against the beliefs, these beliefs are rubbed down, a situation that can eventually result in the complete breaking down of a particular belief, and maybe even the whole system as these shattered beliefs tug against other beliefs.[93] Rather than situated in the middle of the web of beliefs, interested in maintaining and positioning particular beliefs in an increasingly coherent and stable manner, those involved in transformative church theology position themselves on the edge of belief and experience, particularly noting and responding to the areas in which friction is

91. Cf. Barry Taylor, "Converting Christianity: The End and Beginning of Faith," in Pagitt and Jones, *An Emergent Manifesto of Hope*, 167.

92. Lonergan also notes that his theological method is linear, moving from one stage to another. "After research, which assembles the data thought relevant, and interpretation, which ascertains their meaning, and history, which finds meanings incarnate in deeds and movements, and dialectic, which investigates the conflicting conclusions of historians, interpreters, researchers, and foundations, which objectifies the horizon effected by intellectual, moral, and religious conversion, and doctrines, which uses foundations as a guide in selecting from the alternatives presented by dialectic, and systematic, which seeks an ultimate clarification of the meaning of doctrine, there finally comes our present concern with the eighth functional specialty, communications." Lonergan, *Method in Theology*, 355. Instead of being linear, however, these might be best understood in transformative church theology as existing on a wheel, each connected to each other and each connected to the center, with each contribution interactive at each stage. From this, the interaction could be said to also get to communications, run into friction, and then begin the process of working entirely backwards from Lonergan's proposal, sometimes forcing consideration all the way back to the beginning—a pattern that would well explain the decided interest transformative church thinkers have for N. T. Wright, for example. The potential for such friction to cause a critique, reexamination, and adaptation of church practices themselves is also one of the key problems related to using Hauerwas as a theological source for transformative church theology.

93. This might be a fair way of expressing the current ecclesial situation in much of Europe.

high and potentially destructive. Instead of pursuing a dialectic that attempts a synthesis, these theologians are interested in maintaining the integrity of the web of belief with the experiences of those who believe.[94] As such, this method is not as much a dialectic theology as it a form of "theotribology."[95]

The pursuit of integrity and coherence go hand in hand in pursuit of a holistic theological system. Those who specialize in the pursuit of coherence are necessary as those who pursue integrity continue to tug and shift beliefs on the edge of the web. While this can occasionally be done with little impact or disorder, sometimes the adjustments requires strong tugs that if not addressed by the broader pursuit of theology could undermine the ideals of diachronic and synchronic justification. If people ignore the goal of integrity, then systems of theology develop that are both wholly coherent and entirely wrong. If the goal of coherence is ignored, then systems of theology develop that might make sense in the light of experience but have severe weaknesses that would undermine the goal of unsurpassability in increasing ways, and that would also not take the importance of revelation in the belief system into sufficient regard. Understanding transformative church theology as theotribology in the pursuit of theological integrity offers a constructive approach for continual development and allows for more incisive critiques of this movement.

94. Lonergan, *Method in Theology*, 246 writes, "There are finally, the gross differences due to the fact that historians with opposed horizons are endeavoring to make intelligible to themselves the same sequence of events. With such gross differences dialectic is concerned. The cause of gross differences is a gross difference of horizon, and the proportionate remedy is nothing less than conversion." While there are differences acknowledged even still, the conflict is not between converted and unconverted, but within the converted model itself as it is experienced.
95. *Tribology* being the formal name for the study of friction in science.

Moltmann's Method

As mentioned earlier, the study of Moltmann is certainly one that has occupied scholars and students for much of the last fifty years. As attempting yet another thorough study on his method would be superfluous as a minor section in a larger project, I will here only suggest particular themes that are important to this present work.[96] For the sake of some general information, I will also provide a very brief overview of his work and the primary interpreters I will be using in addition to my own reading of his work.

Moltmann found theological superstardom with his 1964 publication of *Theology of Hope*. He followed this text with *The Crucified God* and *The Church in the Power of the Spirit*.[97] The method in these was to examine theology through a single lens, in doing so helping to see the overall insights and connections such a lens can bring to broader theology. In the midst of these, as well as between all of his major texts, he published smaller volumes, many of which were on ancillary themes, helping further elucidate the practical or social implications of his larger works.

In the late 1970s, he switched his methodology. Beginning with *The Trinity and the Kingdom of God*, Moltmann wrote what he has termed "systematic contributions to theology."[98] They are contributions in both offering his perspectives and in seeking to

---

96. Each of the themes I will note are themselves worthy of more specific research than is possible in this present project. These should be included along with, not in contrast to, Moltmann's own list of "personal approaches" found in Moltmann, *Experiences in Theology*, trans. Margaret Kohl (Minneapolis: Fortress Press, 2000), 303–8, in which he notes political theology, the theology of the cross, and Orthodox theology as key orienting guides in his Trinitarian theology.

97. Jürgen Moltmann, *Theology of Hope*, trans. James W. Leitch (Minneapolis: Fortress Press, 1993); Jürgen Moltmann, *The Crucified God*, trans. R. A. Wilson and John Bowden (Minneapolis: Fortress Press, 1993); Jürgen Moltmann, *The Church in the Power of the Spirit*, trans. Margaret Kohl (Minneapolis: Fortress Press, 1993).

98. Jürgen Moltmann, *The Trinity and the Kingdom*, trans. Margaret Kohl (Minneapolis: Fortress Press, 1993), xi.

provoke discussion by other scholars and students. They are also contributions in that Moltmann understands systematic theology as "only one contribution to a greater shared theological whole."[99] One might better understand these as "musings on theology," as Moltmann's goal is not to contribute a compiled dogmatics, but to consider the themes related to each topic, essentially, as they occur to him and as he finds such themes undeveloped in Christian theology.

Which raises the question, what is the goal of theology for Moltmann? When asked about his method, he generally replies that he does not have a method. Yet, there must be some guiding factor in how he writes, an implicit method, even if it does not explicitly limit Moltmann within such. In my reading of Moltmann, four distinct elements stand out that, other than the first, I have not seen highlighted elsewhere as a guiding factor in his writings. I argue these provide a substantive orientation for understanding his work in light of the present concerns. These underlying elements include his interest in experiences, his eco-theology, his "hypersovereign" approach to the study of God, and a persistent interest in the liberation of the oppressor.

Experiences

"Theology," Moltmann writes, "has at its heart only one problem: God."[100] This is not, obviously, a problem God has with himself, but rather a problem that we have with God, which while it may take on a variety of intellectual and logical dimensions, ultimately is an issue related to our experiences of life. God is, we assert, who God is and yet our lives are, we experience, not always, or even often, in keeping with this theology that we assert. Susanna Wesley wrote to her son

99. Moltmann, *Experiences in Theology*, xvi.
100. Ibid., 23.

Charles, after her eldest son had died, "As your good old grandfather often used to say, 'That's an affliction, that God makes an affliction.' For surely the manifestation of his presence and favour is more than an adequate support under any suffering whatever. But if he withhold his consolations and hides his face from us the least suffering is intolerable."[101] This echoes the "wise old theological saying" that Moltmann quotes: "To know God is to suffer God."[102] What are we to do with God? That is, ultimately, the question of theology and a question that Moltmann specially relates to our experiences.

Our experiences, to be sure, are not everything. However, they are significant. They are where we encounter God and it is in our encounters with God that our particular questions and issues become substantive for us, even if not for others. As we often share issues and questions, our wrestling with God in terms of our experiences often resonates beyond our own experiences and thus becomes a useful guide for theological exploration. This is essentially Moltmann's interest in experiences, in which experiences in theology refers to both his own personal encounters as well as the role experience itself plays in the theological endeavor. We might, without stretching the bounds too much, suggest that, in effect, Moltmann is one of the premier connoisseurs of what Wesley scholar Albert C. Outler has called the "Wesleyan Quadrilateral," developing theology through the four fold interaction of Scripture, tradition, reason, and experience.[103] With this, Moltmann likewise shares an interest in

---

101. Charles Wallace Jr., ed., *Susanna Wesley: The Complete Writings* (New York: Oxford University Press, 1997), 180.

102. Moltmann, *Experiences in Theology*, 23.

103. For a substantive discussion of this topic, see Albert Cook Outler, "The Wesleyan Quadrilateral in John Wesley," *Wesleyan Theological Journal* 20, no. 1 (1985): 7–18. This is not to argue that Moltmann is, in effect, Wesleyan; however, in many ways Moltmann expresses much more of a Wesleyan approach and Wesleyan content of theology than what is traditionally seen as Reformed. Moltmann's potential "Wesleyanism" is worth much more study. Cf. Jürgen Moltmann, "Sun of Righteousness Arise! The Freedom of a Christian—Then and Now—for the Perpetrators and for the Victims of Sin," *Theology Today* 69, no. 1 (2012): 16.

"theotribology," wrestling with his own experiences as a German soldier and his experiences as a German after Auschwitz, experiences that provide significant friction for a country that was, otherwise, a historically Christian stronghold.[104]

Ecological Theology

So much of the preaching of the gospel in traditional Evangelicalism has been about personal salvation, ignoring the broader implications of God's work, and in this way Evangelicalism may be emphasizing a limited understanding of doctrine that often lacks a holistic love. Moltmann shares that David Yonggi Cho, of the Full Gospel Church in Korea, told him, "I must repent, because I only preached the salvation of the soul. There is also social salvation and the salvation of the creation."[105] He learned there is salvation and renewal wherever there is life. Cho told him this change in his awareness came about by Moltmann's influence. This overall approach, with its emphasis on a holistic love that encompasses all of creation, reflects what I see as Moltmann's postmodern approach. Throughout his works, it seems that he has a working understanding of premodernism, modernism, and a new approach that I consider his approach to postmodernism. These approaches to the world reflect in each era's approach to theology. "In the history of the theological doctrine of creation, three stages can be distinguished."[106]

104. Indeed, this suggests a "theotribological" connection with liberation theology as it has been developed in Latin America. In both places, the conflict of oppression arose in the midst of, and was even validated by, a strong church structure. I should note that *theotribology* is a term I created in a blog post I wrote in early 2007 as I was wrestling with Moltmann's methodology. See Patrick Oden, "A Theological Post," Present Matters, entry posted January 27, 2007, http://dualravens.com/presentmatters/?p=1454.

105. Jürgen Moltmann, interview by author, Tübingen, Germany, May 18, 2011, at 1:10:40 into the conversation.

106. Jürgen Moltmann, *God in Creation*, trans. Margaret Kohl (Minneapolis: Fortress Press, 1993), 33.

In the premodern world, humanity was afraid of nature, oppressed by it, and struggled in the face of its power. Thought and society reflected this fear of nature. This fear was dealt with by religions that either glorified nature—a pantheistic approach—or entirely dismissing it—a gnostic approach. For a premodern Christian theology of creation, "the biblical traditions and the ancient world's picture of the universe were fused into a religious cosmology."[107] Both of the two extremes—divinizing nature and entirely disparaging it—were seen as heresies by the early Christians, though there was definitely a form of the latter that shaped practices, if not theological assertions. They understood the transcendent Creator to have a relationship with this world through the Spirit, which led to seeing the world as divinely ordered, guided by his wisdom, though it was "temporally and spatially limited, and contingent and immanent world."[108] Fear of nature gave way to fear of God, so that God's presence in this world gave hope to being sheltered from nature's domination.

As humanity progressed in technology, science, and knowledge of this universe in general, it increasingly lost its fear of nature as it protected itself from nature's influences. With this came a change in how broader culture related to nature. In the modern era, humanity learned how to overcome their fears and indeed surpass much of the power of nature. Nature became something to be subdued and conquered. Technology and science gave insights into the ways of this world, and with this insight came a new stance toward the world, one of domination rather than intimidation. With this came new experiences of human freedom and progress as well as new scales of devastation upon nature and within humanity.

107. Ibid.
108. Ibid.

Modernity conquered nature but left emptiness, waste, and destruction that literally threatens our existence. A Moltmannian postmodern approach seeks the re-integration of nature with humanity and the re-integration of the individual within the community.[109] This is not to return to a premodern ideal that rejects technology or tries to find a vague utopia in the idealization of the primitive. "For all of us, there is only one alternative to the humanitarian ideas of human dignity and human rights, and that alternative is barbarism. There is only one alternative to the ideal of eternal peace, and that is a permanent state of war. There is only one alternative to faith in the one God had hope for his righteousness, and that is polytheism and chaos."[110] Moltmann seeks to take the positives of modernity and in its new place of dominance have humanity step back from the now overwrought pursuits of yet more dominance. He asks, "What must we preserve from the project of modernity, and what must we reject? What must we reinvent, so that the project does not founder?"[111]

The answers to these questions fill his various contributions. "The creatures of the natural world are not there for the sake of human beings," he writes, adding, "Human beings are there for the sake of the glory of God, which the whole community of creation extols. The more human beings discover the meaning of their lives in joy in existence, instead of doing and achieving, the better they will be able to keep their economic, social, and political history within bounds."[112] By participating together in integrated life that no longer pursues dominance or independence, we can begin to both bring

109. See Tim Conder, "The Existing Church/Emerging Church Matrix," in Pagitt and Jones, *An Emergent Manifesto of Hope*, 100, for the emerging view of postmodernity as compared with modernity on nine different aspects of ecclesial ministry.

110. Jürgen Moltmann, "Theology in the Project of the Modern World," *A Passion for God's Reign*, ed. Miroslav Volf (Grand Rapids: Eerdmans, 1998), 15.

111. Ibid., 15.

112. Jürgen Moltmann, *GC*, 139.

healing to the destruction and find new understanding of God who is leading us to an integrity with all that God has done and made.

Hypersovereignty

Descriptions of Moltmann often include the fact that he is a Reformed theologian, or at least a theologian from the Reformed tradition, even as many of his strongest critics tend to come from the Reformed tradition. It would indeed be a misnomer to consider Moltmann as representing the Reformed theology as a whole, as though he were attempting to describe what that is. Moltmann's theology is, to be sure, his own theology, reflecting a wide variety of sources and traditions, including the Reformed tradition but also extending to Catholic, Orthodox, Anabaptist, and other directions. As a thoroughly constructive theologian, he shows a willingness to adopt concepts from any tradition. However, if there is one way that Moltmann can and should be included as exemplifying a Reformed tendency, it is in his view of God's sovereignty. Indeed, God's sovereignty is likely the most decisive element of Moltmann's theology, guiding him both in the questions he is willing to ask as well as in the answers such questions bring. If he is daring in his theological approach it is because, it seems, he is utterly confident that God is sovereign above all and so there is not, after all, very much risk in the quest. This view of God's sovereignty is so crucial to understanding Moltmann's entire theological endeavor, and so total in his theological program, that it is useful to apply the term *hypersovereignty* to his understanding of God.

An example worth noting, which will not be discussed in the later text, is Moltmann's understanding of universal salvation. In *Coming of God*, he writes, "God decides for a person and for his or her salvation, for otherwise there is no assurance of salvation at all."[113]

In other places, he has noted that the issue is not who a person believes in, but rather who God believes in. This leads to a perspective of universal salvation that is not emphasizing an overly optimistic anthropology but rather emphasizes the idea that if God is truly God, and if God seeks to save all, then God will save all or he is not God. He writes, "In the divine Judgment all sinners, the wicked and the violent, the murderers and the children of Satan, the Devil and the fallen angels will be liberated and saved from their deadly perdition through transformation into their true, created being, because God remains true to himself, and does not give up what he has once created and affirmed or allow it to be lost."[114] God is all in all, and God is sovereign over all, not so as to dominate but in being, ultimately, irresistible.

God's sovereignty is, as such, the defining theme throughout all of Moltmann's theology, from the work of creation to the work on the cross to eschatological fulfillment, leading Moltmann to discover how this sovereignty is even able to risk itself while not being, ultimately, vulnerable to dissolution. This is a vital point to make at the beginning of this study, as so many critiques of Moltmann are based on assumptions of his anthropological idealism. Moltmann is not an idealist about humanity, as if a German man of his generation could be so. Moltmann is an idealist about God, and in his idealism concerning God he looks for, and expects to see, God's continuing reforming presence in this world that works even through clearly fallible humanity.

This emphasis on hypersovereignty leads Moltmann toward a highly theo-centric approach to theology that is constantly seeking to understand, first, God's perspective in and for this world, and as

113. Jürgen Moltmann, *The Coming of God*, trans. Margaret Kohl (Minneapolis: Fortress Press, 1996), 245. Cf. ibid., 109.
114. Ibid., 255.

this is understood leading theology toward three orienting ideals: orthodoxy, orthopraxy, and orthopathy.[115] In orthodoxy, the goal is to have a right understanding about God. The historic and traditional proposals about God inform this approach but do not limit it. Some doctrines need reexamination to determine their validity in light of the broader revelation of God. In this, we see Moltmann's pursuit of systematic theology. Understanding God is not simply about having the right philosophy about him. It also entails living in a way that reflects this.

Knowing is doing, and so along with orthodoxy there must be a coordinated *orthopraxy*, a way of life that is empowered by and reflects God in his threeness. In this, we see Moltmann's interests in liberation theology and political theology. Theology can never leave us passive; it entails involvement with God and with God's work in this world, a work that carries with it the need to pursue peace and justice in this world through the means that are available to us. Both of these two emphases are present throughout his works, with his emphasis on orthopraxy being especially strong during the late 1960s and 1970s, which coincides with the most prolific era of his political theology.

Third, there is a need for an orthopathy, a right feeling. This is a posture of expectation and joy, oriented toward life in the fullness of meaning that God opens up for us, which even in times of difficulty provides an emotional peace. This third aspect is likely the least considered in theological discussions, or if considered it is often rejected as being too untrustworthy.[116] Yet, for Moltmann, the issue

115. Jürgen Moltmann, interview by author, Tübingen, Germany, May 19, 2011., 53:00, notes that to know Christ is to follow Christ, adding, "There is orthodoxy, orthopraxy, and since the Pentecostal movement orthopathy. The feeling, the emotions, belong together with the reason. And this was overlooked in the German tradition for a long time."

116. Joy Ann McDougall, *Pilgrimage of Love: Moltmann on the Trinity and Christian Life* (New York: Oxford University Press, 2005), 22 writes, "Contemporary academic discourse no longer

of orthopathy has taken on a crucial role. Orthopathy describes what Moltmann sees as the theological project itself, which bears much in common with Lossky's statement about Eastern Orthodox theology: "Christianity is not a philosophical school for speculating about abstract concepts, but is essentially a communion with the living God."[117] Knowing God is about suffering God and about delighting in God. "When God does not 'hide' his face but . . . lets it shine upon those who are his and his whole creation, life comes alive and is filled with inexpressible joy; for this fellowship with the creative, life-giving God is the very 'fullness of life.'"[118]

He continues,

> In this delight in God, the theology of the people who experience it becomes a kind of intellectual love for God, a "delight in the Lord" and "pleasure in wisdom" (Wisdom 6.21). Thoughts no longer just "flow." They begin to dance and play before God in what we might call theo-fantasy. They also move along with measured steps, in logical progressions, so that they can think God in ways appropriate to him, avoiding inner contradictions an irrational mental leaps, and can experience truth in these conformities. This then deserves the name of theo-ology.

expects that systematic theology will also always be a spiritual theology that can ignite the passions and transform the soul."

117. Vladimir Lossky, *The Mystical Theology of the Eastern Church* (Crestwood, NY: St. Vladimir's Seminary Press, 1998), 42.

118. Moltmann, *Experiences in Theology*, 24.

Moltmann develops this orthopathy as part of his "theology of joy."[119] In effect, this aspect of orthopathy points toward understanding Moltmann's theology as doxological in nature, exploring theology through a lens of God's hypersovereignty as it orients us to become participants with him, in worship. What does it mean, after all, "to glorify God and to enjoy him forever?" We must explore the questions of who God is, how he is to glorified, and what it means to enjoy him, which implies as a corollary that he enjoys us. Evagrius of Pontus wrote, "He who is a theologian prays truly, and he who prays truly is a theologian."[120] Moltmann would, it seem, heartily agree with this, including that such a life of prayer involves the whole reality of life, as we encounter it in ourselves and with others.[121] "Summing up," he writes, "we may say that the beauty of theology lies in its doxology, and delight in God is expressed through joy over existence in nearness to him."[122] This beauty and delight are necessary

---

119. See Jürgen Moltmann, *Theology and Joy,* trans. Reinhard Ulrich (London: S.C.M., 1973). This was published in America as *Theology of Play* (New York: Harper and Row, 1972). Moltmann, *Experiences in Theology,* 25 notes that the "word 'play' does not mean something superficial or casual. It is the profound, unreasoning pleasure in God's presence, which goes far beyond all the purpose-and-profit rationality of instrumentalized human reason. In the image of play, we express the truth that the creation of the world is itself meaningful but by no means necessary. With this image we describe the contingency. The uniqueness of existence, its never-to-be-repeated character. The profound sense of human theology is to participate in the playoff the divine wisdom."

120. See *Treatise On Prayer,* 61.

121. I recently came across an interview in which Moltmann basically says just this. When asked about this quote from Evagrius, Moltmann responds, "You can't say about God to other people what you cannot say to God himself, and therefore prayer is at least a test of theology—but it's certainly more. When I pray, I see the world *sub specie aeternitatis,* with the eyes of God, and so I see it differently from other people who don't have this perspective. I see as wrong things they call 'good' and so on. So, prayer is the ground of Christian faith and theology; but the call in the New Testament is not 'Pray!' but 'Watch!' 'Can you not watch with me for one hour?' Jesus asks in the Garden of Gethsemane. To pray means to open one's eyes and watch what is happening, what is coming, the dangers and the opportunities. Normally we close our eyes when we pray, but the catacombs of Rome show that the first Christians stood and prayed with open hands and open eyes. So, we must learn this new type of praying with open eyes. We need a prayer of hope, an eschatological or a revolutionary prayer by watching." See http://www.thirdwaymagazine.co.uk/editions/jun-2012/high-profile/look-forward!.aspx

122. Moltmann, *Experiences in Theology,* 26.

elements of a "right" theology and so it is, thus, important to discuss the orthopathic elements in each theological topic.

Liberation of the Oppressor

Many call Gustavo Gutiérrez the father of liberation theology. Jürgen Moltmann surely is the grandfather of such theologies.[123] In *Experiences in Theology*, he devotes six chapters to theology that relates to the experiences of the oppressed.[124] However, for Moltmann a theology of liberation is not solely for the oppressed, nor it is solely meant to overturn the societal order, leaving the former oppressors eternally punished for their crimes. Rather, Moltmann writes, "Oppression has two sides. On the one side stands the master, on the other side lies the slave. On the one side is the arrogant self-elevation of the exploiter, on the other the suffering of the victim."[125] He continues developing this theme, adding, "Oppression destroys humanity on both sides. The oppressor acts inhumanely, the victim is dehumanized. The evil the perpetrator commits robs him of his humanity, the suffering he inflicts dehumanizes the victim. Where suffering is experienced in the pain of humiliation on one hand, evil spreads on the other."[126] In the light of the kingdom of God, the oppressed need to be freed from their oppression and the oppressors needs to be freed from their oppressing.[127]

---

123. See Volf, *Exclusion and Embrace*, 105.
124. Moltmann, *Experiences*, § III.
125. Ibid., 185.
126. Ibid.
127. See ibid., 186. Here Moltmann writes, "Because oppression always has these two sides, the liberation process has to begin on both sides too. The liberation of the oppressed from their suffering must lead to the liberation of the oppressors from the evil they commit; otherwise there can be no liberation for a new community in justice and freedom. The goal of these reciprocal liberations cannot be anything else than a community of men and women, free of fear, in which there are no longer any oppressors, and no longer any oppressed."

"It is a deplorable fact that after more than thirty years of liberation theology among the poor in the countries of the Third World," Moltmann writes, "there should still be no comprehensive theology for the liberation of the oppressors among the ruling classes in the countries of the industrial West."[128] There are, to be sure, many reasons for this, not least because the needs of the oppressed are much more apparent. Indeed, the tendency is not to call for the liberation of the oppressor, as though they need yet more positive attention, but rather to call for justice and change. The oppressed themselves see, and yearn for, a visible liberation and participation in their present situations. "The liberation of the oppressed is a moral duty, and in many situations a duty that is self-evident, at least for the oppressed."[129] However, the oppressors do not feel this need, content

128. Ibid., 187. He makes note of the European Kairos Document as an example; however, this primarily relates to the church's obligation to social causes, and particularly a Social Democratic political agenda for Europe. See http://www.kairoseuropa.de/english/Kairosdok-eng.doc. Interestingly, the following "among us" list of those participating includes a variety of different backgrounds, including the middle class and historically oppressed groups (such as women). The appeal for the middle class is not out of a suggestion of oppressors being liberated, but rather is about a middle class that is increasingly experiencing its own oppression, and thus a compelling interest in responding to the perceived contextual problems. Yet, in Jürgen Moltmann, "The Liberation of Oppressors," *Journal of the Interdenominational Theological Center* 6, no. 2 (1979): 71, he writes, "A 'liberating theology of the oppressors' is not simply a transposition of the liberating theology of the oppressed into another situation. . . . Rather, it is the counter-image to that theology. In order to understand that theology, we do not ask ourselves, 'In what respects are we also oppressed?' Rather, in order to understand our own salvation, we ask, "How, why, and in what respects have we shared in their oppression?'" It is insufficient for true liberation for us to tell others what *they* must do, rather we must consider our own selves in our own contexts. Scolding is not a liberative act. A more theological exploration can be found in Glenn R. Bucher, "Toward a Liberation Theology for the 'Oppressor,'" *Journal of the American Academy of Religion* 44, no. 3 (1976): 517–34. Although not related specifically to theology or the church, focusing on the issues involved in education, both George Kent, "Peace Education: Pedagogy of the Middle Class," *Peace and Change* 4, no. 3(1977): 37–42 and Chris Van Gorder, "Paulo Freire's Pedagogy for the Children of Oppressors: Educating for Social Justice among the World's Privileged," *The Journal of Pedagogy, Pluralism & Practice* 14 (2008), http://www.lesley.edu/journal-pedagogy-pluralism-practice/chris-van-gorder/pedagogy-children-oppressors/ are helpful. For Van Gorder, cf. Andrew Christian van Gorder, "Pedagogy for the Children of the Oppressors: Liberative Education for Social Justice Among the World's Privileged," *Journal of Transformative Education* 5, no. 1 (2007): 8–32.
129. Moltmann, *Experiences in Theology*, 186.

in the circumstances that seems to bring benefit and apparent choice. "They are blind," Moltmann writes, "and fail to see the suffering they inflict on their victims. They are blinded, and find many grounds to justify their baseness."[130] It is part of the mission of Christ for the blind to receive their sight, and this is as true in the case of oppression as it is in the case of those who have lost use of their physical eyes. "The scales must fall from their eyes. They must recognize themselves with the eyes of their victims, or better: in the eyes of their victims."[131]

Freedom does not come from only one direction or another, but, in the power of the Spirit, it comes from many directions. Holistic freedom calls all people to a new identity and a new community in Christ. The many directions from which freedom arises corresponds to the many locations where the Spirit is at work, in the many ways that a particular freeing is required. For those who do not see or understand, it requires an opening, a space making, so that they understand the reality of life for all those God works in and among. Those in desperate need already see the rich and powerful, assessing them and judging them. With the needy, the Spirit brings empowerment. Those in power and wealth maintain their peace by ignoring the poor and their plights, or justifying it in some respect. With them, the Spirit must bring awareness. "In order to arrive at the truth," Moltmann writes, "the perpetrators, and those who come after them, are dependent on their victims' memories of their suffering, and the memories of those who come after them."[132] Ultimately, this is not the burden of even the oppressors, for Christ takes up the

---

130. Ibid.
131. Jürgen Moltmann, *A Broad Place: an Autobiography,* trans. Margaret Kohl (Minneapolis: Fortress Press, 2008), 230. It was on a flight back from Mexico, after a conference on liberation theology, that Moltmann first realized there must be a "corresponding theology of the liberation of the oppressors if humanity is to be freed on both sides from the sin of oppression." When he arrived home, he wrote an essay on the topic that was published in several places, with an adapted version included as part of his later *Experiences in Theology.* Cf. Moltmann, *Broad Place,* 397n7.
132. Ibid., 230.

burden of the assumed memories, which went from persecution to awareness of sins to forgiveness and embrace. The oppressors, along their own way, put aside their persecuting, take up the effects of the persecution as part of their own memories, and then let go of these in the salvific work of Christ.

This is a difficult process. Moltmann notes that "the social realization of these ideas is a continual problem and a continual opportunity."[133] Calling for liberation, even describing its goals and reasons, is quite easy. Reflection that brings transformation and action becomes quite more difficult, both to escape the ennui of the status quo and to be willing to take a stance against the entrenched positions and practices that, despite the rhetoric, may often, actively, prevent true liberating freedom for all. Moltmann writes, "The liberation of the oppressors, so that they can arrive at their own human dignity and at true human community with the others, is an experience which requires more than good will: the master has to die so that the brother can be born. Control over others must give way to community with others."[134] Dying to self and letting go of control becomes then a formative goal for Christian communities in contexts of oppressing or domination. Such contexts need not be dramatic in scope, as if there is only a binary of oppression and not-oppression in this world. Societies of competition often embed forms of domination and oppression within otherwise positive goals, casting people against each other for the honor, rewards, power, wealth, or other privileges that come with higher status, more opportunities, or more education.

This is an important issue precisely in terms of how Moltmann's methodology applies to the transformative churches, which have arisen in contexts where the participants are often choice-rich and

133. Moltmann, *CPS*, 106.
134. Moltmann, *Experiences in Theology*, 187.

opportunity-laden citizens of global powers. The expressions of these churches, then, are often asking the question of how to live, what to let go, and how to make space, the sort of questions that oppressors in the midst of liberation should be asking. Moltmann is not simply speaking theologically into such a context of oppressing, he is speaking out of such a context. Both his present context—that of a professor emeritus, living in a wealthy section of an esteemed university town in what is widely considered the wealthiest country of the European Union—and his historic context—that of a German soldier whose country contributed to the ravaging of the world in World War II and committed genocide against the Jewish people in particular—epitomize the context of oppressing that must find liberation.

Indeed, it is my argument that one reason that his theology is so helpful in particular to communities seeking their liberation from oppressing is because Moltmann's theology derives from his own quest for liberation. Moltmann's method is himself. "Theology after Auschwitz" not only seeks to answer where God was for the Jews in the concentration camps, it also seeks to answer where God is now for those who were responsible for such camps, either actively or passively.[135] This has led him away from discussing sin and guilt, which for a German of his generation is always apparent, and toward discussing hope and liberation, a topic of real interest for himself, his neighbors, and family.[136] This quest for his own liberation as an "oppressor" develops as widely as his own sense of self with and before God. This is not to make his theology egotistical or dismiss it as mere psychological musings on his own existential angst. Rather, in developing a theology that liberates his own self, Moltmann

---

135. See Moltmann's foreword in McDougall, *Pilgrimage of Love*, xiv.
136. Jürgen Moltmann, "Sun of Righteousness Arise!," 7–17 for his most recent exploration of this theme, focusing on Luther and justification as a way of orientating a liberation for the perpetrators and victims of sin.

engages questions and issues that are applicable to many in many contexts, both those of the oppressors and of the oppressed.

Indeed, this emphasis on discovering God's liberation for himself is, in a way, a curious counter to much critique used against him. Inasmuch as he is liberated, his theology is validated. Inasmuch as his theology helps provide others, in oppressing and oppressed circumstances, with their own liberation, his theology is validated.[137] It is for this reason that it becomes an especially useful task to discover how his liberating theology may in fact point toward liberation in such contexts as transformative churches.

In addition to his own works, there are key secondary resources worth noting. Richard Bauckham and Geiko Mueller-Fahrenholz have provided very helpful surveys of his overall work.[138] In addition, two other texts on Moltmann—written by Joy McDougall and Ton van Proojien—have been particularly helpful for this study as they both provide a very insightful, and I would argue accurate, reading of Moltmann's work and apply their focus in an especially suitable direction.[139]

My Method

While Moltmann and transformative churches may have overlapping concerns, it is very much the case they have distinctly different styles

---

137. Of course, this is a debatable point, and one that depends on a more holistic understanding of theology that seeks integrity and coherence in orthodoxy, orthopraxy, and orthopathy.

138. Geiko Müller-Fahrenholz, *The Kingdom and the Power: The Theology of Jürgen Moltmann,* trans. John Bowden (Minneapolis: Fortress Press, 2001); Richard Bauckham, *Moltmann: Messianic Theology in the Making* (Basingstoke, UK: M. Pickering, 1987); Bauckham, *The Theology of Jürgen Moltmann* (Edinburgh: T&T Clark, 1995). For Moltmann's eschatology—a central theme throughout all his works—see esp. Bauckham, ed., *God Will Be All in All: The Eschatology of Jürgen Moltmann* (Edinburgh: T&T Clark, 1999) and Peter Althouse, *Spirit of the Last Days: Pentecostal Eschatology in Conversation with Jürgen Moltmann* (New York: T&T Clark, 2003).

139. Ton van Proojien, *Limping but Blessed: Jürgen Moltmann's Search for a Liberating Anthropology* (New York: Rodopi, 2004); McDougall, *Pilgrimage of Love.*

of contribution. With such distinct goals, and distinct methods, it is a difficult task to determine how best to place them into conversation without putting the other on less proficient ground. My goal is not to insist either Moltmann or the transformative churches be read in a way that undermines their own priorities, but rather to allow them to communicate with, and for, each other in a way in which their respective strengths resonate. In what follows, I will describe my method for accomplishing this.

My thesis is that at the core of the theology of both interlocutors is that we are to become in the church who we are to be in this world, a becoming that is wholly oriented toward and by God in keeping with his broader mission of restoration in this world, a work that includes salvation and liberation, leading to sanctification and reconciliation. This has implications involving orthodoxy, orthopraxy, and orthopathy, all of which require coordination of various approaches to knowledge and practice in order to both reflect coherence and integrity with historic Christian theology and the contexts in which such a theology is particularly situated. This is not a dialectic in which I put the thesis of Moltmann's more systematic theology in conversation with the antithesis of a transformative church's more practical theology. I protest against a sharp line between practical and systematic theologies in general and see my interlocutors as pursuing the same basic goals in general. My goal is indeed to discover a synthesis, but through examination of these contributions as different layers or colors that can be then developed into a more complete picture. This coordination can happen best by seeing Moltmann and transformative churches as varied layers within a more holistic exploration. With this, then, my basic approach in what follows will be reminiscent of screen printing, in which a layer of a single color is applied, followed by another layer, and then as many further layers as necessary to represent a finished picture.

In transformative church theology, the uniqueness of various participants does not necessarily lead to a resolved common ground, but indeed open conversation contributes to a whole that is greater than the sum of the parts. Disagreements may persist while prioritizing method and unity. The task of reflection performed by theology interacts with the praxis of practitioners, one not dominating or dismissing the other, but rising like incense to the heavens, carrying with it a sweeter aroma of God's holistic work in our holistic existence. This method, then, assumes that a particularly Christian theology must be a theology that is with and for the church, listening and speaking, and so with this in mind I argue that such a theology must include elements that are not traditionally seen as systematic theology. For systematic theology to be truly systematic about its role, however, it must relearn how to communicate with the church, and for the church to regain its theological moorings so that it has integrity with its history and its context, it must find a way of reintegrating the insights of systematic theology.

This is a general comment on the state of theology and the church in our era as well as a specific comment regarding both transformative churches and Moltmann in particular. Indeed, while my approach here assumes they have significant strengths, they also each have weaknesses that, in my estimation, requires a particular kind of guidance. With this in mind, while this present effort may not be emphasizing a critical examination of either Moltmann or transformative churches—leaving more developed and stronger critiques for others—this project carries with it an implicit critique for both. Moltmann's theology, as a theology of experience, seems to argue for liberation of the oppressor. As such, it is not a theology that ultimately will be judged by how it coheres with academic, indeed so-called ivory tower approaches to theology, but how it provides resources for those in need of liberation, as they too need to better understand, better respond to, and better relate to God in the context of this world.

The transformative churches likewise can be critiqued for their relative size and influence as churches; however, this does not really indicate whether they are on the right or wrong track according to God's identity or work in this world. They require a more effective critique in terms of their overall guiding theology. This is necessary to help provide both support for their aims as well as correctives for the particular kinds of mistakes such churches are liable to make. In other words, while critiques from their own realms are helpful, what Moltmann and transformative churches particularly need is guidance from other realms. Moltmann's theology needs the church to help apply it, and determine how applicable it is, giving it integrity with the world. [140] The church needs Moltmann's theology to help deepen it, and determine how much it has integrity with the revelations of God and with Christian theology in general. Thus, I seek to answer the question whether the experiences of the transformative churches match, with integrity, Moltmann's theological program, and whether Moltmann's theological program matches, with integrity, the experiences of these new model churches.

Traditional approaches to Christian theology often, implicitly or explicitly, divide theology into five categories: contextual, practical, systematic, moral, and fundamental. Such divisions are not, however, inherent to Christianity or to Christian theology, and tend to reflect more the divisions that have arisen in forms of knowledge since the Enlightenment. Even after the Enlightenment, however, we have such major Christian leaders like John Wesley, whose prolific contributions cannot be so neatly divided into one category or the

---

140. See Mary Louise Brink, "The Ecclesiological Dimensions of Jürgen Moltmann's Theology: Vision of a Future Church?" (PhD diss., Fordham University, 1990), 6–8 and McDougall, *Pilgrimage of Love*, 147–49.

other. While there is a tendency to address transformative church theology within the confines of practical theology—for example, Tony Jones—this limits the discussion to boundaries that such churches reject. While Moltmann is often considered as a systematic theologian, or separately as a political theologian, his interests also do not provide rigid or simple boundaries.[141] As the boundaries are difficult to apply, and indeed shift depending on the text, I will not recognize these as separated categories, but as integrated categories that support and inform each other in both Moltmann's works and in transformative church theology as a whole. I believe this approach most accurately reflects the historic approach to theology and the church, as well as what seems to be the necessary way forward in the future for theology and the church, which have been, in general, on poor terms with each other for far too long.

Plan

Moltmann discusses his approach to Scripture and provides a framework for how he interprets the written text in *Experiences in Theology*, his last "Contribution to Systematic Theology." More than just a description of his approach to Scripture this is, indeed, a description of his theological method, and as such will provide the

141. Arne Rasmusson is especially noteworthy for considering Moltmann as a political theologian. While acknowledging Moltmann's posture as a systematician, in contrast to Hauerwas's ethics emphasis, Rasmusson interprets Moltmann's work almost entirely through the lens of his assumed political priorities, and often explicitly dismisses the particular, and actually primary, role of Moltmann's systematic developments. In doing so, he almost entirely misunderstands Moltmann's theology as a whole and thus his critiques fall short as either conceptually misguided or deficient. Arne Rasmusson, *The Church as Polis: From Political Theology to Theological Politics as Exemplified by Jürgen Moltmann and Stanley Hauerwas* (Notre Dame: University of Notre Dame Press, 1995). Bauckham, *The Theology of Jürgen Moltmann*, 99 notes, "Moltmann's political theology cannot therefore be easily detached from the dogmatic theology in which it is rooted." For a more adequate discussion of Moltmann's political theology in the context of his overall work see ch. 5 in Bauckham's text. Cf. McDougall, *Pilgrimage of Love*, 16–18.

overall framework for this present thematic study. He writes, "We shall take our bearings from the following guideline. We shall work out what in the texts furthers life, and we shall subject to criticism whatever is hostile to life."[142] From this guideline he develops eight points relating to a holistic encounter between theology and this world. In order to expand this framework wider and to embed Moltmann's more holistic systematic theology, each of the eight points will be centered around one of Moltmann's key texts in the next three chapters. I will use these texts as frameworks themselves, emphasizing certain elements and questions that can help situate the continuing discussion.

Following a study Moltmann's work, beginning in chapter 5 I will turn to transformative church writings. One approach for this conversation could be to splice in responses to Moltmann's theology throughout my examination. However, this would be using transformative church theology as more of a secondary resource, rather than letting it have its unique voice in the conversation. Thus, in each section I will discuss more fully one of Gibbs's and Bolgers's eight attributes of the transformative churches. This will, then, tie together the respective guideline from Moltmann's *Experiences in Theology*, the emphasized Moltmann text, and the transformative church priorities. In doing this, I suggest they will resonate with a shared and integrated theme that comes into focus as each layer is considered in light of the others.

One strong critique of this approach, however, is that the Gibbs and Bolger book is now relatively old. Even Jones's major study can be considered somewhat suspect, as while he published his dissertation only in the last year, his research in specific communities was conducted five years prior. Because of this, I will utilize an

---

142. Moltmann, *Experiences in Theology*, 149.

additional thematic guide along with Gibbs and Bolger. The other key text I will use was published in 2012, and thus is as recent as possible. Jon Huckins is a participant and leader in a missional community based in San Diego, California, and his text *Thin Places* describes that missional community in terms of six "postures."[143] These postures reflect a similar impulse to the Gibbs and Bolger framework, and as such provides a contemporary validation that this present discussion is not oriented around already-dated studies.[144] Following the focused discussion on Moltmann, and the transformative church voices, I will finish each section with a coordinating theological assessment that takes its guidance from all the contributors.

Figure 1.2 shows a visual representation of my plan:[145]

---

143. This book is also especially useful to me as I have visited this community and am friends with a few of the participants. Another equally relevant text is J. R. Woodward, *Creating a Missional Culture: Equipping the Church for the Sake of the World* (Downers Grove, IL: Praxis-IVP, 2012). In many ways, Woodward's book is more substantial and, indeed, theological; however the Huckins text is more focused and offers a more immediately useful framework that more adequately aligns with Moltmann's guidelines.

144. Another very recent text worth mentioning, which likewise is in many ways theologically superior to the Huckins text, is Roger Helland and Len Hjalmarson, *Missional Spirituality* (Downers Grove, IL: IVP, 2011). For my review of the latter text, see Patrick Oden, "Drinking from the Fountain That Runs with Gold," Comment, entry posted July 20, 2012, http://www.cardus.ca/comment/article/3387/drinking-from-the-fountain-that-runs-with-gold/. Huckins thus serves as a succinct representative of the present state of the movement; I am not suggesting his is a clearly superior work. His text is also especially useful as it is most directly reflecting the shared practices of a specific Christian community.

145. In his foreword to McDougall, *Pilgrimage of Love* (xiii) Moltmann wrote that "before writing each book, each chapter, and each presentation I construct a graphic diagram of the concepts, the lines of thought, the connections, and the equivalents, in order to gain clarity."

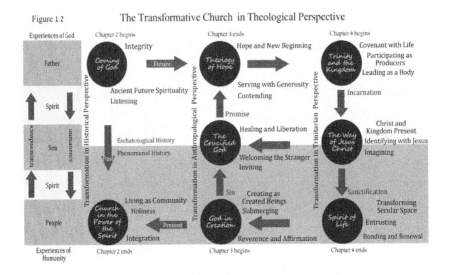

Figure 1.2   The Transformative Church in Theological Perspective

With this broadened conversation, I seek to develop a starting point that can help orient continuing research, research that includes examining the transformative church in light of its historical context. While many have discussed the transformative church within the confines of its philosophical milieu, it has not been adequately situated in terms of its similarity to other radical renewal movements throughout history. Further, as mentioned earlier, these radical movements often have the character of liberation movements, taking a specific kind of shape in contexts of oppressing. What does such a comprehensive liberation of the oppressor look like in light of historic, contemporary, and theological considerations? This is a very important task but one that requires building connections and themes, thus requiring much more space than this present work allows. Because of this, the historical and liberationist goals will have to wait for another time. This present study focuses on the comprehensive approaches of the transformative churches and the comprehensive theology of Jürgen Moltmann, thoroughly exploring these together. Such as study will suggest that becoming a beloved community is a holistic theological task that, in the power of the

Spirit, results in the people of God resonating with the life of Christ in and through this world. This is an embedded church, living together in light of God's promises in the midst of the world he loves.

2

Transformation in Historical Perspective

As this is a thematic study of Moltmann's theology, my concern is not the order in which Moltmann wrote, nor the order in which traditional systematic theology develops a cohesive study of God. Rather, my broader goal is to build a case for a program for liberation of the oppressor that can inform transformative churches, suggesting these as the communities in which a transformative messianic life can take shape. Such communities can give practical expression in return, suggesting more themes and examples for reflection. These lives, then, express God's transformative work and this work resonates outward in this world. To build this model of transformative orientation, I will use a framework that Moltmann constructs in *Experiences in Theology.* There, Moltmann notes the key in his interpretive approach to Scripture is the criterion of life, and delineates nine elements of this schema.[1] I assert that it is a helpful framework for theological interpretation in general as well, especially

---

1. Jürgen Moltmann, *Experiences in Theology*, trans. Margaret Kohl (Minneapolis: Fortress Press, 2000), 149–150.

inasmuch as liberation is ultimately concerned with life over death in all the various ways these conflict.[2] Each major section in the next three chapters will focus on one of these elements and emphasize a particular major text written by Moltmann.

The schema has a richer element of organization upon further examination, and this divides the sections into three distinct chapters each addressing a core aspect of theological inquiry. First, each has a Trinitarian pattern. While the whole of Moltmann's oeuvre is robustly Trinitarian, arguably as much or more so than any other theologian in the Western theological tradition, particular texts may not be so. Different texts seem to highlight different trinitarian persons in different ways. The present organization highlights this tendency by placing the texts in a threefold pattern, with each person finding a particular focus in each chapter, each adding to the substantive theme for each chapter.

This present chapter covers transformation in historical perspective, with the question of history in its past, future, and present forms at the center of focus. In short, the question of history is a question of integrity. How do our present experiences interact with God's eternal perspective? How does God's eschatological perspective interact with our determinative experiences of time and space? Eschatology is history, in effect, pushing us to understand the impact and flow of time in distinct ways depending on our perspective—a divine relativity. Thus, Moltmann's primary work on eschatology is not simply about future events but about interpreting our present and past in light of God's perspective and involvement. An eschatological perspective, then, radically shapes our perception of reality at every stage, and this perspective is at the root of understanding every other doctrine. I will thus devote the first half of this chapter to examining

2. See Jürgen Moltmann, *The Gospel of Liberation*, trans. H. Wayne Pipkin (Waco: Word, 1973), ch. 4.

Moltmann's primary eschatological work, *The Coming of God*. This eschatological focus highlights the role of the Father and the role of the Son, with a surprising lack of focus on the role of the Holy Spirit.[3] It is a focus on understanding our experiences in light of God's work, the future determining the past.

What do we do with this perspective within our present experiences? That becomes the key question for God's gathered people. It is likewise where we find Moltmann's first substantive emphasis on the Holy Spirit. This emphasis on our present experiences and expressions in light of the Spirit in, with, and among us thus points the discussion toward Moltmann's primary work on ecclesiology, *The Church in the Power of the Spirit*, in the second part of this chapter.

The Transformative Life Part One: *The Coming of God*

"What furthers life is whatever ministers to the integrity of human life in people and communities."[4]

In this section, I begin where Moltmann himself so often begins: at the end, with eschatology. Indeed, for Moltmann this end is not at all the end, but a beginning.[5] In this new beginning, we find the courage and faith to press onward even when circumstances overwhelm us or life weighs us down with unanswerable questions.

3. Surprising because *Coming of God* was the next major work written by Moltmann after his groundbreaking *Spirit of Life*. It seems the building pneumatological tension that we see throughout his early contributions, which did not have a separate book on pneumatology in the initial plan, finds a cathartic release in the *Spirit of Life*, so much so that *The Coming of God* hardly mentions the Spirit at all.
4. Moltmann, *Experiences in Theology*, 149, italics removed.
5. See Jürgen Moltmann, *In the End—the Beginning: The Life of Hope*, trans. Margaret Kohl (Minneapolis: Fortress Press, 2004). He notes, ix, that he took this name from T. S. Eliot's poem "East Coker," adding, "I have chosen it as way of expressing the power of the Christian hope, for Christian hope is the power of resurrection from life's failures and defeats."

This new beginning, this life of hope, is at the heart of the yearning for liberation among those who feel the chains of physical oppression. Sometimes they are able to overcome, but this does not solve the crisis. History is filled with movements in which the oppressed take power and become oppressors themselves, taking revenge on their former oppressors, or simply becoming the new oppressors over their one-time compatriots. Confronting liberation from both sides undermines the oppressive power structure itself and replaces it with a new way of living with and for each other, with and for this world. The goal in light of God's work is not to switch sides, but to enter into a new way of living.[6]

Rather than emphasizing the end, with the future ahead of us in a linear perspective of time, Moltmann sees God's comprehensive work as being outside the linear flow of our experiences, and thus capable of being embedded within our experience of God even now. This moves away from thinking of eschatology as being the future or being the end, for conceptions of the future bring with them anticipation—often fear or resignation—rather than hope. "The future offers no special reason for hope, for the past predominates, inasmuch as that which is not yet, will one day no longer be."[7] We anticipate the future in light of our current expectations and our past experiences.

In such anticipation, a person will protect the future by securing power in the present, coaxing the determinative reality towards a desired result but still constrained within the rigid bounds dictated by the past. "Because what is future is already latent in the tendencies of process, these tendencies cannot, either, bring anything astonishingly new. In this concept of time, the future enjoys no primacy and really

6. See Richard Bauckham, "Eschatology in The Coming of God," in *God Will Be All in All: The Eschatology of Jürgen Moltmann*, ed. Richard Bauckham (Edinburgh: T&T Clark, 1999), esp. 14–16.
7. Moltmann, *The Coming of God*, trans. Margaret Kohl (Minneapolis: Fortress Press, 1996), 25.

no 'principle of hope.'"[8] Because our experience of time exists on the phenomenal level, from our perspective we indeed look ahead to a future influenced by past and present. Our experience of time is irreversible and always contingent. Potentiality turns into reality, but reality does not turn back into potentiality. This experience does not, and cannot, define time itself. In contrast, a holistic Christian eschatology brings hope to the end by also speaking of eschatology as beginning, a new beginning in the midst of history, a beginning constructed by the future.

Moltmann thus suggests two aspects within eschatology that emphasize "beginning," moving away from the more popular interpretations that emphasize eschatology as "end times."[9] First, rather than thinking of eschatology solely in terms of future, eschatology is understood as *advent*.[10] "The expectation of the *parousia* is an advent hope," Moltmann writes. This advent hope involves "Christ's coming presence in glory."[11] This coming presence is—in light of Christ's transcendental future—a "messianic note of hope" that imbues the present with the future, rather than suggesting a temporary absence of Christ until a later, future, date.

According to Moltmann, time already incorporates a future that we have not yet experienced, but that already exists.[12] "The future as God's power in time must then be understood as the source of time."[13] This transcendental future does not abolish time, nor does

---

8. Ibid.

9. He writes, "The notion of linear time is not in fact biblical," adding a few paragraphs later, "the reduction of eschatology to time in the framework of salvation history also really abolishes eschatology altogether, subjecting it to *chronos*, the power of transience." This leads him to ask, "Is 'temporality' really 'the essence of eschatology'?" Moltmann, *CoG*, 12–13.

10. Cf. Brad Sargent, "*The Good News for* Marin, California," in *ViralHope: Good News from the Urbs to the Burbs (and Everything In Between)*, ed. J. R. Woodward (Los Angeles: Ecclesia, 2010), 30.

11. Moltmann, *CoG*, 25.

12. Interestingly, this is not counter to many contemporary approaches to time in physics.

13. Moltmann, *CoG*, 26.

it remain outside of time. It can enter time as we experience it, but is in no way limited to time as we experience it. It is eternity itself, which is more comprehensive than our experience of time. The transcendental future can bring reality and potentiality together in a new relationship in which reality can open itself up and be transformed into potentiality, a new reality breaking forth from it, one that moves outside the contingent flow, while at the same time incorporating that which came before within its meaning.

Indeed, in light of transcendental time, we might say that the future impregnates the present with a new potentiality.[14] Death itself is no longer the decisive experience of life, defining everyone's future as a determined event. Advent brings with it new birth and new life, a hope in resurrection that bears the power of the coming God, and thus opens up categories of eschatology that are transformative within our experiences and beyond our experiences. Eventually, this transcendent history will wholly define our experiences. The *eschaton* thus "means a change in the transcendental conditions of time. With the coming of God's glory, future time ends and eternal time begins."[15] This power of the coming God doing a new thing within our experience of time is the category *novum*. Such work is not outside of time nor dependent upon it.

For such messianic religions as are dependent on God's self-revelation, "the category *novum*—the new thing—is the historical side of their eschatological openness to the future."[16] Even declarations of judgment—God's consistent expression of justice—are embedded in prophetic declarations with messages of hope: a new reality will be borne out of the experiences of suffering, a restorative advent of

14. Thus connecting the more traditional use of the term *advent* in the narratives of Christ's birth with its eschatological meaning.
15. Moltmann, *CoG*, 26.
16. Ibid., 27.

God's redemption. With this in mind, Moltmann notes two specific characteristics of the category *novum* in the prophetic literature. The first is that "what is new announces itself in the judgment on what is old. It does not emerge from the old; it makes the old obsolete. It is not simply the old in new form. It is also a new creation."[17] Second, the anticipations of the "new future which God has promised to create casts back to the analogies of history."[18] In casting back to such analogies, however, this is not hearkening back to a restoration of what was, but pointing to how such analogies are prototypes to what is yet to be, partial expressions of a more expansive reality of God's continued work. Such are indicators, prologues, or suggested models of what God is doing.

The hope is thus not in the past, a sentimental return to the "good old days" but a hope in the future, in bringing to fruition that which was seen in part, in the past. God's work hearkens back to his earlier involvement, while it is ever expansive in the broad place of his continuing plans. This is why, as Moltmann notes, "the category *novum* dominates the eschatological language of the whole of the New Testament."[19] Moses, Elijah, and the others were forebears of the messianic mission, but Christ was not just another Moses, Elijah, or any other figure. Nor was the resurrected Jesus simply a revivified Jesus. Moltmann writes, "The new thing . . . the *novum ultimum*, is the quintessence of the wholly other, marvelous thing that the eschatological future brings."[20] The old works do not determine this "new thing" but neither is it entirely separate from them. The resurrected Christ is new to history yet contains with him the history of the crucified Christ, transfigured in light of God's eschatological

17. Ibid.
18. Ibid., 28.
19. Ibid.
20. Ibid. Moltmann adds, "What is eschatologically new, itself creates its own continuity, since it does not annihilate the old but gathers it up and creates it anew."

work, containing both the presence of phenomenal and transcendental history. God is, Moltmann reminds us, "faithful to his creation."[21] As such, the creation is new in expression, gathering up the old within its new trajectory.

This messianic moment redeems the future from the power of phenomenal history. For in that history, power "is exercised by the mighty."[22] Moltmann continues, noting that the oppressors "have to extend their victorious present into the future in order to augment and consolidate their power."[23] Perceptions and potentialities of the apparent future help determine identity for many, precisely because of the uncertainty that a self-empowered identity brings. Power must be established, protected, and expanded in order to secure a perceived identity in light of phenomenal history's suggested dangers, which are often, though not entirely, contextually formed.

It is only the "messianic moment" that offers an alternative to this determinative flow. The determinative flow is that in which the known past flows into the expected future, causing men and women to become anxious, responding with either resignation or by attempting to project power. But in that "messianic moment," "the laws and forces of the past are no longer 'compulsive.' God's messianic future wins power over the present. New perspectives open up."[24] These new perspectives open up the possibility that our love for life can exceed our fear of death. It is this latter element that drives so many attempts to establish our own future, often not only by seeking our own potential but by undermining competition by negating others, or by becoming apathetic to them.

Divisive individualization characterizes this negation and apathy. "Individualization," Moltmann writes, "dissolves the sustaining

21. Ibid., 29.
22. Ibid., 45.
23. Ibid.
24. Ibid.

relationships, making each of us the artificer of his or her own life, and exposing us to the pressure of growing competition."[25] These dissolved relationships are not only with those in our immediate context, but with all people, looking around us, behind us, and ahead of us. With individualization, there is no wider context beyond ourselves, with neither memory nor hope giving us sustenance in our identity that must be, in modernity, defined for one's isolated self. Those that cannot compete, then, are themselves discarded, ignored, or isolated, seen as offering neither gain nor competition. They become nonentities to those who define life by their attempts to establish identity in the context of history's seemingly inexorable flow, one that leads to death for all. The only real hope, then, is in the resurrection.

In the experience of Christ, the resurrection gathers all people into the power of the messianic moment even now; as such people live in the light of the Spirit's in-breaking of history. "Only the love which passionately affirms life understands the relevance of this hope, because it is through that that this love is liberated from the fear of death and the fear of losing its own self."[26] Rather than losing one's own self, thus always being anxious about the encroaching identity of others, and feeling vulnerable and fragmented, thus being easily subverted, the person who lives in the light of the resurrection is secure in their identity as being alive in Christ. The substance of Christ gives substance to each person, securing their future as participants with the open fellowship of God. This security frees people to live with openness in their particular contexts. "The resurrection hope," Moltmann writes, "makes people ready to live their lives in love wholly, and to say a full and entire Yes to a life that leads to death. It does not withdraw the human soul from bodily,

25. Ibid., 51.
26. Ibid., 66.

73

sensory life; it ensouls this life with unending joy."[27] We say yes to death only in light of resurrection hope, which allows us to no longer fear death nor be determined by false forms of identity that we think might protect us from death. "In this resurrection dialectic, human beings don't have to try to cling to their identity through constant unity with themselves, but will empty themselves into non-identity, knowing that from this self-emptying they will be brought back to themselves again for eternity."[28] The transformative process of letting go of the apparent need to force identity upon the world and becoming free to live in the eternal identity provided by God is the very definition of the liberation of the oppressor.

Instead of developing eschatology in light of these two mutually interactive experiences of history—the phenomenal and the transcendent—the relatively recent trend, especially in North American theology, has been to see God as operating solely within phenomenal history, according to our timelines. This leads us to a determinative end of this present history, which is where eternity then begins. Eternity is a temporal reference, where time has no end, a linear extension into infinity. This, then, leads to linking much of eschatology with some kind of millenarianism, and with it an embrace of the apocalyptic.

Those without faith see only the power of destruction in the future and experience fear. Those with Christ, however, have hope. "God's will for life is greater than his will for judgment. God's Yes outweighs God's No. . . . Consequently believers discern in God's No a hidden Yes, and sense in judgment his coming grace, and see in the end of this world the beginning of the new world God will create."[29] In the end is the beginning. This concept, for Moltmann, extends

27. Ibid.
28. Ibid., 67.
29. Ibid., 229.

very deeply in his eschatology, and is the key for understanding his views on judgment. Things are, and will become, genuinely bad. God is genuinely good. In the friction of these realities, Moltmann finds his theology. It is also in the friction of these realities that people have a choice of whether to contribute to the bad or to participate in the messianic renewal of all things. In choosing this latter, they become a messianic people who represent the transcendent history in the contexts of present experiences, thus, even now, making the turn toward that which is eternal and whole. [30]

It is not enough to speak of an eschatology that is only concerned about humanity. "Human life is participation in nature."[31] Therefore, human redemption includes redemption with nature. Thus, "Christian Eschatology must be broadened out into cosmic eschatology, for otherwise it becomes a Gnostic doctrine of redemption, and is bound to teach, no longer the redemption of the world but redemption from the world, no longer the redemption of the body but a deliverance of the soul from the body."[32] Moltmann is particularly interested in the physicality of God's work, insisting theology is not separate from holistic understanding. This physicality constantly grounds Moltmann's work, literally and figuratively.

Bouncing off the thoughts of Johann Tobias Beck, Moltmann develops his idea of eschatological ecology, rejecting the annihilation of the world. With this, 1 Cor. 15:28 is a key verse: "When all things are subjected to him, then the Son himself will also be subjected to the one who put all things in subjection under him, so that God may be all in all." Moltmann notes, "If God is 'all in all,' then

---

30. Eschatology thus has two sides. Moltmann, *CoG*, 255 writes, "God's judgment, which puts things to rights, and God's kingdom, which awakens new life." Cf. Miroslav Volf, "Enter Into Joy!," in *The End of the World and the Ends of God,* ed. John Polkinghorne and Michael Welker (Harrisburg, PA: Trinity, 2000), 271–77.
31. Moltmann, *CoG*, 260.
32. Ibid., 259.

the fellowship in God and fellowship in the world are no longer something separate or antithetical."[33] This concept draws upon the idea of mutual *perichoresis*, in which God and humanity interpenetrate each other. God does not absorb humanity within himself. Rather, the unity and the difference of the various diverse forms are preserved. Space, which is the self-limitation of God, becomes imbued with the fullness of his presence so that all things are within God and God is within all things.[34]

At this point, it is necessary to look again at the concept of eternity itself. What is this that is breaking into our present experiences, provoking transformation, and orienting liberation toward integrity with God and all of creation? In 1 Cor. 15:51-52, Paul writes, "We will not all die, but we will all be changed, in a moment, in the twinkling of an eye, at the last trumpet." In a moment, ἐν ἀτόμῳ, in an atom, becomes Moltmann's "atom of eternity." From this, Moltmann develops his concept of eternity within time. The fullness of time is in this moment. This is

> the completion of history and creation, its perfecting into the kingdom of glory in which God himself "indwells" his creation. If God himself appears in his creation, then his eternity appears in the time of creation, and his omnipresence in creation's space. Consequently, "time shall be no more"; it will be gathered up, fulfilled, and transformed through the eternity of the new creation.[35]

This is not the same as an end of time. Rather, God emerges within time and folds time upon itself. Time is the seed in which eternity blossoms.

He continues with an insight into our religious interest: "Eternal life has nothing to do with timelessness and death, but is full-filled

---

33. Ibid., 278.
34. Cf. Moltmann, *The Trinity and the Kingdom*, trans. Margaret Kohl (Minneapolis: Fortress Press, 1993), 109–11.
35. Moltmann, *CoG*, 280.

life. Because in historical time we experience fulfilled life only in the form of moment-like eternity, we develop a hunger for a wholly and completely unclouded fullness of life, and therefore for the life that is eternal."[36] Reorienting this hunger to embrace God's eschatological history is that transformative task, one that transforms both oppressed and oppressor. In such transformation, the promise of God is embraced as the true reality of life. This promise is the hope in participating even now in the experience of God's eternity. God's promise of wholeness transforms our values and orients the transformed person toward integrity with all God's people and all of his creation.

Time and space are one, thus agreeing with Moltmann's contention that these are not two different realities but rather two different forms of the same reality. "In the Christian understanding of God, God's eternity is something other than the mere negation of temporality—if it is the fullness of creative life—then it is possible to conceive an opening for time in eternity."[37] How is this possible in theological terms? There are two possibilities. One way is God's self-determination in terms of his creative resolve. "God resolved to be Creator of a world different from his Being, with a time different from his eternity."[38] The second is the self-restriction of God in which God made a place for his creation by withdrawing his presence from this primordial space. Space and time become a balloon of sorts, inflated within the context of God's eternity.[39]

With the eschatological moments there is an inbreaking of God's fullness within this world, corresponding to but not equivalent to the beginning of creation. "The end of time is the converse of

36. Ibid., 291.
37. Ibid., 281.
38. Ibid.
39. This is my analogy, not Moltmann's, which came to mind as I read this text and tried to conceptualize his meaning.

time's beginning. Just as the primordial moment springs from God's creative resolve and from the divine self-restriction on which God determined in that resolve, so the eschatological moment will spring up from the resolve to redeem and the 'derestriction' of God determined upon in that."[40] Using the balloon analogy again, God does not deflate the balloon, but instead eternity enters it, filling it with the same reality as was previously outside of it. The "atom of eternity" is where God's fullness enters into what was once separate and "outside" of God's being. The moment will extend to all moments, filling all with life and joy. Forward-moving, irreversible time become cyclical, as the cosmos interpenetrates the Divine, and the Divine interpenetrates the cosmos.

Eternity thus itself is the *perichoresis* of God and his creation. "The preferred images for eternal life are therefore dance and music, as ways of describing what is as yet hardly imaginable in this impaired life."[41] This idea of a created space is more than just a call for a physical room to use or a making of time for others in activities. There is a significant resonance of both God's initial act of creation and his eschatological renewal of his creation in the active opening up of space for others in the Christian community. "If in a community," Moltmann writes, "we take over responsibility for others, these others exists in a certain way in us. . . . In human community we mutually open up for each other the spaces of freedom through love, or we close them through intimidation. We are presence, space and dwelling for one another."[42] We create space by allowing others to participate with our identity and presence, to give them room for participation within the spaces we might otherwise attempt to fill or dominate.

40. Moltmann, *CoG*, 294.
41. Ibid., 295.
42. Moltmann, *CoG*, 301. Cf. Jürgen Moltmann, *Two Studies in the Theology of Bonhoeffer*, trans. Reginald Fuller and Ilse Fuller (New York: Scribner, 1967), 44–47.

Such participation together is a reflection of God's actions; it is the living out of the transformative life. This opening up of space by God entailed the risk that humans would use their freedom against God and against themselves, orienting themselves to pursue their own ends, rather than God. "Through the space conceded by God, creation is given detachment from God and freedom of movement over against him."[43] But in the created space, "the dwelling space God conceded to them," God enters "through his Christ and his Spirit, in order to live in it and to arrive at his rest," overcoming the separation caused by sin which leads to a system of oppression.[44] Restoring the likeness of God that is the process of *theosis* involves more than just ethical or moral realignment. There is a creative and creating aspect, a liberating space making in which we participate as a community to give room for others, and in doing this finding more and more space for our own participation and expansion. This orients us toward God's consummation of history, when we will "fully love God and fully love ourselves and fully love others and dwell in the world as God designed for us." At that point, "we will be at one with God, with self, with others, and with the world."[45]

The Transformative Life Part Two:
The Church in the Power of the Spirit

"What furthers life is whatever ministers to the integration of individual life into the life of the community, and the life of the human community into the warp and weft of all living things on earth."[46]

---

43. Ibid., *CoG*, 306.
44. Ibid., 306–7.
45. Scot McKnight, "Scripture in the Emerging Movement," in *Church in the Present Tense: A Candid Look at What's Emerging*, by Scot McKnight, Peter Rollins, Kevin Corcoran, and Jason Clark (Grand Rapids: Brazos, 2011), 120.
46. Moltmann, *Experiences in Theology*, 149, italics removed.

The identity of God gives integrity to all living things through their participation in his eschatological reality, which we perceive as transcendent history. The only ultimately cohesive form of identity is that which has integrity with God's identity, as it is only God's identity that provides an eternal coherence to each person within their hopes and fears, and each person with another. The awareness of this transcendent history, and the encounter with it at death, provokes fear and anxiety if one is not in a substantive relationship with the Triune God. This relationship is breathed into our phenomenal history through God's actions in our experiences of history, atoms of eternity that fill and renew, advent experiences that invigorate that which has stalled or become destructive. This is God's messianic movement into human history, and those who participate with God in this messianic re-creation participate with him, and with each other, as a messianic people in this world, testifying to life rather than death, community rather than isolation, hope rather than despair, faith rather than anxiety.[47] The church is the gathering of those who participate together as this messianic community.

In *The Church in the Power of the Spirit* Moltmann provides a substantive study of the church, though certainly he highlights the topic of community in Christ throughout all his books. In what follows, I will discuss the pertinent themes of this text that relate to our present study.[48] Having studied the source of our integrity—our life oriented with God—we can now look at the structures that

---

47. See Jürgen Moltmann, *History and the Triune God: Contributions to Trinitarian Theology,* trans. John Bowden (New York: Crossroad, 1992), 109.

48. Cf. Richard Bauckham, *Moltmann: Messianic Theology in the Making* (Basingstoke, UK: M. Pickering, 1987), ch.5. Tony Jones, *The Church Is Flat: The Relational Ecclesiology of the Emerging Church Movement* (Minneapolis: The JoPa Group, 2011), 124 remarks, "While the emerging church movement has much to learn from Moltmann's entire corpus, his ecclesiology is particularly pertinent to this study. . . . Moltmann's ecclesiology offers particular possibilities to the American church in an era in which lay participation is waxing and the potency of mainline denominations is waning."

develop this integrity in the context of others. This is not only a messianic movement outward, to those who are not yet in communion with God, but also a formation process together, a messianic development of those still finding integration with God in this present experience of history. This is important because God cannot be oppressed by us, even though we may assume positions and approaches that seek this as an implicit goal. Our pursuits of identity radically affect other people, however, so it is in the context of a shared community that such attitudes and actions most explicitly reflect our status either as oppressors or as liberating and transformed participants with God. This is a historically determined community that perceives both transcendent and phenomenal history, acting as a continued incarnation of God's mission within this present world.

Thus, it is within the setting of a gathered community that the need for present liberation confronts us, revealing the ways in which such liberation should develop, and the kinds of community that can form when all involved are dedicated to a community of messianic liberation. Learning and practicing this liberation in the community we call the church, we become transformed into the kinds of people who continue to live in these patterns throughout our lives, a messianic people in this world who are participating with God's eschatological newness to help bring renewal to all those we encounter. The transformed people resonate as the transformative community. The integrity we develop in light of God's transformational reality extends to all who encounter us, "for we are the aroma of Christ to God among those who are being saved and those who are perishing."[49]

---

49. 2 Corinthians 2:15. Jones, *The Church is Flat*, 161 notes 2 Cor. 5:18-20 as well, suggesting that a relational ecclesiology can be understood in light of the doctrine of reconciliation found in those verses.

In the preface, Moltmann notes his intent for this text. It is as radical in its proposal as it is simple in his declaration. Moltmann seeks "to point away from the pastoral church, that looks after the people, to the people's own communal church among the people."[50] In effect, this is itself a liberation goal, turning the church itself away from a mode in which a small segment of leaders exercise paternal domination—in the name and purpose of care—and toward a mode in which the gathered community finds sustenance and formation together, each member with a role of responsibility and each with a role of discovery, together forming a path of transformative discipleship.

What is the nature of this discipleship? This is the particular mission of the Spirit since the beginning of our history, reaching into the work of Jesus, and through the earliest days of the church even until our day. Concerning this, Moltmann writes, "The tradition to which the church appeals, and which it proclaims whenever it calls itself Christ's church and speaks in Christ's name, is the tradition of the messianic liberation and eschatological renewal of the world."[51] Understanding this tradition in light of the Holy Spirit, then, demands that we cannot see this is as a static or single event. Indeed, seeing a specific point of history as being the moment for God's entire revelation brings us back to the danger of epochal oppression.[52] The Spirit continues to work in each era and this messianic work

---

50. Jürgen Moltmann, *The Church in the Power of the Spirit*, trans. Margaret Kohl (Minneapolis: Fortress Press, 1993),, 8., xx.

51. Ibid., 3. Cf. Michael Frost and Alan Hirsch, *The Shaping of Things to Come: Innovation and Mission for the 21st-Century Church* (Peabody, MA: Hendrickson, 2003), 209.

52. The obvious argument against this statement would be the person of Jesus, whose presence as God among us constitutes a form of entire revelation. However, while we can say Jesus was himself, in himself, a complete revelation, the era in which he lived does not have epochal priority, as indicated by the almost entirely misguided attempts throughout history to remake the present church into an exact model of the earliest. It is the mission, not the epoch, that should define our own communal identity.

is always applied in contextual ways as the experiences of suffering, oppression, and forms of faithlessness are also always contextual.

This same Spirit "leads to the fellowship of Christ and consummates the messianic Kingdom."[53] Like history in general, the Spirit brings what is new within the contexts of what came before, not vacating tradition, but constantly enlivening, reshaping, gathering, and building anew. "Anyone who enters into this messianic tradition," Moltmann writes, "accepts the adventure of the Spirit, the experience of liberation, the call to repentance, and common work for the coming kingdom."[54] With this statement, Moltmann is essentially describing what it means to be part of the church, this messianic people who represent God's transformation and newness in the midst of each society, and in the midst of all of creation, becoming a people who resonate this transformative reality, a reality that reflects the Spirit's work in the messianic mission of Christ.[55]

In keeping with the messianic moments of Christ's life, death and resurrection, the church must continually orient itself toward Christ in any given context, each person finding their identity in Christ rather than any form of unrest or finite responses to such existential or societal angst.[56] This is not spiritualizing such palpable forms of disquietude, but rather beginning with the fact that is only in Christ that we gain a transcendent orientation that allows our responses to find integrity in light of God's holistic renewal. "It is only where Christ alone rules, and the church listens to his voice only, that the church arrives at its truth and becomes free and a liberating power

53. Moltmann, *CPS*, 3.
54. Ibid.
55. Cf. Michael Frost and Alan Hirsch, *ReJesus: A Wild Messiah for a Missional Church* (Peabody, MA: Hendrickson, 2009), 11.
56. Cf. Jürgen Moltmann, *The Spirit of Life*, trans. Margaret Kohl (Minneapolis: Fortress Press, 1992), 201.

in this world."[57] The church is a participant in the messianic renewal of Christ only as far as it is oriented toward Christ in light of its contextual experiences.

In the power of the Spirit, the church is the messianic representative of Christ in its context, proclaiming the name and filling the content of understanding about Christ by how it conveys its mission. Christ is the ultimate subject in the church in this way. Moltmann writes that "every statement about the church will be a statement about Christ."[58] He goes on to note that every statement about Christ thus implies a statement about the church. However, the finitude of the church itself—it is a representative of Christ, but one that is often bashed and battered by the storms that rage in each age—means that Christ is not synonymous with the church, but rather the orienting concern about which the church must constantly reorient itself in light of the unrest of its contexts.

This mission is a messianic mission, and the messianic mission is "not to spread the church but to spread the kingdom."[59] This places Moltmann's ecclesiology in the context of his broader theology, as the kingdom is understood as a holistic testimony to the full work and being of God. The church has a role in the work of God, but it is not itself the goal of the work of God. Thus the church, and its practices, are liable for critique in light of the overarching eschatological purposes of God's messianic mission in this world. This messianic mission, ultimately, is the only real source of ecumenical unity as it is only in light of the transcendent history of God that we find integrity with ourselves and with others. Those who are drawn into, and adapt themselves toward, the messianic mission "are becoming the church of the coming kingdom of God."[60] The

57. Moltmann, CPS, 5.
58. Ibid., 6.
59. Ibid., 11.

eschatological reality gives definition to the church as the church of Christ, and in this integrity of definition the church carries the people and the society into discovering the kingdom of God in their midst.

Moltmann proposes three dimensions in which the suffering and death of the Messiah Jesus press forward in the life and mission of the church. A church "which sees itself as the church under the cross" should "perceive all three of these dimensions."[61] The first is a liberation from the compulsion of sin. This is not a legalistic form of holiness or separateness, which confirms the power of compulsion of sin rather than providing liberation from it.[62] Instead, the cross and resurrection demonstrate the power of God over those forms of bondage, proclaiming their finite status in light of God's transcendent entry into our history, and calling for a holistic expression of holiness that reflects God's identity in this world.[63] The guilt that results from the compulsions of sin was the guilt that Jesus took upon himself at the cross. This is, Moltmann suggests, why he was silent at his own trial, as he reckoned himself with the transgressors (Luke 22:37). Moltmann goes on to note that the trial has been reopened in light of the resurrection, which justifies his righteousness and with him the righteousness for all who believe in him. In this new trial, which seems to be the history of our era since the resurrection, "the church has to appear as witness," and "the real question at issue is the question of the divine righteousness."[64] Jesus had no witnesses at his original trial and so gathers witnesses on his behalf, witnesses to the resurrection who can testify to his righteousness.

---

60. Ibid., 13. Cf. Moltmann, *Theology of Hope*, trans. James W. Leitch (Minneapolis: Fortress Press, 1993), 333.
61. Moltmann, *CPS*, 86.
62. See ibid., 89.
63. Cf. Patrick Oden, *It's a Dance: Moving with the Holy Spirit* (Newberg, OR: Barclay, 2007), ch. 5.
64. Moltmann, *CPS*, 87.

THE TRANSFORMATIVE CHURCH

The next dimension of the messianic mission is "the liberation from the idols of power."[65] This is a political liberation, though not liberation through the normal channels of revolutionary politics, which likewise justify the very system they are purportedly fighting. The cross, after all, represented the taking on of the guilt of blame by three distinct forces in his era. Christ took on unrighteousness in light of the religious reasons as he was put on trial by the Jewish leaders. He took on the rage of the zealots—those who sought structural changes in their society and the fears of those who sought to prevent such changes—by not being chosen for freedom, as they instead chose Barabbas, one more beneficial to their cause. He was crucified by the Romans to quell unrest, to be a sign for those who sought freedom not to seek it. Because the "idolization of political power and the religious legitimating of economic, social and political conditions of rule are compulsions which no people and no society and hardly any political movement escapes," those in the church are compelled to undermine oppressive and oppressing structures, even those which may suggest a compatible goal.[66] The *Pax Romana* is an enticing pursuit, after all, and can take many forms, with many justifications, in a given society. The *Pax Christi*, in contrast, stands against oppression and oppressing, projecting a peace based on freedom and hope.

With this form of peace, with their stand *for* the people, the messianic community confronts the second danger that comes with seeing politics and religion together. In light of the cross, political action is always "from below," which is the only form of action that itself resists becoming oppressive because it stands with the outcasts and rejected. As a messianic people, those in the church do not identify with the powerful or seek symbols of strength and

65. Ibid., 89.
66. Ibid., 90.

wealth to legitimize their claims for the kingdom, but instead share solidarity with the people who have no power. Moltmann writes, "Wherever remembrance of the crucifixion of Christ revived in the church, it produced estrangement from the religious legitimation of the political authorities and solidarity with the people whom they were humiliating and persecuting."[67] This is not political separation or isolation, a suggestion that religion and politics should not mix. That suggestion is likewise to legitimate the political powers as holding a segment of ultimate authority on many key issues related to life and thriving. This fellowship is "called into life by Christ's self-surrender" and "serves to reconcile the world through solidarity with the suffering of the people and through participation in the representative work of Christ."[68] Rather than being a source of power and domination, acceding to the structures of oppression and oppressing even if seeming to confront the present power holders, the messianic community testifies to the Messiah from the place of the forsaken and rejected, which is the place of the cross.

The messianic mission is one of identifying also with the godforsaken, those who experience squelched lives and dashed hopes, for it is these who have run out of choices in terms of the standard religious, social, and political options as they stand in present society. "Fellowship with the crucified Jesus is practiced where Christians in solidarity enter the brotherhood of those who, in their society, are visibility living in the shadow of the cross; the poor, the handicapped, the people society has rejected, the prisoners and the persecuted."[69] This means that the fellowship with Christ does not simply encourage including the poor in our services or reaching out to them or giving them what we think they require, acting in paternal

67. Ibid., 92.
68. Ibid., 96.
69. Ibid., 97.

ways. Rather, this fellowship insists on involving ourselves in true solidarity, seeing them not as objects to fix but as people included in our fellowship, the fellowship of Christ.

Indeed, it might even be said that it is not our choice to include them in our fellowship with Christ but to seek their fellowship so as to be included with Christ who is already with them. This then becomes a church that is not only proclaiming Jesus as Lord but also indeed actually expressing such in its formative structures. As Moltmann writes, "Church must first of all reflect and represent the lordship of Christ in itself."[70] A particular church reflects a particular kind of lord, which is not always the lord it claims to serve.

Participation in the messianic mission orients the community toward those outside the church as well. When the church is oriented toward the mission, rather than the mission being oriented to the structures of the church, then "the question is not how people or happenings outside the church respond to the church, but how the church responds to the presence of Christ in those who are 'outside', hungry, thirsty, sick, naked and imprisoned."[71] The church, if it is to be the church of Christ, is integrated into the mission of Christ, as the messianic people, participating in the ministry of Christ in their contexts. As Jesus himself ministered outside the confines of clearly established religious settings, with a clearly regulated polity, so too does the body of Christ reflect this. *Ubi Christus, ibi ecclesia* is the continuing definition of the church, with the prioritization being on the pneumatological presence of Christ's continuing mission in and for this world, rather than the object-oriented possession of Christ that people must attend to within the confines of the church. Moltmann writes that "it is a matter of the church's integration in Christ's promised presence."[72] As the Spirit mediates this presence

70. Ibid., 106.
71. Ibid., 129.

now, the church exists where Christ is present and Christ is present in the manifold ways the Spirit is working inside and outside of established ministry settings.

The individualized assertions of identity based on fragile egos finds confrontation and alternatives in the context of those who are free within their identity in Christ, free to be whole and thus free to enter into community with others without competition or destruction. This arena of freedom is the messianic community, the church of the free people who are seeking freedom for others. This freedom does not only involve freedom from others, it also involves freedom for one's own self, as it is the false form of identity that perpetuates a slavery to one's own actions.[73] The ego always attempts to form identity in contrast with others. When churches perpetuate seeking meaning in differentiation, which involves a heightening of one's own sense of self and a depreciating of others, they not only point away from the messianic renewal of all life, they also offer a false form of justification for oppression and suppression, baptizing false forms of identity in the name of Christ, even as Christ himself rejects such attempts.

Instead of perpetuating such finite, and ultimately destructive, responses, a liberating church is a fellowship of persons "free from ego-identity; a fellowship of the justified, who no longer have to justify themselves on the basis of their own characteristics; and hence a fellowship of the unequal and different, held together by free and courteous recognition."[74] In this fellowship, the liberation of oneself and the liberation of others is a continual process, enabled by community, which both highlights continued conflicts and provides

72. Ibid.
73. See ibid., 222. Cf. Romans 7 and 8.
74. Moltmann, *CPS*, 188.

substantive responses. Such liberation is the very definition of the transformative life enabled and oriented by the Spirit of God.

In short, the messianic community is not one of rhetoric nor is it limited to existential debates about distant forms of salvation. In the messianic community, liberation is the expression of sanctification, the enacting of holiness in the processes of our daily existence, transforming a people in the messianic community so they can be messianic people in the midst of their contexts. "Christianity," Moltmann writes, "is not yet the new mankind but it is its vanguard, in resistance to deadly introversion and in self-giving and representation for man's future."[75] The church is, then, the anticipatory community, representative of the new ways of living and being together in this world. It is the community whose orientation is not finite forms of power, wealth, or oppression, but rather is found in the eschatological integrity of God himself, a transcendence that then orients the participants to have increased integrity with God, with each other, with all those in their contexts, with all of creation itself.

In his identity, God's integrity extends to all his creation and thus those who seek integrity with him participate together in transformative integrity with all of creation. "If Christian anticipation is directed toward the resurrection and eternal life, then it will encourage everything in history which ministers to life, and strive against everything that disseminates death."[76] Those who seek this life are "therefore determined by anticipation, resistance, self-giving, and representation."[77] They orient themselves toward a renewal of life and orient themselves away from destruction of life. Because life is not within our ability to define or perpetuate, such orientation

75. Ibid.
76. Ibid.
77. Ibid.

cannot be ego oriented, structured upon finite forms of identity and perpetuating the structures that are based upon promoting one person's, or one group's, identity in contrast to others. Instead, the community gains legitimacy only "by the Messiah and the messianic future, so that through their profession of faith, their existence and their influence, people, religions and societies are opened up for the truth of what is to come and their powers are activated for life."[78] The messianic people are within society, joined in a messianic fellowship committed to finding identity in light of the identity of Christ, proclaiming the messianic promise of life and living in the ways of life, transforming unredeemed structures from within.[79]

The messianic community, then, "is the fellowship which narrates the story of Christ, and its own story with that story, because its own existence, fellowship and activity springs from that story of liberation."[80] This is why conceptions of church are wrong when they see themselves as centers of worship or the arbiters of faith or the location of religious activity. This messianic fellowship is much more than that; it is a transformative community, with such transformation driven by a "fellowship of hope, which finds freedom for the perspectives of its society through the perspectives of the kingdom of God."[81] This messianic fellowship is one that "liberates men and women from the compulsive actions of existing society and from the inner attitudes that corresponds to them, freeing them for a life which takes on a messianic character."[82] This messianic fellowship entails an ecclesiology that organizes itself according to these themes, with its practices shaping and reinforcing the story, the hope, and

---

78. Ibid.
79. Moltmann, *CPS*, 212 writes, "The certainty of faith does not separate men and women from the world, but leads them into deeper solidarity with unredeemed creation, in so far as this faith is itself hope for the redemption of the body."
80. Ibid., 225.
81. Ibid.
82. Ibid.

the liberation of a renewing people of God, orienting itself according to the messianic mission inaugurated by Christ. This mission is not one of words but "experiential, communal and enacted."[83] And it is only as such that a community participates in the mission of Christ through the power of the Spirit and it is only inasmuch as they participate in this mission that such a community truly is the church of Christ.

83. Tim Morey, *Embodying Our Faith: Becoming a Living, Sharing, Practicing Church* (Downers Grove, IL: IVP, 2009), 49.

3

———

Transformation in Anthropological Perspective

Two reluctant German veterans of the Second World War provided what is arguably the most substantive way forward for Protestant theology after Barth and Bultmann seemingly closed the chapter on the Enlightenment theological project. These veterans, Moltmann and Pannenberg, could thus be accurately described as postmodern theologians, though not in the more conventional use of the term as describing forms of continental deconstructionism. They each would resonate more with the forms of postmodern thought discussed above, though not intentionally so and not entirely so. They each sought to construct a theology after Barth and both, in their own way, point to substantive themes in how this can be done.

Pannenberg attempted his reorientation of theology through the topic of history, pointing to ways in which history can and should be a source for theological engagement.[1] For Moltmann, however, the topic of creation points toward a new theology, one that is inclusive of nature. Moltmann's way forward after modernity is an integrated approach that proposes a way to reshape community with each other, with God, and with all of creation. Modern attempts at domination and dismissal resulted in either devastation or disillusionment, a theology that veered more toward Gnosticism's devaluing of physicality than Jewish inclusion of it in understanding the work of the divine. For we are a physical people, in a physical world, participating in a linear experience of time that does not exclude God, nor encompass God. Finding our identity restored within this comprehensive awareness of God's creation is the only way we can find a holistic, hope-filled, perspective about how then we shall live, and in finding this perspective we can begin to live in transformative ways that reflect this hope.

This is, essentially, an anthropological focus, though not one that emphasizes human potentiality or progress in an idealist sense. Rather, following Moltmann's strong emphasis on God's sovereignty and work as the defining characteristic for our identity, we find true anthropological understanding only through an understanding of God's reality and work in this world. In other words, it is through God's work that we understand ourselves. In this chapter, I focus on God's work as it particularly relates to understanding our context, our crisis, and our hope. It is through this work that we find transformation in anthropological perspective, answering what God's work means for us as people in this world.

---

1. Although itself a highly interesting study of personal interest, Pannenberg's contributions in this respect are far outside the bounds of this present work. See F. LeRon Shults, *The Postfoundationalist Task of Theology: Wolfhart Pannenberg and the New Theological Rationality* (Grand Rapids: Eerdmans, 1999), for further discussion about Pannenberg's method. See Patrick Oden, "Spirits in History," in *Interdisciplinary and Religio-Cultural Discourses on a Spirit-Filled World: Loosing the Spirits*, ed. Kirsteen Kim, Veli-Matti, and Amos Yong (New York: Palgrave Macmillan, 2013) for a discussion of Pannenberg's use of history specifically, especially as it relates to the idealism of Hegel's historiography and new models of historiography.

This work initiates in the very creation of the *cosmos*. As part of this creation, we find our integration with God's work in us as we are integrated in God's whole work, a holistic embrace of divine activity that gives us meaning in light of all that has been created. This is, essentially, a pneumatological focus. Moltmann emphasizes that when he is talking about God in creation, he is talking about the Spirit's initiating and sustaining work in particular. In this chapter, I will thus begin this divinely oriented anthropological discussion more closely, beginning with a study of *God in Creation* and addressing how we can reshape community with creation in light of the Spirit's continuing work.

The initial work of creation quickly becomes a topic of restoration, as a humanity made very good become divisive and destroyers as they seek identity without God. So much is this the case that it seems the evil introduced to the world becomes itself the defining experience for the world, a world groaning in subjection and a humanity lost in suffering or lost in causing suffering. There is few better illustrations of this in world history than the context of the Holocaust. Where indeed was God in light of Auschwitz? That is a profoundly anthropological question, as it strikes to the heart of our experiences and our relationships with each other. Yet there is no way we can justify God's identity as God in light of this question without considering God's place and role in even this most pernicious event. Where is God in the midst of suffering? He is there in the midst of it. This is the God who was crucified, who enters into our humanity and our human suffering, confronting false forms of meaning and identity, taking on the fury of such, experiencing forsakenness in its most stark forms. Thus, the second part of this chapter will turn to *The Crucified God* and look how we can reshape community with the victims and casualties of this present experience of life.

Finally, I will turn to *Theology of Hope* and look at how we dwell with a God who understands, who is with us in this present experience, and who offers a substantive promise for renewal, a hope that defines, ultimately, the shape of this new messianic community. It is, after all, only through hope in God that we can be open to each other and to this world in light of God's hope for us. In the previous chapter, the focus began with an emphasis on God's eschatological work that highlights the role of the Father and the Son, then moved into the Spirit's role in our present experience through the church, thus orienting a historical perspective. This present chapter begins with a focus on the Spirit within the world's history, following the narrative to and through the fall and Christ's work of restoration, ending with a focus on God's promise as the destiny of hope for his people. As in the last chapter, I shall develop these themes through the interpretive lens of life that Moltmann proposes in his *Experiences in Theology*.

The Transformative Life Part Three: *God in Creation*

"What furthers life is whatever spreads reverence for life and the affirmation of life through love for life."[2]

In light of God's identity being the only coherent source of identity for people and all of creation, the goal for those who participate in God's transformation can no longer be domination or subjection or control, but rather living in light of God's creative love. Identity is formed in light of this new stance, and the whole identity of a person becomes involved in community with people and everything. Moltmann has noted that this is the "greening" of his theology. "Since *God in Creation* I find this very important," he says; "modern man

---

2. Jürgen Moltmann, *Experiences in Theology*, trans. 149, italics removed.

wants to become the ruler of the earth, subdue the earth, but this is a great misunderstanding. We are part of the earth."[3] This brings to mind one emphasis of Blumhardt, who also had a "green" theology. "Blumhardt had a special relationship to the earth," he says. "You find traces in Barth and also in Bonhoeffer. Be faithful to the earth. Bonhoeffer said to his fiancé, 'Our wedding should be a yes to the earth.' And this is a situation when Berlin was in ruins, his fiancé was far away." He then added, "Or like Martin Luther planting an apple tree. If the world would come to an end tomorrow that is a yes in the face of the no, and the yes is stronger." Love is a constant yes to life, a stance of hope and a stance of believing in the potentiality of someone or something. This hope, this love for life, points toward the eternal nature of salvation but is not limited to a distant moment of judgment.

True love, God's love, sees time with all its moments, so that someone who loves believes in redemption from the past, experiences of acceptance and fruition in the present, and hopes for sharing a holistic community into the future. This is the messianic promise. Moltmann notes that for Paul, "The raising of the crucified Jesus is the beginning of the End-time process of the raising of the dead, and with that the new creation of the world."[4] With this in mind, the body of Christ is the body of Jesus who was raised from the dead and the body of Christ that is the church. This is the community of the risen Jesus, where the Spirit who participated and participates throughout creation manifests through the gifts that "are the energies of the new eternal life."[5] This work of the Spirit emphasizes the

---

3. The following quotes are from Jürgen Moltmann, interview by author, Tübingen, Germany, May 18, 2011, beginning at 1:08:25. Cf. Jürgen Moltmann, *Sun of Righteousness, Arise! God's Future for Humanity and the Earth*, trans. Margaret Kohl (Minneapolis: Fortress Press, 2010), 79–82.
4. Moltmann, *God in Creation*, trans. Margaret Kohl (Minneapolis: Fortress Press, 1993), 66.
5. Ibid., 67.

"bodily character of the gifts . . . because it is in the new bodily obedience that they are experienced."[6] The fear and anxiety that arise from experiencing this world in a bodily manner find redemption and redirection in the work of the Spirit, leading the individual and the community to live in new ways with this world, pointing toward and exhibiting the renewed life. As men and women no longer see the world as something that defeats them, but something within which they are integrated as part of the holistic work of God, then they no longer have to define themselves over and against creation or their contexts, but see their definition with the Spirit as being itself part and parcel with the Spirit's holistic work in their specific context. The messianic people become integrated in the ecology of their location as they participate in the energies that evokes a messianic love for their whole contexts. This is a redemptive presence, not a dismissive, dominating, or destructive presence.

Moltmann notes three "concentric circles" that he sees in the writings of Paul that arise from this redemptive reality. First, the "children of God, who have already been seized by the first energies of the Spirit, long for liberty."[7] They receive a new direction but still experience the weight of this phenomenal history's determinative flow. Second, this longing for liberty means a longing for redemption from "the body of death."[8] Suffering still exists, and in many ways is emphasized, as people reject it as the way things should be. Third, "believers are bound together in a common destiny with the whole world and all earthly creatures."[9] The desire for liberty is not, and cannot be, a desire only for one's own liberty, nor even just for human liberty, as the Spirit who evokes this is working to bring renewal to the entire world. Moltmann writes,

6. Ibid.
7. Ibid., 68.
8. Ibid.
9. Ibid.

"The liberty which believers lay hold of in germ through the Spirit is not an exclusive liberty from created being and from the body. It is an inclusive liberty, for these things too."[10] These "things" are nonhuman creation. Creation, after all, did not begin with humanity, and so what came at the end of the creation narrative in Genesis is the beginning of the new narrative: "It starts with the liberation of the human being and ends with the redemption of nature."[11]

The closing off from the world that occurred in many premodern and modern theologies closed the community of Christ from fully participating in the broader work of God, resulting in new forms of bondage, ones with religious and theological justification, rather than new expressions of liberation.[12] "The human being who is closed in upon himself finds his correspondence in the nature that is sealed off and therefore dies. The person who has been opened up for a new hope for life finds his correspondence in the nature which has been thrown open for its own future."[13] We are saved with the world, or we die with the world. We experience shared destinies of either slavery or liberty. If we separate ourselves from the holistic work of God we embrace a slavery of nature and thus of our own selves, which will be reflected in forms of community that are oppressive, dismissive, competitive, or disintegrating.

If we join with the holistic work of God, seeing ourselves in light of the ecological movement of God's holistic activity, then we put aside fear and anxiety and take up thanksgiving. An oppressive community becomes a eucharistic community.[14] The eucharistic

10. Ibid.
11. Ibid.
12. See ibid., 69. Here Moltmann writes, "The messianic knowledge of the world starts from the expressed hope of faith in the raised Christ and sees a correspondence to this in the sadness and longing for liberty of imprisoned creation."
13. Ibid., 69.
14. See ibid., 69–71. He writes of the intended identity of a person, "To express the experience of creation in thanksgiving and praise is his designation from the very beginning, and it is also the content of his life in is consummated form. The human being does not merely live in the world

community, then, exists within this world with an attitude of thanksgiving for the continuing work of God, celebrating God's continuing redemption of this fallen world as part of this redemption process. This is the song and dance of life, a celebration and a feast that sees what is possible in the Spirit rather than what is determined by the past.[15] Once again, the *novum* and advent of creation exhibit an ecclesial principle, arising from the beginning of creation and drawing us to its eschatological fulfillment. This ecclesial principle is one of liberation, and is derived both from eschatological perspective on God's transcendent future and God's holistic work of creation, thus deriving from both our future and our past to orient us in an integrated way within our present as a messianic people.

The initial work of creation is without analogy, a new reality formed from the creative purpose of God, with the beginning being "the sheer, unqualified precondition for all happening in time, rather than the beginning of time itself."[16] With this in mind, Moltmann affirms the idea of *creatio ex nihilo*, noting that the act of creation is without any presuppositions or prior substance. It is not a making, it is a creating. This creating is an exclusive act of God, deriving not from any preformed substance, but rather "out of" a negation of substance. That which was not became what is. There was not, according to Moltmann, a preexistent something named nothing, but rather it really was a lack of anything, nonexistence itself. There is nothing equivalent we can perceive or imagine that would fit this category. We can form and shape, but do not create. Creation only

---

like other living things. He does not merely dominate the world and use it. He is also able to discern the world in full awareness as God's creation, to understand it as a sacrament of God's hidden presence, and to apprehend it as a communication of God's fellowship. That is why the human being is able consciously to accept creation in thanksgiving, and consciously to bring creation before God again in praise."

15. See ibid., ch. 11.
16. Ibid., 75. See also ibid., 74. Here Moltmann writes, "Wherever and whatever God creates is without any preconditions. There is no external necessity which occasions his creativity, and no inner compulsion which could determine it."

derives from the actualizing imagination of God himself, a "divine resolve of the will to create" rather than an impersonal emanation of his essential nature.[17] This means that creation is arbitrary in a way, though this word tends to suggest meaninglessness or impersonal chance. Creation was a decision of the Triune God to express a new thing and to have a formative relationship with it in eternal communion.[18]

This excludes a supposed arbitrariness, for the God who is free has chosen in his freedom to create. Rather than an arbitrary movement of divinity, a personal God has made an expression of a particular creation an expression of his personal identity.[19] This identity then gives definition and communicates the goodness and integrity that forms the basis of this creation. God created something new, and that newness is wholly derivative from God's expressed self.[20] Indeed, this is not just new creation, it is declared good and humanity is declared very good. One perceives even an aesthetic goodness in all of what God has done, an aesthetic goodness that God celebrates within himself, inviting others to this celebration, this feast of new life.[21]

Creation is re-created. It is here that the doctrine of *creatio ex nihilo* presses forward as a necessary doctrine in Christian theology, as God's determinative authority asserts itself over determinative history. In the context of Creation, the seeming determinative force is that of Nothingness, the Void. If God is merely a participant in the swirling chaos, a sustainer but not encompasser or Creator, involved but not definitive for what exists, then he is among this swirling chaos, not

17. Ibid., 75.
18. Ibid., 76, where Moltmann writes, "Creation is not a demonstration of his boundless power; it is the communication of his love, which knows neither premises nor preconditions: *creatio ex amore Dei*." See also Moltmann, *GC*, 82–86.
19. See ibid., 80–81.
20. Ibid., 85, where he writes, "In his creative activity, God employs his inner, divine self."
21. See ibid., 76.

defining it but being himself defined by it. Moltmann writes, "If the idea of the *creatio ex nihilo* is excluded, or reduced to the formation of a not-yet-actualized primordial matter 'no-thing', then the world process must be just as eternal and without any beginning as God himself."[22] This is either relegating God to a secondary status in the order of the universe, thus re-asserting the gods of nature over and against the One God of Genesis, or depersonalizing God to be the process, not the person, in the midst of creation's endless cycle.

The God who creates and interacts with his creation expresses continued interaction through the messianic intervention, and this intervention expresses God's original creative ideal, which includes liberation. God's particular work with the Son and with the Spirit gives this liberation a substantive orientation.[23] In other words, there is not just a goal to keep in mind—the goal of God's creative act—but humanity also must align with the method, the "how" of creation. "Our purpose," Moltmann writes, "should be to find a deeper understanding of the creative God."[24]

Moltmann asserts the *creatio ex nihilo*, but that opens up another question. What, in light of God's presence, is this "nothing" in which God created? God determined that he would create, and in this determination enacted a change in his own self. As the determinative presence and identity, it was only by acting first within himself that anything could begin to be newly created. "Before God issues creatively out of himself," Moltmann writes, "he acts inwardly on himself, resolving for himself, committing himself, determining himself."[25] Part of this inward action was an act of withdrawal, a making of space so that nothing could be present in order that a new, created something fills it. This self-withdrawal is a choice by

22. Ibid., 78.
23. See ibid., 90–93.
24. Ibid., 85.
25. Ibid., 86.

God to create a space in which his creative work can fill, move, and shape.[26] God withdraws in order to make a space in which he can be extroverted in his work, working outward into a nothingness that has been itself created by his voluntary withdrawal. Moltmann applies the term *zimsum* to this self-limitation in the process of creation, following the proposal of Isaac Luria. It means "a concentration and contraction, and signifies a withdrawing of oneself into oneself."[27] In this way, we can see the Philippians hymn as reflecting not simply a work of Jesus in his own self-humiliation that brings glory, but also a consistent pattern in the work of God from the time of Creation. *Zimsum*, it might be said, is the *kenosis* of the Father in the activity of creation. Moltmann notes that theologians have discussed this throughout history, as they "saw that when God permitted creation, this was the first act in the divine self-humiliation which reached its profoundest point in the cross of Christ."[28] A pattern of God in creating becomes a pattern of the Son in redemption and a pattern of the Spirit in re-formation.

In both creation and redemption, the nothingness is not over and against God, but something that God is able to enter, create, and renew. In the original creation, God fills the void with something new. In his work of redemption through history, that which is pointing away from God leads to the emptiness that is not God, and God seeks to overcome such nothingness. Moltmann writes, "If we compare the processes of creation as they are described, we can see initial creation as the divine creation that is without any prior conditions: *creatio ex nihilo*; while creation in history is the laborious

---

26. Ibid. Moltmann writes, "It is only a withdrawal by God into himself that can free the space into which God can act creatively."
27. Ibid., 87.
28. Ibid. See also ibid., 89. Moltmann writes, "The movement from God's initial self-limitation to his eschatological delimitation in respect of his creation can best be grasped if we compare the process of the original creation with the process of the new creation.". Cf. Moltmann, *The Trinity and the Kingdom*, trans. Margaret Kohl (Minneapolis: Fortress Press, 1993), 202–22.

creation of salvation out of the overcoming of disaster."[29] God's creation out of nothing is the initial affirmation of his creation against that nothingness, an affirmation that continues as God works in the processes of history to reorient this creation away from its trajectory toward death and emptiness. God has invested himself in the cosmos, and invested himself in a particular way.

God "pervades the space of God-forsakenness with his presence."[30] This is not an authoritarian imposition against his creation, annihilating what he made. Instead, it is a renewing act to bring what is now oriented back toward nothingness into a continued relationship with God's presence: the messianic mission that carries forward the original intent of creation. "God overcomes sin and the death of his creatures by taking their destiny on himself; and he overcomes in his own eternal Being the Nothingness which lies heavy over sin and death."[31] God turns himself against the nothingness that threatens his creation, the determinative trajectory that is a sin-oriented history, which is most fully expressed in the acts of oppressing and oppression that on the one hand push people toward their loss of self, and on the other hand carry others forward into a wrong projection of self, each expression an affront to the creating God.

God, though he is able, does not play the part of the oppressor in contrast to this world, but carries forward as the Creator, sustaining and recreating that which is oriented away from his eternal identity. This orients, then, his mission in a particular way. Those who seek to join with him must also be oriented in this particular way if they are to be participants rather than opponents of his method for creation and salvation. In identifying themselves in the Son's act of obedience,

29. Moltmann, GC, 89.
30. Ibid., 91.
31. Ibid., 90.

humanity becomes participants with this mission inasmuch as they continue to be oriented toward the method of God in his redemptive works. God who created by self-limitation, into which space could be made for the existence of other participants, carries this mission of creation forward through "inexhaustible patience and his active capacity for suffering as the root of his creative activity in history."[32] God remains open to others even as they close themselves off to him, confronting their nothingness with his fullness.[33]

He chooses his creation, even when his creation has chosen against him. "By enduring this breach of communication, God keeps their future open for the beings he has created; and, with that future, he also keeps open the possibilities for conversion, or a new direction, which it offers."[34] God does not only keep open the possibility, however, as though his creatures must make the long trek back into his graces. He does not create then withdraw back into himself, away from the nothingness and then away from what fills the nothingness. He engages both the original state of the nothingness and, in the midst of history, the nothingness toward which determinative history is now oriented. He opens up creation and he opens up history.

This is a proactive opening, a participatory work of God in God invites humanity to participate with him, as images of his self within his creation. People find fullness in their lives as they are oriented back toward God's life and into the mission that he pursues through his creation and redemption. "As the image of God on earth, human beings correspond first of all to the relationship of God to themselves and to the whole creation."[35] This image reflects the inner relationships of God to himself, and manifests outward to creation. This then is the very essence of being for men and women, who

32. Ibid., 211.
33. See Moltmann, *TK*, 105–13.
34. Moltmann, *GC*, 211.
35. Ibid., 77.

can correspond to God in their love and openness to the other, not seeking domination but seeking the fullness of the other. "As God's image, men and women are his counterpart in the work of creation. The human being is the Other who resembles God (Ps. 8.5)."[36]

This likeness, Moltmann notes, should start as an insight about God. "It first of all says something about the God who creates his image for himself, and who enters into a particular relationship with that image, before it says anything about the human being who is created in this form."[37] We are like God in that we can be in relationship with God, corresponding to God in our relationship to the rest of creation, and a counterpart with God in providing response and interaction with him, appearing in this way as the goodness of God—the splendor of God—among each other and among all of creation. It is in this identification with God himself that we participate first as relational beings with an orientation toward freedom and love with and for each other. This substantiates our identity as created beings within this world.

That impulse with which God created becomes our impulse in participating with him in this creation. As God's image, with his likeness, we can be people who love wholly and freely, without having to define ourselves over and against each other or over and against nature itself. God's image in humanity, then, takes shape as we encounter that which is in and around us as well.[38] Moltmann writes, "The whole person, not merely his soul; the true human community, not only the individual; humanity as it is bound up with nature, not simply human beings in their confrontation with nature—it is these which are the image of God and his glory."[39] God, who needed no others outside of his triunity to give definition to his

36. Ibid., 77–78.
37. Ibid., 220.
38. Cf. Phil. 2:5.
39. GC, 221.

106

identity, created freely and opened himself up to the free response of his creation. In doing this in our own context, we become participants with God, resonating his image within and around us, enlivening rather than stifling, invigorating rather than depressing.

It is the expression of God toward this world, a turning toward all of creation, that not only invites but indeed ontologically insists upon a humanity that, together, reflects back to him the self-similar expression of his own creating identity. God, in creating, creates a cosmos of community that enters into relationship with him and, by definition, with each other as a holistic image of God. This image is carried in always particular instances, in always specific contexts, an infinite complexity of eternal relating that encompasses each person into the whole mission of God. The term *expression* is an apt one here, as this word often more specifically refers to our facial features. God's openness toward this world is, as Moltmann reminds us, often indicated by the idea that he turns his face toward us. He writes, "The face of God is a commonly used symbol for God's turning to men and women in kindness, for his attentive mindfulness and his purposely directed presence."[40] When we perceive someone face to face, we are seeing them as distinct individuals, of value and worth and specific identity, and as counterparts, another like us. Indeed, the formation of a healthy psychology comes, initially, from the recognition of the faces of others, the face of mother and father, our personal creators and sustainers, whose orientation toward us with open freedom orients us to become people who are free to be who we should be.[41]

This activity of God in turning toward us is itself the decisive reality in which we participate or we resist, but even in our resistance,

40. Ibid.
41. See James Loder, *The Logic of the Spirit: Human Development in Theological Perspective* (San Francisco: Jossey-Bass, 1998), ch.4–5.

we cannot escape the ultimate intent of God. "Human sin may certainly pervert human beings' relationship to God, but not God's relationship to human beings."[42] God's relationship to human beings, however, changed from open participation with God into the trajectory of redemption, a re-creation. It is this process that encompasses the mission of God, involving humanity within its way of redeeming the whole world, giving significant insight into the fullness of God, our own identity, and leading to the promise of ultimate rest in and with God.

The Transformative Life Part Four: *The Crucified God*

"What furthers life is whatever heals broken relationships and liberates life that has been oppressed."[43]

A critical theology of the cross makes criticism of the church a radical venture, as each church must be oriented to the crucified Christ in order for it to be, indeed, a Christian church. The cross is "the criterion of their truth and therefore the criticism of their untruth."[44] In this way, then, the church is a microcosm of humanity in general, given identity by this particular Christ and only in this identity finding substantive identity for continuing life. The reality of this man Jesus orients the life of the church, the man who died in a particular way with a particular mission. This transformative mission invites those who are broken, breaks those who are oppressing, and gathers together friends and strangers into the shared fellowship of

42. Moltmann, *GC*, 233.
43. *Experience in Theology*, 149, italics removed.
44. Moltmann, *The Crucified God*, trans. R. A. Wilson and John Bowden (Minneapolis: Fortress Press, 1993), 2. He writes, "When churches, theologians and forms of belief appeal to him—which they must, if they are to be Christian—then they are appealing to the one who judges them most severely and liberates them most radically form lies and vanity, from the struggle for power and from fear. The churches, believers and theologians must be taken at their word. And this word is 'the word of the cross.'"

God. The goal of Moltmann's text *The Crucified God* is to understand this work of Christ as it relates to the very identity of God and to understand God's continued presence with us in our suffering. Here he addresses most fully the driving question of much of his theological life: the question of Auschwitz. Such a question is, essentially, the question of the Other, the Other that is God, the Other that we may dismiss or alienate. Alternatively, it is a question of ourselves as the Other, the ones who are excluded, wondering where God is in our experiences of persecution, suffering, and exclusion. The testimony is that the Other is with us, not Other at all unless we are asserting ourselves in contrary ways to the mission of God.

Those in the church cannot appropriate this mission for their own benefit or to further their own goals. Moltmann writes, "The crucified Christ himself is a challenge to Christian theology and the Christian church, which dare to call themselves by his name."[45] Inasmuch as they may try, they distance themselves from Christ in the process and thus establish their own markers for the knowledge of good and evil. Thus, an ecclesiology that embeds oppression is antichrist, orienting itself in contrast to the mission of Christ, representing Christ in name but opposing this mission in practice. The cross confronts such oppression and in its absurdity offers a constant challenge to attempts to develop theology. Moltmann writes that it is "the cross alone, and nothing else" that is the test of Christian theology, "since the cross refutes everything, and excludes the syncretistic elements in Christianity."[46] Only a theology that takes the cross seriously, with all its challenges and confrontations, firmly establishes the mission of Christ as Christ himself initiated it.

45. Ibid., 3.
46. Ibid., 7

This substantive contribution must be transformative rather than serving to justify societal expressions of domination or distortion. Because the effects of sin have long (almost since the beginning) become established in individuals and in the institutions such individuals develop, a Christian theology of the cross confronts both these internal distortions and the external structures, a holistic encounter with particular contexts for what they are.[47] A theology of the cross looks inward and outward and it orients theology vertically and horizontally. "There is no vertical dimension of faith opposed to a horizontal dimension of political love, for in every sphere of life the powers of the coming new creation are in conflict with the powers of a worlds structure which leads to death."[48] In the incarnation and on the cross, God oriented our vertical theology in a horizontal manner, and oriented our horizontal theology in a vertical manner. If we are to serve God, we are to serve Christ, and

---

47. See ibid., 23. Here Moltmann writes, "Personal, inner change without a change in circumstances and structures is an idealist illusion, as though man were only a soul and not a body as well. But a change in external circumstances without inner renewal is a materialist illusion, as though man were only a product of his social circumstances and nothing else." Moltmann has often been critiqued for lacking a substantive discussion of personal sin. See Joy Ann McDougall, *Pilgrimage of Love: Moltmann on the Trinity and Christian Life* (New York: Oxford University Press, 2005), 123 and 162–64. This, however, is an argument from silence, suggesting that Moltmann's tendency to emphasize societal and structural sin implies a gap in his theology of personal sin. However, as this quote suggests, Moltmann certainly appreciates the importance of personal sin as a matter for theological and ecclesial discussion. However, as he is apt to ignore that which is fruitfully discussed elsewhere, his writings tend to emphasize the political and social aspects of sin rather than the inner and personal. Moltmann responds to this critique in his foreword to McDougall's book, xiv, noting, "When I searched for a 'theology after Auschwitz' in 1972, I followed the path of Christ's passion and his descent into hell into such depths of evil that the concepts of sin, guilt and godlessness were struck out of my hands." He goes on to note that "a robust doctrine of sin was not possible for me thus far." In my conversation with him, he notes agreement with Pannenberg's understanding of sin as a relational orientation—sin being egocentric rather than the exocentricity modeled by God—adding a particular nuance that to egocentricity must be added the expression of sin in which one gives oneself wholly to another insufficient identity. Exocentricity must be rooted in our identity with God, in our fullness as a person before God—not rooted in either ourselves or another person or group. See Jürgen Moltmann, interview with the author, Tübingen, Germany, May 17, 2011, beginning at 40:18.

48. Moltmann, *CG*, 24.

if we are to serve Christ, we are to serve the people who Christ served, a messianic mission of hope that embedded itself upon the ultimate symbol of oppression, participating with the suffering as the suffering. Transcendent Christian theology finds its relevance in the same place the transcendent God established his identity in contrast to worldly forms of domination and control. "The crucified Christ became the brother of the despised, abandoned and oppressed."[49] A Christian theology must orient itself around the same concern, a concern that then embeds the church within the particular instances of despising, abandonment, and oppression in its particular context.

If a community aligns itself with Jesus, they are aligning themselves with those who are unlike themselves. This is a principle of fellowship with those who are different, who are outsiders. These outsiders do not have the ability, or have abandoned such attempts, to compose a self-justification that orients itself around establishing identity in the context of a society's attempts to define meaning.[50] "By alienating the believer from the compulsions and automatic assumptions of an alienated world, Christian identification with the crucified necessarily brings him into solidarity with the alienated for this world, with the dehumanized and the inhuman."[51] Those who bear witness to Christ express this witness in solidarity with Christ in fellowship with those who have abandoned or have been excluded from false forms of righteousness.[52]

The primary element of the theological challenge of the cross is that it undermines assumptions of power, control, and honor. Because such assumptions are part of our establishment of identity within the structures of our context, the cross then confronts us as a negation, a violation of who we want to be in light of our

49. Ibid., 25.
50. See ibid., 27
51. Ibid., 25.
52. See ibid., 28.

contextual approval. The cross is antidesire, not the fulfillment of notions of enlightenment or transcendence. "It is," Moltmann writes, "the suffering of God in Christ, rejected and killed in the absence of God, which qualifies the Christian faith as faith, and as something different from the projection of man's desires."[53] This is faith because it is not something we would want, for ourselves or for our perceptions of God. If we want the cross, we do not understand the cross.[54] If we understand the cross, then we understand that the cross itself negates even religious attempts to define and establish God, so we are alienated even from our religious attempts to define ourselves in light of a conception of God that emphasizes only his power and dominance.

Those who seek to align themselves with God, then, align themselves with this Christ, which is not an existential alignment but a real expression of identity substantiation.[55] "To the extent that men in misery feel his solidarity with them, their solidarity with this sufferings brings them out of their situation."[56] Those who have no identity, or who have only meager scraps and wallow in sins to cover their gap, are given the identity that Christ maintains. The powers of this world do not rob God of who he is—only God has the power to forsake himself—so he is able to establish himself on the side of those who are in need of substantive identity and being. With this, if men and women "understand him as their brother in their sufferings,

53. Ibid., 37.
54. Cf. Matt. 20:20–28. Moltmann, CG, 38.
55. See CG, 41. Here Moltmann writes, "But the more the church of the crucified Christ became the prevailing religion of society, and set about satisfying the personal and public needs of this society, the more it left the cross behind it, and gilded the cross with the expectations and ideas of salvation. . . . This is to maintain the significance which the cross has come to have in the context of the process of one's own salvation, one's own faith, and one's own theory of reality, and to suppress and destroy the unique, the particular and the scandalous in it." We assert on the cross our own understanding of good and evil, and modify our understanding of the cross to fit what we already think we know to be true. The fruit that was taken from the tree is put back on the cross, with equally unfortunate results.
56. Ibid., 51

they in turn do not become imitators of his sufferings until they accept his mission and actively follow him. He suffered on account of the liberating word of God, and died on account of his liberating fellowship with those who were not free."[57]

For those who are in need of a substantiating identity, Jesus becomes their brother in their brokenness and exclusion. They are already on the cross, rejected and despised. For those who have options and can assert their identity upon or against others, the cross becomes a challenge, not about moral legitimacy but about eternal identity. This makes the cross an eschatological reality, and to follow Christ means to follow this crucified Christ outside the bounds of contextual identity formation. "It is," Moltmann writes, "a call into the future of God which is now beginning in Jesus, and for the sake of this future it is not only necessary but possible to break one's links with the world which is now passing away and abandon a concern for one's own life. The call to follow Jesus is the commandment of the eschatological moment."[58] The issue of identity is important to make because with that in mind, the cross is not simply about suffering, which can bring honor and acclaim. Instead, the suffering of the cross disputes the forms of honor and acclaim, as well as traditional ethical authority. This was not an argument over who was right about what was wrong, but an argument about who had the right to establish identity and control over people's lives. The cross was an intersection of human attempts to establish identity and the act of God's resistance to such attempts, putting himself at the crux of the matter.

This was an ultimate stance of rejection. Jesus was abandoned not only by the world but also by the Father, situated on the cross in the place of all those who have been both rejected and distant from God. "To die on the cross, means to suffer and to die as one who is an

57. Ibid.
58. Ibid., 55.

outcast and rejected."[59] It is the place of curse, of religious and social alienation. Jesus becomes a stranger to those who seek to establish identity through social or religious means. Those who follow Christ either meet him where they already are, on the cross of their own sufferings, or they go with him to the place of rejection, suffering a rejection and bitterness that comes with forsaking alternative forms of identity. The image of the God who suffers, the Messiah on the cross, dying at the hands of multiple human expressions of identity and power—religious, political, physical—establishes a break. Jesus cannot be syncretized.

He was confronted by and confronts the attempts to assert the knowledge of good and evil as determined by human perspective, an attempt that is, in essence, always about dismissing the need for God as he is. "If he sees and believes God in the actual suffering and dying Christ," the God who actually is, "he is set free from the concern for self-deification which guides him toward knowledge."[60] A substantive and adequate theology of the cross will create, by necessity, a contrast between the identity in Christ and an identity that finds substance in the political, social, cultural, or religious orientations within a given society. A theology of the cross "right down to its method and practice, can only be polemical, dialectical, antithetical and critical theory."[61] A theology of the cross is "also crucifying theology, and is thereby liberating theology."[62] By liberating theology, it liberates those who experience rejection, dismissal, and abandonment. The cross is, one might say, an invitation to the stranger to participate anew.

Such a theology also seeks to liberate those who are finding their identity through forms of inadequate theology that imbue syncretic

59. Ibid.
60. Ibid., 69. See especially ibid., 71.
61. Ibid., 69.
62. Ibid.

notions within theology, fruits of the tree that suggest knowledge but lead to death. The cross, in contrast, is the work of the new Adam who rejects the fruit of the knowledge of good and evil as suggested by the many contextual purveyors, and instead faces the void for what it is, a confrontation, ultimately, between good and evil, and being and nonbeing. On the cross, Jesus experiences the fullness of forsaken identity. This is, then, the place Christian theology also must start. [63] The cross is a crossroads.

Jesus was rejected by the establishment who sought to rob him of his personhood and identity. He was dishonored, in Roman terms, and cursed, in Jewish terms, a nonperson treated as one rejected by the society in which he was born. It need not have been this way. He could have found honor, glory, and fame within the identity structures offered by his context—the very essence of the temptations in his wilderness experience. In his rejecting of such forms of identity, Jesus asserted his identity in obedience to the Father, suffering the determinative consequences of such an assertion in his context. Moltmann writes that a theology of the cross "does not state what exists, but sets out to liberate men from their inhuman definitions and their idolized assertion, in which they have become set, and in which society has ensnared them."[64] It liberates by presenting an alternative, like with the tree in the Garden.

The cross is also, then, the crossroads of a Christology from above and a Christology from below. The theological difficulties of the cross return us to the most basic questions of human and divine identity. Who are we and how do we commune with God? Moltmann writes, "The question about God which it assumes is that of finite being seeking the infinite being of God which imparts permanence."[65] Humanity seeking infinity—fullness in Moltmann's

---

63. Ibid., 70.
64. Ibid., 72.

conception—is the perspective in which we encounter the cross, where we encounter the negation of that search in the forsakenness of Christ. That is the natural end of the human attempt to determine identity, both a dying human and the death of God on a cross. Only an answer "from above" can then carry this further, but the experience of this answer involves the willingness to face the negation from below, the deresolution of self and forms of identity that continue to thrust attempted answers to feebly address our negated questions.[66] The answer that comes from above is oriented toward our stance below, with the obedience of Jesus on the cross an answer and a testimony to the human situation.

The cross is the place we let go of our attempts to formulate an answer from below to the existential problem of our finitude. This is a stance of absolute faith, letting go of what makes sense in order to embrace God's future. "By confessing Jesus as the Christ, faith also confesses that this future of his is real. Its confession of Jesus does him justice when it also anticipates the future for the sake of which he existed, died and was raised."[67] Thus, in faith we let go of what we know and can apprehend, only seeing the vision of the broken, cursed, and outcast, letting go of forms of attempted dominance that seek to assert our identity, asserting our proactive answers to the problem of our own self upon the world.[68] We forsake our own self—including all forms of oppression and domination that assert our identity for its own sake—for the sake of God who is the only one that can contribute substantive selfhood. One must "accept the openness of one's finite existence in order to recognize its fulfillment of one's own openness."[69] This openness is a place of negation without the resolution of one's entire substantiation. It is

65. Ibid., 89.
66. Ibid., 106.
67. Ibid.
68. See ibid., 213.

a risk, putting our risk in God rather than ourselves. This is a risk because on the cross God negates human philosophy about the divine and Jewish anticipation of the messiah. This is a God who experiences suffering and a Messiah who is broken by the established oppressors.[70]

Because of this, Moltmann writes, "this means that for Jesus there cannot be disciples of his teaching as there were in the case of Socrates, and after the death of Socrates."[71] Jesus intentionally embedded his ethical and religious teaching within the context of the events of his life, and the central event of this was his suffering and death on a cross. By personalizing his teaching in his obedience on the cross, he committed his teaching to the judgment of his future. Ethics and eschatology, past and future, humanity and divinity are also forsaken with Jesus on the cross. "Jesus," Moltmann writes, "associated his eschatological word with his human person and his vulnerability, and therefore with the fate which overtook him."[72] This event is, thus, also the crossroads of determinative history and eschatological history. Which has the final say? Which history determines identity of Jesus and identity in general?

His death then instantiates both his teaching and Christian theology in general, uniting his proposals for how we are to live and what we are to expect. Salvation does not come from domination, nor the establishment of identity through competition or contrasting with others. Jesus did not defend himself in the trials that sought to establish his identity in the context of human proposals. Jesus commits his whole identity to the Father, even facing ultimate forsakenness in doing so, the loss of his entire human and divine identity. This then, is a problem for theology. It is where theology

69. Ibid., 89. Ibid., 109n20 notes that "this openness-fulfilment pattern was continually used for the verification of revelation."
70. See Ibid., 215–19.
71. Ibid., 122.
72. Ibid., 123.

stops and then starts again in an entirely new conception of reality and identity. "The death of Jesus on the cross is the centre of all Christian theology. It is not the only theme of theology, but it is in effect the entry into its problems and answers on earth. All Christian statements about God, about creation, about sin and death have their focal point in the crucified Christ."[73] This man on a cross is the face of the God who sustains our own identity. "When the crucified Jesus is called the 'image of the invisible God', the meaning is that *this* is God, and God is like *this*."[74]

The objection to this image of a man crushed and broken, suffering both physical pain and the emotional pain of alienation, being the image of an almighty God is obvious. However, this objection continues to insist that phenomenal history determines meaning and that human systems of identity formation substantiate God. This is precisely what Jesus is rejecting. By dying on the cross, Jesus is asserting that human validation or achievement does not form identity but that identity is formed in obedience to God.[75] In the event of the cross, God identifies with the rejected and outcast, participating in the place of the sinner, while at the same time dismissing the notion that human systems even have the ability to reject and cast out a sinner who deserves death.

The cross confronts false or temporary forms of peace by refusing to accept it as true peace. As such, a theology of the cross can never be merely a private faith or a nonpolitical faith, as the very reality of the cross is both public and political, taking a side with those who are outsiders. The cross stands against those who are proposing alternative forms of identity and society based on assumptions that may overlap, in part, with the kingdom preached by Christ, but

73. Ibid., 204.
74. Ibid., 205.
75. Cf. Dave Kludt, "The Good News for Los Angeles," in *ViralHope: Good News from the Urbs to the Burbs (and Everything In Between)*, ed. J. R. Woodward (Los Angeles: Ecclesia, 2010), 43.

that always seem to exclude as many as they include. This leads Moltmann to write, "Faith in the crucified Christ is in the political sense a public testimony to the freedom of Christ and the law of grace in the face of the political religions of nations, empires, races and classes. Between faith in Christ and the deified rulers of the world, the person cults and the social and political fetishes of society, Jesus himself stands."[76] Indeed, this very definitive and confrontative nature of the cross is why the cross is at the heart of a liberation of the oppressor possibly even more than at the heart of a liberation of the oppressed (for whom the resurrection bears more substantive hope). The cross is a choice, a choice by Jesus to be crucified and a choice by the various political factions to crucify him.[77] Just as Moltmann noted that the pursuit of the liberation of the oppressor is a dangerous task, so too "the recollection of his crucifixion is something both dangerous and liberating."[78] It is dangerous because it involves the dominant identifying with the forsaken, to include themselves among the godforsaken—the strangers in society and before God—in order to participate with Christ.

Jesus did not just identify with the godforsaken in their struggles, he was forsaken himself on the cross. The testimony of his death suggests pain and struggle, both external and internal suffering, an act of obedience that led into crisis, not into immediate victory. Moltmann writes that we can "understand it only if we see his death not against his relationship to the Jews and to the Romans, to the law and to the political power, but in relation to his God and Father, whose closeness and whose grace he himself had proclaimed."[79] The cross seemed to indicate that God rejected the message Jesus preached

76. Moltmann, *CG*, 145.
77. Ibid. Moltmann here writes, "Christianity then poses the question, for resolution by open trial: Christ—or Caesar?"
78. Ibid.
79. Ibid., 146.

just as Jesus was himself rejected. However, while this is not ultimately the case—as the testimony of the resurrection validated Jesus—the experience of the cross *was* the experience of God encountering ultimate rejection and the decisive experience of being apart from God.

As the Spirit is the Spirit of life, and the presence of God is the source of life, the death of Jesus was not simply a rhetorical or symbolic gesture. In death, Jesus was forsaken as God by God; otherwise, he could not have truly experienced death.[80] The experience of Jesus was one of rejection, where his pain and death was seemingly decisive about his authority and message. Indeed, it was decisive, but not in how Jesus was wrong. Instead, it was a decisive moment in understanding who God is, what God is doing, how God is doing it, and whom God is including. Those who are forsaken, who are poor in Spirit, are blessed because in their forsakenness Jesus identifies with them; these are the people whose life share his own experiences and those are the people with whom he was cast. They are blessed because then, with Jesus, his future becomes their future.

The Transformative Life Part Five: *Theology of Hope*

"What furthers life is whatever leads to the new beginning of life in hope."[81]

The cross is not the end. If the cross was the end for Jesus it would have been the end of his mission and it would have been the end of the testimony his disciples had about him. The cross was a crossroads. As a crossroads, the cross is a substantive work of God that reveals

---

80. See ibid., 151.
81. Moltmann, *Experiences in Theology*, 149, italics removed.

God's work and reveals God himself, orienting humanity toward a particular trajectory in this work. The cross *was* the end of life, end of the life of Jesus and end of the validations that alternative forms of identity seek to provide. Those all lead to death, the death of oneself and the deaths of others. In the work of God on the cross, however, the trajectory did not end with death, but passes through the cross to offer hope, a hope that begins by negating alternative forms of identity and the accompanying determining effects of history. On the cross, all are gathered together. Broken relationships are healed in the light of the cross and the cross orients a new way of liberation. Again, however, this is not an isolated work. The work of the cross is a substantive work of healing and reconciliation because of the work of God that defines it, the eschatological history that breaks into the world in the resurrection and resonates the definitive eschatological history of God throughout all of his work in, with, and for this world. This is our future and it is our hope. It is where hope begins.

In his beginning, for Moltmann, was the end—the study of eschatology as the formative basis of hope. His text *Theology of Hope* was the book that launched him onto the global theological scene, not only for academics but also for a broader readership. While reading Bloch's considerations on hope, Moltmann was struck how this theme was so inherently part of the Christian story and yet so unconsidered in theological studies and church life.[82] Yet the work of God in this world is a work that should bring hope to those who struggle and who are discouraged by life experiences.[83] This book sought to view all of theology through the single lens of eschatology

---

82. See Moltmann, *Theology of Hope*, trans. James W. Leitch (Minneapolis: Fortress Press, 1993), 9.

83. Ibid. Moltmann here writes that "for me, the God of promise and exodus, the God who has raised Christ and who lets the power of the resurrection dwell in us, is the ground for active and for passive hope." Indeed, in my book *How Long? The Trek Through the Wilderness* (Newberg, OR: Barclay, 2011) I sought to bring this theology of hope into a more conversational and contemporary context, looking at it through the lens of an emerging church community and the exodus narrative.

and did so with the unifying theme of hope as that which reaches into our lives from the work of God.

As a book on eschatology, one might assume that his later book, *The Coming of God*, has essentially superseded the earlier, and as I have already covered that book in the previous chapter, that it might seem extraneous to discuss yet another version of Moltmann's eschatology. For some, it might make sense to talk about *Theology of Hope* in order to discuss the development and possible refinement of his overall theological program from his first major work to one of the last of his "Contributions." Yet, as this present work is a thematic study, rather than one focusing specifically on Moltmann's own trajectory—which has been well treated in other texts—my goal here is to see how his *Theology of Hope* can add a unique element to, ultimately, a comprehensive liberation of the oppressor and, more immediately, a program for transformative ecclesiology.

Essentially, *The Coming of God* derives from *inquiries from above*, looking at the work of God from God's own perspective, attempting to discern the nature of the cosmos through the revelation that has been given to us about God's perspective, and in that revelation to understand how God seems to be bringing ultimate resolution to the seemingly unformed and chaotic. With his *Theology of Hope*, however, we have what might be called an eschatology that derives from *inquiries from below*, an eschatology that seeks to understand God's work from our own perspective, and leads us to consider what this means for us as individuals, as people in general, and as a specific community seeking to participate with God's work. This places it quite usefully within the flow of study that began this chapter with the topic of creation and then discussed the event on the cross. *Theology of Hope*, along with *God in Creation* and *A Crucified God*, helps comprise a thematic study of creation, salvation, and re-creation from below, a liberation theology from an anthropological perspective that informs a transformative community.

Eschatology from an anthropological perspective does not mean a projection of our identity or desires into the future—though many develop eschatology in this way. Instead, eschatology from an anthropological perspective understands the process of God's work and asks, then, what this means for those of us whose lives are still oriented within a seemingly determinative and certainly phenomenal history.[84] How should a theologically adequate eschatology shape our priorities, expectations, and interactions? Moltmann answers that question in this first major work, a question that arises out of Moltmann's own struggles to come to terms with the identity of God, and the identity of his people, after World War II, and especially after Auschwitz.[85]

Eschatology that is one of hope embeds the experience of life within the promise of God.[86] It is only in light of this promise, and

84. See Moltmann, *TH*, 16–19. I should note that "eschatology from an anthropological perspective" is my term, not Moltmann's, and I suspect Moltmann would not be entirely comfortable with that description of *Theology of Hope*. My suggestion here is that while both *Theology of Hope* and *The Coming of God* are oriented in a similar direction, Moltmann develops his themes in different ways, first addressing more of what it means for us in his first book, and then filling out more deeply the themes related to God's perspective in the second. I would suggest that it is in themes of God's experiences and an overall perspective on history that Moltmann has adapted and developed more over the last few decades, while his anthropological comments on hope, and what it means for our participation with God and with others, has remained more constant. Moltmann's increasing embrace of a kind of universal history, here adapting the proposals of Joachim of Fiore, lead him closer to Pannenberg's proposals of revelation in history. Moltmann's developing understanding of history is worth its own specialized study. For a worthwhile, yet brief, examination see Laurence Wood, *Theology of History and Hermeneutics* (Lexington, KY: Emeth, 2005), 197–224.

85. I would suggest that, in this, Moltmann is using the Blochian theme of hope to respond to the Blumhartian despair, revitalizing Cristoph Blumhardt's themes in many ways, however without the naïve assumption of inherent human progress that had been demolished first in the trenches of World War I and second, decisively in the concentration camps of World War II. Moltmann, *TH*, 25 writes, "Hope alone is to be called 'realistic', because it alone takes seriously the possibilities with which all reality is fraught. It does not take things as they happen to stand or to lie, but as progressing, moving things with possibilities of change." Cf. Jürgen Moltmann, "The Hope for the Kingdom of God and Signs of Hope in the World: The Relevance of Blumhardt's Theology Today," *Pneuma* 26, no. 1 (2004): 4–16.

the God who promises, that life can be oriented in light of what is hoped for but not yet experienced. Moltmann writes,

> In order to attain to a real understanding of the eschatological message, it is accordingly necessary to acquire an openness and understanding vis-à-vis what "promise" means in the Old and New Testaments and how in the wider sense a form of speech and thought and hope that is determined by promise experiences God, truth, history and human nature.[87]

This real understanding of the eschatological message is provided by promise inasmuch as God himself defines his work through promise, initiating his work, declaring it certain before it is completed, and then defining relationships with people based upon their reception and response to the promise.

This model is an example of God's work being self-similar across scales, so that the broad and expansive exodus narrative shares a commonality with the event on the cross, the work throughout history sharing a commonality with the work in specific lives.[88] As such, Moltmann suggests that the doctrine of the revelation of God is itself embedded within eschatology: we know God because of what he promises and what he accomplishes—which is different than approaching revelation through asserting philosophical proofs or projecting humanity's questions about God and self.[89] God is the God who says he will act and then does act.

Moltmann notes three conclusions that come from this understanding. First, "God reveals himself as 'God' where he shows himself as the same and is thus known as the same. He becomes

---

86. For a critical study of Moltmann's use of promise in, especially, *Theology of Hope*, see Christopher Morse, *The Logic of Promise in Moltmann's Theology* (Philadelphia: Fortress Press, 1979).

87. Moltmann, *TH*, 41.

88. Cf. Morse, *The Logic of Promise in Moltmann's Theology*, ch. 4.

89. See Moltmann, TH, 43.

identifiable where he identifies himself with himself in the historic act of his faithfulness."[90] God is God when God acts as God says he will act. This is palpable involvement in historical situations. God asserts his determined intent in contrast to history's determining flow. Moltmann writes that "God himself" "cannot then be understood as a reflection on his transcendent 'I-ness' but must be understood as his selfsame-ness in historic faithfulness to his promises."[91] Our understanding of God, then, comes from his faithfulness in accomplishing the acts that he is determined to accomplish.

In our participation with God we do not encounter a static entity who awaits our arrival, or a topic that can be described by a description of characteristics or facts, but "a name of promise, which promises his presence on the road on which we are set by promise and calling."[92] In this way, God is, in essence, continually determining himself. God puts his own Godhood at risk—risking whether he can be faithful and if he will be faithful. Is God who God says God is? We have hope because in God's promises God is involving his own identity. This is the second aspect of faithfulness. In his faithfulness, God "keeps faith with his promises and thereby remains true to himself."[93] Knowledge of God then is also dynamic, as it comes to understand God in light of his work in history—the past promises and past faithfulness—but does not constrain knowledge of God to facts about the past.[94] True knowledge of God is expectant, awaiting, involved as it applies the lessons of the past to present situations. To know God is to risk God with God. This risk with God then risks our own selves as we commit to the knowledge of

90. Ibid., 116.
91. Ibid.
92. Ibid., 117.
93. Ibid.
94. See ibid., 118. Here Moltmann writes, "Just as the promises are not descriptive words for existing reality, but dynamic words about acts of a faithfulness to be awaited from God, so knowledge of God cannot consist in a resume of the language of completed facts."

God in our participation that reflects the reality of the promise rather than the reality of the determinative history. "It is a knowledge," Moltmann writes, "that oversteps our bounds and moves within the horizon of remembrance and expectation opened up by the promise, for to know about God is always at the same time to know ourselves called in history by God."[95] As an expression not of what we say or what tradition we affirm, but how we live, knowledge of the promise participates with God as this knowledge transforms our participation in this world.

Third, "the guarantee of the promise's congruity with reality lies in the credibility and faithfulness of him who gives it." This avoids abstraction in that it unites a hope in God for himself with hope in what God himself promised will happen. Hope is substantive because it is hope in the God who is faithful and credible, and this hope is in God's coordination of his identity with his action, a hope that is in God himself and also in what God commits himself to, a substantial hope in his practiced lordship, in his accomplished peace and his asserted righteousness. Hope then derives from the faithfulness of God in the past combined with an expectation that this God of the past is the God who is promising in the present for a particular future in which God remains true to himself. Our experiences are not determinative for God, but rather God creates what is new in the midst of experiences, the fulfillment of the promise. In this fulfilled expectation, a person embodies hope and resonates the declaration of God's identity, which is yet again confirmed. This does not exhaust knowledge about God but points even to further and deeper and richer fulfillments as the promise itself is never ultimately exhausted.

This orientation of faithfulness with the identity of God then makes the promises a part of our faith, an awaiting, and a trajectory within that awaiting that orients itself toward what we know already

95. Ibid.

about God's promises and his identity. In holding onto the promise, we do not put the trust in our own identity, nor are we the force to confront those who oppress us, but align ourselves with God. That is the risk of promise, and in God's identity is the source of our hope. This hope brings with it new experiences and "brings the human spirit to an ever new and restless transcending of itself."[96] The oppressor, in contrast, is committed to determinative history and its experiences and its end.

Oppression is setting ourselves up as the guarantors of our own expectation or of the expectations of others, dominating so as to accomplish in and of ourselves the establishment of our own identity. Oppressors set themselves up against God as they oppress those who he desires to have freedom. They array themselves against the promise as they lead others into alternative forms of identity and as they depress someone's awareness of God's promises to them. As God sets his identity up as the essential guarantor of the promise, opposing liberation (in a true sense, not an apparent sense) is opposing God's identity itself. In confronting his identity with their own, then, oppressors face judgment, as their identity cannot be sustained in that confrontation.[97]

The promise of God is the fulfillment of God, as God will do what he says he will do. The hope confronts circumstances in light of God's declarative identity and confronts oppressors as those who are not in line with God's identity or his promises. This means, then, that hope is not an otherworldly, ethereal, or mystical hope, but a present hope in awaited fulfillment of God's work in our contexts. As a specific promise for particular people, this hope is not a general hope, some kind of vague religious sentiment concerning

96. Ibid., 120.
97. On a personal note, at this point of writing, my wife came into the room and said that we needed to go to the hospital. That weekend, on Easter Sunday, my beautiful little girl Vianne Rose was born.

a notion of the divine. The particularity of the specific God who works in specific ways in specifically promising specific expressions of faithfulness leads to specific responses in specific contexts as people are oriented within the trajectory of this promise. The particular promise then gives a particular hope to specific people whether they experience oppression or act as oppressor, leading to a life of change. In the resurrection, there is new life in light of Christ's continuing promise.[98] Participation in this life with Christ brings realization of the hope contained even in our present experience of life.[99]

The identity that Christ promises to his people, then, substantiates each particular person as a particular subject in God's particular mission. They do not lose their identity, becoming a drone in a collective. Rather the promise of resurrection is a process of a person becoming who they fully can be. The hope in God is hope in one's own future in which a person achieves identity and blossoms into fullness. The resurrection leads a person past the work of the cross, in which history and the past finds resolution, and into the future where a person can truly be who they are in the community of others who are similarly becoming. "Communion with Christ," Moltmann writes, "the new being in Christ, proves to be the way for man to become man. In it, true human nature emerges, and the still hidden and unfulfilled future of human nature can be sought in it."[100] The goal of much oppression, to secure one's own identity, power, and position—to secure one's self in a particular context and project one's security into the future—invariably leads to death, and thus dissolution of that goal. That was the earliest deception of sin, the taking of the fruit to assert one's own identity and bypassing God.[101]

---

98. Moltmann, *TH*, 194 writes, "The Christian hope for the future comes of observing a specific, unique event—that of the resurrection and appearing of Jesus Christ."

99. Ibid., 189.

100. Ibid., 196.

Only the way of the cross includes the path to resurrection, and only by participating with the crucified God do we then have a substantive hope for not only salvation *from* but indeed and more importantly, salvation *into*. This salvation *into* includes those ultimate goals for which oppressing tends to be concerned—issues of fulfillment, identity formation, security. Because the cross entails the loss of identity, the resurrection is about more than resuscitation of that old identity into becoming a more successful version of the same. Jesus does not valorize who we were but awakens us to new possibilities in accordance with who we were always meant to be. "For freedom," Moltmann writes, "is nothing else than being open for the genuine future, letting oneself be determined by the future." Yet, while the Spirit of resurrection can thus be called the power of the future, the resurrection is not *futuram* but an advent, a *novum* of new life, a new way of living.

This new way of living involves participating not in our determinative future but participating in Christ, "from the knowledge and recognition of that historic event of the resurrection of Christ which is the making of history and the key to it."[102] The cross opens a person up to be a new person, emptying and forsaking; the resurrection is the promise of filling, of new life. Thus, the resurrection "means recognizing in this event the latency of that eternal life which in the praise of God arises from the negation of the negative, from the raising of the one who was crucified and the exaltation of the one who was forsaken."[103] This recognition is important because hope implies not yet experiencing that which one

101. Obviously a statement like this would raise objections concerning the historicity of the Garden narrative. Whatever the historical basis, the narrative intent of the story was to assert a particular kind of action/response that is at the root of human alienation from God and self. It is this narrative intent that is my concern.
102. *TH*, 212. Cf. ibid., 229.
103. Ibid., 211.

hopes for, so the oppressor then has to let go of that which is palpable for the sake of the not yet fulfilled. Hope is not static. Hope initiates movement.

This movement has three elements. First, it reorients one's concerns away from previously held priorities and toward that which is promised but not yet experienced. Hope is, thus, risk. It risks not pursuing what promises more immediate satisfaction and contextual respect. It is risking a life with the Spirit who draws us through our present, transforming us and pointing us to the resurrection that is the history and the future with Christ. "Just as the urge of promise is towards fulfillment, as the urge of faith is towards obedience and sight, and as the urge of hope is towards the life that is promised and finally attained, so the urge of the raising of Christ is towards life in the Spirit and towards the eternal life that is the consummation of all things."[104] This is a new thing that places us within a new trajectory, and so we can speak of life with the Spirit as a new way. Who we are is no longer coinherent with our contexts but with the fullness of reality that is found in God. Either we derive our identity from our contexts or we resonate identity within our contexts.

As we are awakened to new possibilities in this participating with God, we are also awakened to the frictions, free but also experiencing the suffering of the latent freedom in circumstances that are not yet amenable to new ways of life. "In the darkness of the pain of love," Moltmann writes,

> the man of hope discovers the dissension between the self and the body. In the struggle for obedience and for what is due to God in the body, he discovers the contradiction of the flesh and his subjection to the hostile powers of annihilation and death. In beginning to hope for the triumph of life and to wait for resurrection, he perceives the deadliness of death and can no longer put up with it.[105]

104. Ibid., 213.
105. Ibid., 213–14.

130

As an isolated struggle, this perception would only lead to resignation. Thus, hope carries with it not only the promise of new life but also the promise of realization in God, and with God participation with others who likewise experience the friction and the unwillingness to put up with the experiences of death in their particular contexts. We are not left alone. We are gathered together.

Hope being what it is, we do not currently experience the fullness that is promised but wait for the fulfillment of the promise in which we experience God who is all in all. As such, the "universal and immediate presence of God is not the source from which faith comes, but the end to which it is on the way."[106] Hope is, thus, a trajectory. In this trajectory, hope both discloses the context of self and situation for what it is, and then points toward resolution of these in the way of formative transformation through participation with Christ.[107] Hope points to what is possible for each person and certain in light of God's identity as God. This is a future impregnated with promise that gives each person a place in the transforming and intentional work of God.

In this work, a person learns from God who they are, becoming true to themselves as they are led into the history that God determines from an eschatological perspective. Moltmann writes, "The real mystery of his human nature is discovered by man in the history which discloses to him his future."[108] This future is not limiting, forcing a person into becoming an automaton in the service of either the past or some rigid and limiting future, which leads to resignation to the determination of the past or the vagaries of fate. Instead, this trajectory opens up possibilities. In the *novum* that is resurrection, a person is led toward a new freedom of awakened potentiality.[109] In becoming open to God, a person is then and only then truly open

---

106. Ibid., 282.
107. See ibid., 285.
108. Ibid., 286.
109. Ibid.

to their own self and to this world, not determined by their context but remaining free to be whole within their context. "Hoping in the promised new creation by God, man here stands *in statu nascendi*, in the process of his being brought into being by the calling, coaxing, compelling word of God."[110] This openness is a continuing trajectory of transformation as the new and the free pushes aside the old and binding.

God gathers in order to orient his people toward himself and the future for which he is working. As this path gathers together people from all backgrounds, the blameworthy and the blaming, it entails another basic human need, that of community: noncompetitive, nonauthoritarian community where identity is derived by sharing in the identity of Christ, so that each person becomes substantively able to participate as a free person among others, celebrating diversity in an infinitely complex unity. This participation with God enables a person to participate in the work of God to help free others into the resonating life with God, giving an active and exocentric component to participation in the promise. Truly believing in the promise entails acting in accordance with the promise as reality. Hope is, thus, a mission.

Indeed, it is this concept of hope as mission that helps orient theological anthropology, and with this helps orient hope as a liberating reality. The dominant question of anthropology "arises in face of a divine mission, charge and appointment which transcend the bounds of the humanly possible."[111] This orients the question of humanity in light of God's work, not in light of humanity's inherent potential or ability to progress. "Self-knowledge here comes about in face of the mission and call of God, which demand impossibilities of man. It is knowledge of self, knowledge of men and knowledge of

110. Ibid., 287.
111. Ibid., 285.

guilt, knowledge of the impossibility of one's own existence in face of the possibilities demanded by the divine mission."[112] Rather than resignation, however, this mission of God that delineates the contours of hope both confronts a person with their inability to bring about their own liberation, while at the same time inviting the person to a hope that is, ultimately, a hope with God.

The mission and call "reveal and open up to him new possibilities, with the result that he can become what he is not yet and never yet was."[113] Yet, I should add, this is who such a person truly is; they are becoming in full that which their previous forms of identity only revealed in fractured parts. That is the liberating promise to the oppressor: not simply to stop doing what is wrong because it is wrong, but to stop oppressing both because it is destructive and because it is futile—it can never achieve what it promises and it is only through the promise of God that fulfillment can be attained. Only the mission of God fulfills this promise and this mission gathers all people into a new way of being in, with and for this world. There is no hope in Egypt. The slaves are set free and set on a new path. They join together in new, shared hope that entails participating in God's risk, trajectory and mission. This participation is transformative, forming the people and, through the people, forming the context as the people share with others the promise and the hope that they have received from God.

112. Ibid.
113. Ibid., 286.

4

Transformation in Trinitarian Perspective

What makes a thoroughly Christian theology of liberation, and thus a theology of transformation, so distinctive is, in essence, what makes Christian theology itself so distinctive. We speak of a God who acts, who is involved, and who seeks and calls people toward reflecting his action. We also speak of a particular God who exists in a certain way and, in this way of existing, liberation is not simply an ancillary trait. God loves because that is who God is. God liberates because that is who God is.[1] Liberation is, then, an ontological category in Christian theology, and transformation is its continuing expression. It is not something we are called to do, but a people we are called to be, a liberating people who reflect the liberating God. It is only this liberating experience that leads to a transformative community. Just as liberation is at the root of God as a triunity, so too we discover the

---

1. In saying that God is love and God is liberation, it must be stressed that the reverse should not be prioritized as definitions. Our conceptions of love and conceptions of liberation do not define God. Rather these gain their substantive content through his expression and definition. This means, oftentimes, our conceptions must be adapted and thickened in order to be more integrated with God and with God's creation.

roots of the transformative identity as a new orientation in light of God's unified threeness.

We are, after all, created in the image of God, and it is thus through better understanding the identity of God that we better understand who we are to be. This is who we are called to be because this is the identity that God is seeking for his people, actively involved in this world to form them into becoming, truly, a likeness of him in this world. Indeed, this instinct that theology is intimately involved in transformation is that which led Moltmann to begin his "systematic contributions to theology" with a text on the Trinity, rather than the long-hoped for ethics of hope that he had in mind since the early 1960s and that friends and colleagues eagerly awaited.[2] That ethics had to wait for more thorough theological development, as "everything done and suffered must conform to what is believed, loved and hoped for."[3] If we commit to believing, loving, and hoping for vague or diffuse realities, we express our faith in similarly diffuse ways. What we believe, truly believe, affects how we live, and our very understanding of the Trinity is not an auxiliary belief but a substantive orientation that should guide all of our life together.[4]

2. See Jürgen Moltmann, *Ethics of Hope*, trans. Margaret Kohl (Minneapolis: Fortress Press, 2012), xi.

3. Ibid., xiii.

4. Arne Rasmusson, *The Church as Polis: From Political Theology to Theological Politics as Exemplified by Jürgen Moltmann and Stanley Hauerwas* (Notre Dame: University of Notre Dame Press, 1995), 179–83 points in this direction, emphasizing the similarities of Hauerwas and Moltmann in defending "a sort of eschatologically-oriented Trinitarian theology." Adding that while they may not agree in detail, "their general positions point in similar directions." And yet, while this similarity of direction can be maintained in a general sense of affirming the Trinity and its implications for an embodied theology, Rasmusson seems unconcerned with the particularities that both distinguish Hauerwas from Moltmann in this topic and, in essence, provide the substantive foundation for Moltmann's moves that differentiate him from Hauerwas. This distinction is almost certainly most clear in terms of their relative pneumatologies, of which Rasmusson, 179 notes, "Hauerwas' explicit use of pneumatological language is meager, but it is implicit in his ecclesiological account." A Trinitarian theology with a meager pneumatology is not, I argue, a substantive Trinitarian theology, and in relegating pneumatology to a functionally implicit role, Rasmusson is, in essence, relegating a substantive, holistic Trinitarian doctrine to an auxiliary role behind a more dominating Christology. This

In this chapter, I will examine the transformative life in a Trinitarian perspective, so as to best understand how our lives are transformed by, and become resonating transformative partners with, the three persons of the Trinity. I will begin with *The Trinity and the Kingdom*, follow with *The Way of Jesus Christ*, and finish with *The Spirit of Life*. As with the previous sections, this emphasis follows Moltmann's framework in *Experiences in Theology*, which he likewise finishes with a strong Trinitarian orientation.

The Transformative Life Part Six:
The Trinity and the Kingdom

"What furthers life is whatever ministers to God's covenant with life, and whatever breaks the covenant of human beings with death."[5]

In *The Trinity and the Kingdom*, Moltmann orients his Trinitarian theology as intentionally moving away from either the premodern emphasis of Trinity as substance or the modern emphasis of Trinity as subject.[6] This move is made because the former requires a return to older cosmologies that are no longer maintainable after the Enlightenment. In regard to the latter, Moltmann writes, "Anthropological thinking is giving way to the new, relativistic theories about the world, and anthropocentric behavior is being absorbed into social patterns."[7] Such relativistic theories can be expressed as pure relativism, as continental deconstructive

suggests that the difference between Hauerwas and Moltmann may be seen as a functional binarian theology contrasted with a more holistic Trinitarian theology—thus leading them to see and understand the work of God, and thus the call upon God's people, in sharply different ways.

5. Jürgen Moltmann, *Experiences in Theology*, trans. Margaret Kohl (Minneapolis: Fortress Press, 2000), 149–50, italics removed.
6. Moltmann, *The Trinity and the Kingdom*, trans. Margaret Kohl (Minneapolis: Fortress Press, 1993), 18–19.
7. Ibid., 19.

postmodern thought tends to do, or it can turn another direction, into relationality, which is where Anglo-American postmodernism tends to lead, and is indeed where Moltmann turns in his proposals for a social understanding of the Trinity.[8] At the root of this approach is Moltmann's intent to consider the Trinity through the lens of the revelation of Christ—who is our access not only to the Trinity itself but indeed the source of debate about the Trinity. Jesus speaks of God in terms of relationship—he is the Son of the Father—and such relational thinking seems to be the mode of expression throughout Scripture—establishing God's people in relationship with him in familial, covenantal, and indeed even affective ways.[9]

Such considerations of the Trinity, then, lead naturally into our own relating with and for each other. Rather than being separated topics—where the considerations on the Trinity and the doctrine of the church are considered each in their own and often isolated ways—a social understanding of the Trinity leads us to see identity itself as relationally determined and relationships as part of our transformative ideal.[10] In becoming, we come together. This moves Trinitarian thinking from an abstract concept to one that is central for our participation with God and with each other, guiding us to think ecologically as part of the context of God's overall work and our part within it.[11] Of course, Trinitarian thinking has always had an effect on our ecclesiology—implicitly if not always explicitly—and it is such historic influences that Moltmann seeks to address and correct.

Relationship implies mutual influence. A social understanding of the Trinity, then, requires us to reexamine the assumption of God's

---

8. See Veli-Matti Kärkkäinen, *The Trinity: Global Perspectives* (Louisville, KY: Westminster John Knox, 2007), 59–64, for a brief and excellent study of the rise of social Trinitarian thought in Christian theology.

9. Moltmann, *TK*, 19.

10. Ibid.

11. See ibid., 19–20.

impassibility.[12] Such an assumption derives in part from an understanding of what a god must be in order to be God. God, in traditional terms, must be inviolable, not affected by transience or susceptible to loss. This then leads to an understanding of salvation—a sharing in the divine source of being—as likewise reflected in impassibility. An ecclesiology that assumes an impassive God reflects a particular kind of community, with a myriad of corollary doctrines that tend to deemphasize love as a formative guide. A God who cannot suffer, after all, is a God who cannot really love—and in protecting God from forms of suffering, earlier approaches to Trinitarian thought essentially depersonalized his identity by essentially negating his expression of self through love.[13] Thus, it is important to understand the pathos of God in a way that reflects his revelation—a revelation of how this particular god interacts in this world—and so Moltmann begins his text by seeking "to develop a doctrine of *theopathy*."[14]

A theology of God's suffering is connected to questions about our own suffering—in both how God experiences suffering and how we can explain our experiences of incomprehensible suffering. "It is in suffering," Moltmann writes, "that the whole human question about God arises; for incomprehensible suffering calls the God of men and women in question."[15] Suffering that is a consequence of sin or guilt is understandable, but if this is the only understanding of suffering, then we ignore the suffering of the innocent and dismiss the idea of the suffering of God. Indeed, even as a punishment for sin, the experience of suffering is only of a limited value, as such suffering often far outweighs the guilt, and indeed allows suffering a form of permanence through its justification.[16] Moltmann suggests a form

12. See ibid., 22–25
13. See ibid., 38.
14. Ibid., 25.
15. Ibid., 47.

of suffering that is not about the punishment for guilt but rather involves the experience of love, so that God suffers because he loves, because one who loves experiences pain as others suffer. Moltmann writes, "The experience of suffering reaches as far as love itself. The love which creates life and quickens it is the positive thing; it is against this that the negativeness of suffering and death shows up and is perceived."[17] Love experiences the suffering of those who suffer as it refuses to justify suffering as deserved, instead seeking to overcome such suffering.[18]

God determines God's identity by himself, an identity that is free in both its self-realization and self-communication. Instead of God being determined by some conception of godness—definitions of divinity that are established as defining who can and cannot be divine—God himself defines his own being and, inasmuch as he defines his own being, determines the nature of divinity for himself.[19] This is freedom. Like with suffering, however, deficient definition can limit an understanding of freedom, seeking to define it over and against others. "Freedom as it truly is, is by no means a matter of power and domination over a piece of property."[20] Freedom that is of God is a freedom of love—though this too raises conceptual problems. Moltmann notes Barth's attempt to relate God's freedom and love as complementary realities. However, in mediating between these two expressions of identity one runs into either an arbitrary element or a tautology. As Moltmann puts it, "Either God loves as one who is free, who could just as well *not* love; or his freedom is not distinguished from his love at all, and he is free as the One who loves."[21]

---

16. Ibid., 52. Note how this would violate such passages as Exod. 21:23-25, let alone Matt. 5:38-42.
17. Moltmann, *TK*, 51.
18. Ibid.
19. See ibid., 52–56.
20. Ibid., 55.
21. Ibid., 56.

An alternative to this approach is to see the coordination of freedom and love expressed through the ideals of community—freedom as friendship. [22] "This freedom consists of the mutual and common participation in life, and a communication in which there is neither lordship nor servitude. In their reciprocal participation in life, people become free beyond the limitation of their own individuality."[23] This freedom is revealed in the Trinity itself—a unity of reciprocal interactions—and is extended as freedom in offering such fellowship to men and women, making them God's friends. Such friendship then frees others by creating an open space and maintaining this space for the reciprocal love. "Through his freedom," Moltmann writes, "he keeps man, his image, and his world, creation, free—keeps them free and pays the price of their freedom."[24] This freedom is his openness, being free to be who he is and is not, thus, vulnerable to dissolution by the nonresponse of others. It is precisely because his identity is secure in himself that he is, however, vulnerable to suffering.

Moltmann bases his theology of divine suffering on the identity of God as love—orienting this identity in terms of relationship. This move develops with six underlying theses. First, "Love is the self-communication of the good."[25] Good is not self-contained but

---

22. In using such language as *friendship*, and equating such freedom for relationality as reflected within the Trinity itself, Moltmann is vulnerable to charges of either an overrealized anthropology or an underrealized understanding of the Trinity, where people are included within the fellowship that is the Trinity itself. Moltmann certainly does not imply this, and his use of the term *friendship* may be loosely, and contextually, related to the Eastern Orthodox emphasis on the energies of God. Thus Moltmann is essentially using Orthodox language, arguing for *theosis*, a unity with God in which we participate in the energies of the Trinity but not the essence. Indeed, it is the fulfillment, not dissolution, of our own essence to relate in full to God and to each other—a unity that derives from freely expressed diversity. Cf. Moltmann, *The Way of Jesus Christ*, trans. Margaret Kohl (Minneapolis: Fortress press, 1993), 261.

23. Moltmann, *TK*, 56. Although Moltmann has been criticized for a lack of a thoroughgoing doctrine of sin and, with this, a developed anthropology, it is here that one can see his perspective, which may be illuminated by seeing the similarity between Moltmann and Pannenberg in understanding sin ultimately as an issue of identity.

24. Ibid.

exocentric, the passionate regard for others that involves the expression of one to the other for the benefit of the other. Passion here is not equivalent with earlier, often monastic uses of the term, which involves destructive passions. Love is an unselfish and positively transformative passion for the other. Second, "Every self-communication presupposes the capacity for self-differentiation."[26] Love cannot be solitary nor can it simply absorb the other or be absorbed by the other.[27] God, in eternity, is expressed in his self-differentiation and his self-identification, taking on the burden of that which seeks to violate or subsume this—and guiding his creation toward its own fullness of identity in him. Third, by "deciding to communicate himself, God discloses his own being; otherwise his decision would not be a self-communication of the good which he is."[28] This disclosure of his inner being—exposure of his true self to the vagaries of this world—is an expression of the love that finds pleasure in self-communication. God delights in sharing himself. In opening himself up to the other, and in allowing himself to suffer the response of the other, God might even "need" the other—though not to secure his existential identity but to fulfill his own delight. God's identity as love is God's self-communication—a communication of love that seeks reciprocity.

This leads to the fourth thesis of God's identity as love. "God is love means in Trinitarian terms: in eternity and out of the very necessity

---

25. Ibid., 57.
26. Ibid.
27. Here we have the different emphases of identity in Moltmann and Pannenberg. Pannenberg tends to emphasize the former as sin—leading toward his strong antiauthoritarianism, while Moltmann tends to emphasize the latter, leading to his priority of liberation. This is not a disagreement but rather a distinction of theological emphasis as it relates to identity. "The image of the individual who takes himself or herself to be the center of his or her life aptly describes the structure of sin." Wolfhart Pannenberg, *Human Nature, Election, and History* (Philadelphia: Westminster, 1977), 26. Cf. Wolfhart Pannenberg, *Anthropology in Theological Perspective*, trans. Matthew J. O'Connell (Philadelphia: Westminster, 1985), ch. 3.
28. Moltmann, *TK*, 58.

of his being the Father loves the only begotten Son."[29] The Son is like the Father, other in identity but not in essence, and their love is the love of the "like for the like," a love that is necessary as part of their being. As this love goes out it is creative and brings forth bounty, no longer necessary but free. Such love goes beyond the like, and seeks more than the like—it seeks an echo and reciprocity in the free response of others, calling these others to life and thus also to the fullness of love. The expression of love that exists in the Trinity is extroverted into creation—in its foundation and in its redemption—a mutuality of divine love that draws all of creation into its embrace. The history of creation, then, involves "the tragedy of divine love" but also, with its redemption, "the feast of divine joy."[30] Fifth, "With the creation of a world which is not God, but which none the less corresponds to him, God's self-humiliation begins—the self-limitation of the One who is omnipresent, and the suffering of the eternal love."[31] God gives creation space and he gives creation time—involving a patience and a withdrawing—a self-limitation that allows creation its own identity, and suffers as such an identity that orients itself away from God's identity.

It is important, again, to note that what is at stake is not God's identity. Rather, God is able to suffer because his identity is secure. This suffering is part of his creative love. God's love defines his participation. It is the source of his vulnerability and the source of his passion— that in his participation he suffers the loss and celebrates the mutuality that emerges from his continued love for and with the

29. Ibid. It is noteworthy that Moltmann does not here, or in these theses, have a notable role of the Spirit. We see echoes of the Augustinian understanding of the Spirit as the bond of love between the Father and Son, but not fully realized as a person with a distinct identity or relationship. See Joy Ann McDougall, *Pilgrimage of Love: Moltmann on the Trinity and the Christian Life* (New York: Oxford University Press, 2005), 60–67 for a discussion of Moltmann's pneumatological development. We see the direction of Moltmann's developing pneumatology in *TK*, 104–5.

30. Ibid., 59.

31. Ibid.

world. This love suffers so it can redeem, and redeem in a way that allows the other a space of reciprocity and freedom of love in return. God takes on what is broken so that what is broken can be wholly renewed in creative love.

Sixth, "This means that the creation of the world and human beings for freedom and fellowship is always bound up with the process of God's deliverance from the sufferings of his love."[32] Love that is willing to suffer is not willing to be content with suffering. Such love finds fulfillment in the redemption of the beloved, liberating and renewing them, finding bliss in a revived way of being, where their identity is secured in the source of identity and, as such, they find freedom to be wholly who they are in communion with one another and with God. Liberation is about redeeming the other as well as themselves, entering into the suffering to make the love wholly realized. God loves, and so liberates his beloved for his own sake, for the sake of his love, which finds its own completion in the restoration of what was distant and enslaved. God's compassionate suffering is the expression of God's passionate love within the history of his creation, participating among us so that we can participate with him.

It is here, then, that a discussion of unity can proceed. Having established God's identity as love and love as self-communication, what then is the nature of the Trinitarian unity? There are two possible major errors in understanding God's identity as Trinity, and each of these relates to how we conceive of his unity and his diversity. On the one side, there is modalism—where God is one and there are three expressions of his identity. On the other side, there is tritheism, in which three gods are joined together as one. From the earliest days of the church, there has been a strong tendency to risk the former rather than the latter, affirming the identity of

32. Ibid.

God as one and then discovering how to understand the role of the separate persons in this unity. Moltmann takes a different course and is willing to risk the charge of tritheism in pursuing what he calls a more biblical foundation to theology.[33] The testimony of Scripture in this regard leads toward an understanding of the Trinity expressed in relationship and it is a testimony of which we do not have a complete revelation.

This unity then is "the eschatological question about the consummation of the Trinitarian history of God."[34] As such, "The unity of the three Persons of this history must consequently be understood as a communicable unity and as an open, inviting unity, capable of integration."[35] Neither homogeneity nor a single, absolute subject are capable of communication, as communication requires at least two distinct subjects of interaction. Such interaction need not insist on separation, however. God is one in his unity, in his unitedness—"at one with himself"—in the fellowship of the Father, Son, and Spirit. These are not distinguished from each other as separate, but rather their unity is as much a defining reality as their threeness—a unity that is not formed around an exterior philosophical concept or established in one person alone. Instead, the unity in love—the reciprocating self-communication of one to the other—"must be perceived in the *perichoresis* of the divine Persons."[36] This perichoretic interaction of the Trinity expresses further in the

---

33. See ibid., 149. Here Moltmann argues that beginning with God's absolute unity and then moving to the threeness is proceeding from philosophical logic. One can counter with the idea that one God in Christian faith is not preceded by philosophical inquiry as much as testimony of the Jewish Scriptures, with passages like the *Shema* especially noteworthy in this regard. However, it is also the case that while Jewish testimony supported the idea of monotheism, this was not entirely unique to Jewish theology. On the other hand, the concept of Trinity is unique—the idea that we can have three persons as one God—and is driven by the testimony of the New Testament.
34. Ibid.
35. Ibid.
36. Ibid., 150.

works of salvation the "opening of themselves for the reception and unification of the whole creation."[37] This pushes against a dichotomy between God's immanent identity and his economic identity, and instead leads toward a mutuality of insight in which God's works invite us toward response and in this response gain understanding of God as he is.

Distinguishing between the economic trinity and the immanent Trinity, Moltmann argues, attempts to better define God's liberty and God's grace. God's actions in this world are not necessitated in his being itself—which is wholly sufficient in itself—and so such volition in salvation is a distinguishing choice. We should not interpret such grace as an indication of our inherent worth or necessity to God. Such a distinction between liberty and grace, however, ignores the ontological reality of God as love—with love being the expression of his liberty and liberty the expression of his love.[38] He is not compelled to act; he is being himself in his actions. "Love is self-evident for God," Moltmann writes, "so we have to say that the triune God loves the world with the very same love that he himself is."[39] This love for the world loves the whole of the world with the infinity of his love—a love expressed in a unity with himself and with his activities. The two expressions—the economic and the immanent—"form a continuity and merge into one another."[40] These can be distinguished only in doxology—the praise of the Christians as a community celebrating together the life of the God who is.

An experience without expression in response can never be a liberating experience, as it stays only a rhetorical or intellectual reality. Thus, our experiences of the work of God insists on expression in response to God. This expression draws us into the life

37. Ibid., 157.
38. Ibid., 151–54.
39. Ibid., 151.
40. Ibid., 152.

of the God-who-is, a reciprocal embrace of his identity, expressed in praise and trust and mutuality. In participating with God, we "are transformed into the thing perceived" through wondering perception.[41] The knowledge of God who reaches out to us is the good news toward us, and our response to this God awakens understanding of who he is as himself—a responsive theology in which we respond to the *kerygmatic* message and return that which was experienced, a mutuality of responsiveness that ties us together with the immanent Trinity.

God recognizes us, and we recognize God. In our response, we see the integrity and coherence of God's work with God as he exists eternally. In this mutuality of response "is the love story of the God whose very life is the eternal process of engendering, responding and blissful love. God loves the world with the very same love which he is in himself."[42] The unity that is established in self-communicating love is expressed eternally in the *perichoresis* of Father, Son, and Holy Spirit. This then cannot be analogous to a relationship either with oneself or as a pattern of lordship over others. Instead, it "only corresponds to a human fellowship of people without privileges and without subordinances."[43] The community of Christ reflects the experience of the Trinity as a self-communicating community based on mutuality, respect, affection, and love.[44] The more such a community resonates the work of the Spirit, the more such a community reflects the experience of the Spirit in both immanent and economic forms as a covenant community within its context.

In regard to the Father, Moltmann resists the idea of the Father as being "the universe's highest authority," and modeling a patriarchal form of leadership upon the creation.[45] God is, again, Father in

41. Ibid.
42. Ibid., 157.
43. Ibid.
44. Ibid., 157–58.

respect to the Son. "It is solely the Father of Jesus Christ whom we believe and acknowledge created the world."[46] Our perspective of the Father, then, derives from our relationship with the Son, and in fellowship with the Son, one enters into relationship with the Father, not as patriarch but as "Abba."[47] This is a theological expression of an intimate relationship, expressing the identity of God in loving relationship with the Son, and through the Son we are included in this relationship. Creation itself is the expression of the whole of the Trinity, so we cannot think of the Father as being the patriarch of the world, but as the Father in the inner-Trinitarian identity. This is important, as by defining the Father relationally in terms of the Son, not in terms of the world and in terms of monarchy, our models of community shift emphasis.[48] Instead of legitimizing forms of rule and relations that legitimize dependency, helplessness, and servitude, seeing the Father as the Father of the Son pushes against expressions of dominance in his name, as we are in relation with the Father in our relationship with the Son, not representatives of the Father and the Son to others.[49]

Instead of domination, then, the community formed around such a relationship is inviting and expressing freedom. This expression of freedom in relationship replaces models of domination and control, and in this freedom of being defined in relationship with the Trinity we see the kingdom of God.[50] In this, we see a mutuality and reciprocity that involves others. "The Trinitarian Persons do not merely exist and live in one another; they also bring one another mutually to manifestations in the divine glory."[51] Such mutuality of

45. Ibid., 163.
46. Ibid.
47. Ibid.
48. See ibid., 164; 171–74.
49. See ibid., 191.
50. Cf. Neil Cole, *Organic Leadership: Leading Naturally Right Where You Are* (Grand Rapids: Baker, 2009), 164–65.

magnification that involves total openness to the other and trust with the other—dwelling within each other—is the foundation of their unity; they are communicating eternal life to and with the other, not divided by their differences but able to express a perfection of unity precisely because of them.

These are not three different individuals or modes of being, but three in one, forming a unity in their eternal "circulation of the divine life."[52] They are each expressed in full, magnified and emphasized by the others, in their eternal relationship. Unity is not the lordship, where one defines the others, but is in relationship, where each celebrates the other in perfect harmony. In this harmony, God is free to be wholly himself. In this freedom, God invites others to discover such wholeness and freedom, undermining all other demands to define oneself in contrast to others.

The kingdom, then, is nothing other than the extension of God's exocentric identity expressed in, with, and for this world—an inviting identity that draws others into such freedom, and transforms them into expressing the selfsame mutuality in, with, and for this world. This mutuality is the very essence of love—a love that seeks to enliven the other and to resist forms of decay and death that might strangle the true freedom and identity of others from finding inclusion in a celebratory relationship of mutual magnification. In terms of the Father, the world is created open to the future—a future that is not determined by death but is preserved and made continually open for its future in the kingdom of glory. In the creation of the world, God is glorified. This expression of glory substantiates the expectation of

51. Moltmann, *TK*, 176.
52. Ibid., 175.

glory.[53] God sustains and transforms the world so that his glory is ever and increasingly evident.

Time itself is an expression of his grace—an expression of his divine patience in, with, and for this world, giving it space in its becoming—maintaining hope despite humanity's apostasy and withdrawal into other—deficient—forms of identity.[54] The self-restriction of the Father—the patience of love—is not a loss or violation of God's identity but an expression of it, making space for the other in the transformation toward real liberty. "Where it is the Father of Jesus Christ and not 'the great Lord of the Universe' who preserves the world through his patience, the liberty of created beings is given space and allowed time, even in the slavery they impose on themselves."[55] Those who are free, however, express this same patience and love for their contexts—contexts limited by finitude and so limited in scope but not in love, as their freedom is given space in the love that exists eternally in God.[56]

God's work in his creation is one of liberation, of freeing his creation from the bondage of sin and death so that in its freedom, the creation expresses in full the bounty of a free relationship with God. God who is free in himself expresses the fullness of freedom in his love toward and with the world, calling others to express this freedom. Moltmann writes of his conception of this kingdom, one that is oriented around the identity of God as Trinity, "The Trinitarian doctrine of the kingdom is the theological doctrine of freedom. The theological concept of freedom is the concept of the Trinitarian history of God: God unceasingly desires the freedom

53. See ibid., 212. Here Moltmann writes that "the kingdom of glory must be understood as the consummation of the Father's creation, as the universal establishment of the Son's liberation, and as the fulfillment of the Spirit's indwelling."
54. Ibid., 209–12.
55. Ibid., 210.
56. Ibid., 219.

of his creation. God is the inexhaustible freedom of those he has created."[57]

In participating in this freedom, people are able to participate in relationship with God in a free and freeing way. Such participation is "friendship" with God.[58] In freedom as friends, God's people express their freedom with boldness and confidence. They share this expression in their contexts, praying and acting in ways that express the God-given liberty. This is a "concrete expression of freedom" that God desires, not one that is hidden or separated, but one that is enacted and inviting—resonating this freedom for and with others. Such freedom is not fully experienced in either history or a particular person all at once, leading to stages of resonance of God's freedom that lead to "strata" of the experience of freedom. There is the experience of freedom as servants, the freedom of children, and the freedom of God's friends that correspond to the history of God's work in creation.[59] This trend does not push aside the previous stage, but includes and expands its meaning. The freedom of the kingdom of God is the freedom of servants who have become heirs who are becoming friends with God, expressed in particular contexts and eternally in relationship.

Life expresses itself as filled with God's love, enlivening and creating, participating in free mutuality with God and with others. This transformative reality is "the process of maturing through experiences that are continually new."[60] Men and women experience wholeness and freedom in the present, finding fulfillment in the "unhindered participation in the eternal life of the triune God himself, and in his inexhaustible fullness and glory."[61] This is hope that both

---

57. Ibid., 218.
58. Ibid., 221.
59. Cf. Jürgen Moltmann, *History and the Triune God* (New York: Crossroad, 1992), 91-109.
60. *TK*, 221–22.
61. Ibid., 222.

challenges and inspires, a hope that shows every other source of identity as deficient, the hope that leads to participatory freedom for all of God's people, celebrating the fullness of life and actively resisting anything that hinders such freedom to live within God's empowering love.

The Transformative Life Part Seven:
The Way of Jesus Christ

"What furthers life is, first and last, whatever makes Christ present, Christ who is the resurrection and the life in person; for in and with Christ the kingdom of eternal life is present, and this kingdom overcomes the destructive powers of death."[62]

In *The Crucified God*, Moltmann wrote about Christ, but that book was not necessarily a thoroughgoing Christology. His goal was to examine the whole of God through the lens of the cross, and in doing this better come to terms with the issues of suffering, pain, and exclusion that seem to populate our experience of history—a history that we dogmatically would otherwise argue God himself is responsible for causing. The anguish of Auschwitz, which exceeds the capability of words to describe, is a theological challenge. If confronted, such anguish seemingly leads us either to atheism or to retreat behind the barrier of faith, not letting the world confront God and, in essence, restricting God's confrontation with the world. With *The Way of Jesus Christ*, Moltmann turns more directly to the person of the Son, asking what this life and work mean for our lives as individuals and as a gathered people, in the past, present, and through the consummation of the future. This is not a bit of historical trivia to

62. Moltmann, *Experiences in Theology*, 150, italics removed.

reflect on, but rather a way of being in and for this world, a way of becoming, a way of participation with God and with others.

In asserting the way of Jesus as the way of messianic expectation, it is important to insist that our Christology must include within it the Jewish perspective on the Messiah. This is the heart of the hope expressed throughout the Old Testament and continues to underlie the hope contained in our participation with God.[63] Messianic hope is not an idealistic hope, as if humanity were progressing in its collective identity and that circumstances will likewise reflect the continued path of human becoming in the process of universal history. "History understood as a continuum, as development and progress, can only be the history of the victors, who wish to secure and expand their own power."[64] The Messiah is not, then, the expression of the continuation of determinative history but the hope in the transformation of the conditions that otherwise are without hope. This is, as Moltmann notes, the "revolutionary element in the messianic hope."[65] This messianic hope may develop in two different ways, ways that point to two different forms of ecclesiality.

Such a hope can lead people away from the present, to put stock only in the future, and reflect a sectarian form of revolution, a distancing and denial of the present's substantive reality. This makes life in the present empty of meaning, denying likewise actions in the present and the need to oppose oppression. The hope is one of a "deferred life."[66] In contrast, another way of understanding this messianic hope is "to make the future of the messiah present, and fill

---

63. Moltmann, *WJC*, 2.

64. This is something Hegel, for instance, explicitly affirmed, especially in his celebration of Napoleon as an icon of the World Spirit, and in his willingness to concede the necessity for crushing many "little flowers" on the way to full expression and fulfillment. See Georg Wilhelm Friedrich Hegel, *Reason in History*, trans. Robert S. Hartman (New York: Liberal Arts, 1953), 43.

65. Moltmann, *WJC*, 24.

66. Moltmann notes that this is essentially the perspective of messianic hope in Judaism, though it certainly is expressed in much of Christian theology as well. Indeed, this was precisely the

that present with the consolation and happiness of the approaching God."[67] In the former way, we wait until we can approach God. In the latter, we await the God who approaches us. In this awaiting, we resonate with this transformative reality rather than acceding to the determinative realities that seek to dominate and establish identity for everyone.[68] Christianity as "nothing other than faith of Abraham" derives from this messianic hope and only in this messianic hope serves a role in the mission of God.[69] Such a role, Moltmann suggests, is that of a *praeparatio messianica* of the nations, proceeding from the Messiah himself and expressing the hope of God to, with, and for this world in a way that resonates with this Jewish hope. Such a messianic mission of preparation, then, "requires a profound renewal of the church and a fundamental revision of its theological tradition, for Jesus' sake."[70] This renewal and revision, then, calls for the formative work of the church within covenant communities and in entire communities, a transformative participation with God that resonates the whole work of God deeply and broadly in infinitely complex, particular ways.

Such a way eschews the imperial and chiliastic models that seek to impose domination and monolithic unity upon the church and the world. The way of Jesus Christ is not a triumphing Christology but a Christology of history that involves itself in history as a transformative renewal. The church, then, "must organize itself as the visible community of believers against the impeachments of this world of violence, so that it may show the world God's alternatives."[71]

---

emphasis the Catholic Church, for instance, taught in South American and similar poverty-stricken, oppressed contexts.

67. *WJC*, 26.

68. See ibid., 26–27. He emphasizes here especially the role of the Sabbath as an expression of hope, an expression of rest in the midst of often oppressing demands to give up ourselves in the demands of other identity forming system.

69. Ibid., 36.

70. Ibid., 37.

71. Ibid., 55.

Such an organization is not the model of the Essenes, who separated themselves in remote communities, nor even the organization of the Pharisees, who lived as a separated people within the Roman contexts. It is the model of the cross. The center of this Christology is oriented around the model of Jesus of Nazareth who is also the promised Messiah.[72] Such a model must understand who Jesus was in his context in order to answer the question of who he is, and thus who we should be, in our contexts. This question also insists on understanding our contexts for what they actually are, rather than generalizing vague models that result in vague and generalized expressions.

In this, Christianity must have something to say about "the crises and contradictions of scientific and technological civilization, and the people who suffer under them."[73] Who Christ is for us today becomes a guiding question for who we are to be as the people of Christ in this world today.[74] This leads Moltmann to orient his Christology with three emphases. First, Moltmann develops Christology "in the eschatological history of God."[75] Such a history is a cosmic history, and thus contains both human history and the history of nature, oriented toward God's work of constructing the future—"all created things and conditions are true symbols and ciphers of this future."[76] This approach to history sees Jesus as the Christ who is "on the road" and working in the transformative realities in this eschatological history. This ties together the whole of God's work with the history of Jesus, and orients the work of Jesus as part of the whole history of God's interaction with this world—past, present, and future. This is a Trinitarian history, which expresses the Trinitarian identity.

72. See ibid., 55–63.
73. Ibid., 64.
74. See ibid., 65–66.
75. Ibid., 70. See previously in ch. 2 for the discussion of Moltmann's *The Coming of God.*
76. Moltmann, *WJC*, 70.

The second element that orients Moltmann's developing Christology is "the relationship of Jesus Christ to other people, and his community with them."[77] An understanding of Jesus looks at the cross and more than the cross, noting all of his interactions—especially with the abandoned and the outsiders—involving his identity as a particular person with particular responses in particular contexts as fundamentally informing how we understand him. "We are searching," Moltmann writes, "for an emphatically social Christology."[78] Beginning with the social relations of Jesus gives significant insight into the relations of God with the world, and thus orients the church in its expression of community. Third, Moltmann seeks to examine the relationship of the "divine person Jesus Christ" with God—examining his self-understanding as an expression of his identity—which gives his followers significant insight into God's identity as a whole and God's work in this world. With these orienting elements in mind, Moltmann develops his Christology in light of how Jesus related to the future, in his community interactions, and in his relation to God.[79]

In order to develop his Christology coherently within these orienting themes, Moltmann turns to pneumatology as underlying his Christology—developing a spirit Christology that serves "as the first facet of the mystery of Jesus."[80] It is by starting with pneumatology that Moltmann sees the path for a truly Trinitarian Christology, "in which the Being of Jesus Christ is from the very outset a Being-in-relationship, and where his actions are from the very beginning interactions, and his efficacies coefficacies."[81] The Spirit makes Christ present—from the moment of his birth onward, in

77. Ibid., 71.
78. Ibid.
79. Ibid., 72.
80. Ibid., 73.

his resurrection and in his teaching—in his baptism and in his healing and in his relating to others. Thus, as Jesus was wholly participating with the Spirit, the work of Christ wholly corresponds to the work of the Spirit—a work of the Spirit that is specifically contextual and universal.[82] Moltmann writes, "Jesus appears as the messianic human being in the history of the Spirit of God with him and through him."[83] With this, we can discuss the "condescending" of the Spirit upon Jesus—who in his mortal and fleshly body was vulnerable to all that is in this world. Jesus was not a superman—able to leap tall buildings and stop bullets—nor did he dominat others and insist on reducing them in contrast to his superiority.

He experienced pain and he sought participation, especially with the "least of these," identifying with them as part of his mission. This exhibition of the work of the Spirit in the person of Jesus is the expression of the Triune God in a specific context of history, and gathers together the whole of salvation history in its interpretive schema. Such interpretation, then, opens up into our present and our future as the work of the Spirit reaches "beyond the person and history of Jesus Christ."[84] The history expressed in the person of Jesus is the continuing orientation of the Spirit into our day.[85] "Through Jesus Christ," Moltmann writes, "the Spirit is sent upon the gathered community of his followers, so that his efficacy spreads."[86]

---

81. Ibid., 74. It is such a task that leads Moltmann, it seems, toward a expanding interest in pneumatology as its own distinct study, as a pneumatological Christology assumes, by its very nature, a substantive pneumatology.
82. See ibid., 76–78.
83. Ibid., 78.
84. Ibid., 94.
85. Ibid. Moltmann here specifically argues against relativizing Jesus as "one bearer of the Spirit among others," arguing for the unique character of Jesus' "imbuement with the Spirit, which led to his divine Sonship and his special mission." Essentially, relativizing Jesus and prioritizing the Spirit would lead us into a different kind of binarian theology rather than understanding the history of this world and God's work in it in wholly Trinitarian terms.
86. Ibid., 94.

This message and this efficacy is the gospel of the kingdom of God expressed in, with, and for the world.

This messianic mission has six key elements. First, it is a gospel of freedom. This mission gives hope and liberation to those who are restricted and reduced. Second, it is a message of new creation, insisting that determinative history is not, in fact, determinative. The whole world groans for renewal—and such renewal is indeed to be expected in light of God's redeeming work. Third, such a proclamation is realistic, not idealistic. It brings a new reality to, with, and for this world so that the good news of God is not rehashed views on progress but a real and substantive hope for the poor and excluded. God's partisanship for the sake of the poor gathers together all the left out and excluded as being particular recipients of the hope given in Christ through the power of the Spirit. It is, thus, "only in community with the poor that the kingdom of God is thrown open to the others."[87] If such others refuse or reject such community, they are rejecting Christ.

Fourth, the message of the kingdom is one of conversion, which "leads men and women into the discipleship of Jesus."[88] This conversion is not limited to existential reassessment, and thus private and wholly personal. Such a conversion involves the whole of a person and the conditions in which they live. "That is to say," Moltmann writes, "it takes in personal life, life in community, and the systems which provide and order for these ways of living."[89] Conversion is transformative, holistically and totally. "If it does not happen like this, it does not happen at all."[90] There is no half-hearted, segmented correspondence to the kingdom, in which a person can participate with integrity in the old and the new way of life.

87. Ibid., 102.
88. Ibid., 103.
89. Ibid.
90. Ibid.

This conversion is total because it insists on an orientation that actively opposes forms of identity that are oriented toward death, dissolution, and destruction. With this in mind, it becomes especially useful to note Moltmann's last two elements of the messianic mission. The gospel of Jesus Christ involved both healing and exorcism, physicalized expressions of the stance of life confronting the patterns of death. These two elements suggest, then, that the person of the Messiah reorients a way of living in, with, and for this world that is proactively transformative. This is not a sectarian movement, aloof from the world, but an expression of God's salvation that is proclaiming, and enacting, good news. This is, in other words, a messianic way of life—one expressed in the life of Jesus and one that continues expression in the power of the Spirit.[91]

This new way involves participating in the sufferings of the world as a transformative presence within them. In contrast to much of contemporary society that often organizes life so as to protect against not only suffering but even inconvenience and annoyance—and thus continues models of society and identity structures that leave many outside such protection—the suffering of Jesus is one that actively engages such models and structures, willing to wade into them. In confronting them, people experience the backlash of their self-protection. Such sufferings are, then, neither meaningless nor fruitless. "They are fruitful suffering which, like labour pains, bring forth what is good," and such is the example of Jesus for his followers in each context. "Jesus' call to discipleship leads men and women to break their existing ties and the forces that dominate them, for the sake of the new creation."[92] This then may lead to suffering and persecution as well, a suffering that in the mission of God extends the resonating work of Christ and is a testimony of God's eschatological

91. See ibid., 119.
92. Ibid., 133–34. Cf. ibid., 156.

work. The community of the Messiah who suffered is a community who suffers in, with, and for their context, resonating a new way of living in light of Christ's eschatological work and against any forms of identity or systems that continue to insist on determinative reality for the inhabitants. The fellowship of suffering in the cause of Christ bonds us in community with others who are committed to Christ and to all those Christ is committed to, creating a resonance of the Spirit that is a bond of fellowship in action and devotion.

The significance of such suffering by Christ leads to the salvation of the world, an expression of God's work in history, which is the process of God's eschatological history supplanting determinative history. Moltmann summarizes this process: "The immediate goal is the justification of human beings, but the supervening goal is the justification of God, while the common goal is to be found in the reciprocal justification of God and human beings, and in their shared life."[93] This is not a single event but a process, which begins in the life of God and is expressed in the work of Christ, and which a person participates in through faith, and which leads to new world. This eschatological renewal is experienced even now and finds its completion with the resurrection of the dead and new experience of living. Thus, theodicy becomes doxology, and this is the transformative anticipation of those whose faith resonates in their particular contexts.[94] A hunger for righteousness anticipates God's justification, causing those who participate with God to "weep over the injustice of this world" and perceive this world in light of God's eschatological redemption.[95]

93. Ibid., 183.
94. See ibid., 189. Here Moltmann provides a six point summary of justification: "1. Forgiveness of sin's guilt. 2. Liberation from sin's power. 3. The reconciliation of the God-less. 4. New life in the service of righteousness and justice. 5. The right to inherit the new creation. 6. Participation in God's new just world through passionate effort on its behalf." Cf. 193–95.
95. Ibid., 193.

The resurrection is the expression of eschatology that confronts determinative history in its midst, and as such is "the foundation, goal and praxis of a history of liberation."[96] It is, as such, the final paradigm of humanity. The expression of God's work in, with, and for this world is a persistent struggle of life against death. This praxis of God, then, leads to the praxis of God's people. Such people are oriented by this resurrection hope in their new way of living in, with, and for this world and respond to the world in light of God's eschatological reality.[97] Overall, the experiences of witnessing the risen Christ "awakened in those who experienced them an expectation which was highly tense and which embraced the whole world."[98] A transformative experience led the earliest Christians to become transformed in the power of the Spirit of resurrection and respond to the world as transformative people.[99]

This orients life within a "horizon of expectation."[100] God's people become oriented within the process of his eschatological work, while continuing to experience the contradictions of determinative history in their contexts—yet the hope in the transformative work of God allows them to live within the word of promise, which gives meaning to their participation and contexts. The expectation, then, is not in vain but in keeping with God's creative interaction and commitment, a commitment that seeks complete correspondence with heaven and earth.[101] The resurrection is, then, a "historical hope for the future" that is concerned with "the future in the lives lived by those who belong to the past."[102] The resurrection is not, however, a

96. Ibid., 215.
97. See ibid., 220. Here Moltmann notes three dimensions of response shown by the witnesses of Christ's resurrection: the *prospective*, the *retrospective*, and the *reflexive* dimensions.
98. Ibid.
99. See ibid., 236–45.
100. Ibid., 238.
101. Ibid.
102. Ibid., 239 and 240.

spiritualized hope, a vague embrace of otherness that imbues people with a sense of security in the midst of transitory, and often unfortunate, reality. Christ lives. This is a bodily resurrection that orients toward a physicalized salvation. The experience of the Risen Christ points toward a process of transition, one oriented eschatologically and experienced within its processes.

This is the Way. "Just as Moses led the people of Israel out of Pharaoh's slavery into the liberty of the promised land, so Christ leads humanity out of the slavery of death into the liberty of the new creation."[103] Those who participate with Christ participate in this way, entering into the process of God's renewal of all life and becoming a liberating presence of Christ. The praxis of Christ leads to the praxis of the Spirit in the praxis of the people. This is the experience of resurrection hope. This praxis is the expression of love realized in the flesh, the "transcendent perfecting of love."[104] This love is itself the orientation of the resurrection, leading life to be expressed in love and it is this life of love "that will rise and be transfigured."[105] Such love is oriented by the Spirit, opening up, steering, even limiting the way toward the fullness of life that is expressed, making what is not present or even seemingly possible come into being.[106] The energies of the Spirit are the power of the resurrection among us, and the new way of living initiated by Christ is "the anticipated rebirth of the whole cosmos."[107] A life lived without expression of this resurrection is a life that is devoid of the horizon of expectation that includes the resurrection of Christ.

In the light of the resurrection, however, the promise of God extends to humanity and to the whole world, a promise of renewal

103. Ibid., 257.
104. Ibid., 262.
105. Ibid., 263.
106. Ibid. Moltmann writes, "The horizon of expectation make the sphere of experience accessible."
107. Ibid.

and new life. This horizon of expectation bonds us with the whole of creation, as we are bonding through a shared hope, rather than competing for dominance or competing for the best strategy to address the fate of the world. "Human beings cannot redeem nature, and nature cannot redeem human beings."[108] Thus communities that are framed around either of these hopes—either explicitly or implicitly—will fracture and divide, asserting as they do an insufficient hope in an insufficient identity for the world. In the expectation of hope that is the resurrection hope, nature itself is not subjected to humanity nor is humanity subject to nature. There is a mutuality, a " brotherly and sisterly relationship to fellow creatures," a reality that leads to an understanding of the world after modernity and also insists the church engage in a nondivisive relationship with the world. This is a community of solidarity with all of creation, expressing, in its practices, hope for a context in light of the horizon of expectation.[109]

As the work of God is one that encompasses all that is, "the coming of Christ in glory is accompanied by a transformation of the whole of nature into its eternal discernible identity as God's creation."[110] The church in community with Christ, then, reflects this cosmic lordship in much more than its worship.[111] Such must also define its presence in this world, honoring God as lord of all creation as part of its expression as the church. "The true church of Christ,"

108. Ibid., 272.
109. See ibid., 273. Here Moltmann quotes Isaac the Syrian as a description of this attitude—that is, the attitude of Christ: "What is a loving heart? It is a heart that burns with love for all creatures—men and women, demons, all created things. . . . Immeasurable pity wrings the heart. . . . It can no longer endure even the slightest pain inflicted on a created being. . . . It prays even for the snakes, moved by the infinite compassion which is awakened in the hearts of those who are becoming like God."
110. *WJC*, 280. In following the model of self-similarity across scales, what God does on a cosmic level we can and should resonate within our own spaces.
111. See ibid., 286–87. Here Moltmann notes three dimensions of a cosmic Christology that should be integrated together in order to avoid one-sided emphases that have undermined other approaches.

Moltmann writes, "is the healing beginning of the healed creation in the midst of a sick world."[112] This is a movement that runs from the future to the past, bringing God's eschatological history to bear upon the otherwise evolving determinative history—a course that leads to death and decay. Instead of dominating and competing, the people of God exhibit dignity toward God's creation.

The redemption of Christ, then, involves God entering into this world for the sake of his own identity becoming definitive for all things, reconciling what was broken and would otherwise be wholly lost, and involving his people in expressing this relationship.[113] "An ethic of reconciliation serves the common life of all created beings. It is bound to assume a defensive character, solicitous of life, over against the aggressive ethic of the modern era."[114] It is defensive, that is, for the cause of life, not defensive in isolating or protecting, and thus is an act of resistance against the prevailing values and assumptions that pit nature against humanity or humans against one another. In the work of God, all of creation is gathered together in order to collaborate in the mission of God.[115]

The fulfillment of the work of God in history is brought in the Parousia of Christ. The end-time process that began in the resurrection of Jesus leads to the fulfillment of the promise of the return of Jesus, and this in glory. The reconciliation goes hand in hand with the new creation, intertwining the transformative remembrance with the transformative expectation, deepening each other mutually.[116] The expectation of the coming of Christ orients how we live and what we hope for, actively and transformatively awaiting "the fulfillment of the history of salvation and the

112. Ibid., 285.
113. See ibid., 303–5. Cf. ibid., 307.
114. Ibid., 307.
115. See ibid., 307–12.
116. Ibid., 320.

termination of the history of affliction and disaster, the fulfillment of liberation of the history of affliction and the end of suffering."[117] The people who seek this new reality "should live in the fellowship of Christ and lead their whole life in his Spirit."[118] Those who hope for the fulfillment of Christ remain faithful to the way of Christ, and in living in this expectation, Christ will find them faithful. There is a decided patience in this hope. This patience structures the community of Christ and provides an engaged stillness to those within it.

This expression of faith is about hope in Christ, faithful in the faithfulness of God to honor his promise, no matter what determinative history might suggest. Those who join in this way of expectation and awareness reshape their lives to match the more decisive reality, giving their lives to the light and abandoning the patterns and identities of darkness. This community is made up of men and women who live in active, and transformative, anticipation—an "expectant creativity"—in shaping their lives and their contexts in the light of what God is doing and will do in Christ. Instead of a person holding onto a life oriented wholly by the past and defensive against the present, their life "becomes a life which is committed to working for the kingdom of God through its commitment to justice and peace for this world."[119] This is a messianic expectation expressed in the messianic way of life entering into our communities and resonating the work of the Spirit deeply and broadly, awaiting the fulfillment of Christ by participating with this fulfillment in, with, and for our present contexts. This is a relational ecclesiology, one that gains meaning and content by the messianic nature of God's particular work in particular ways in

117. Ibid., 320–21.
118. Ibid., 339.
119. Ibid., 340–41.

particular people, leading toward the infinitely complex fulfillment of his cosmic plan of redemption. This is the mission of God.

The Transformative Life Part Eight:
The Spirit of Life

"What furthers life is . . . the creative energies of the Spirit in which the uncreated and the created are bonded, and which renew the human life from its foundations, making it immortal in the eternal fellowship of God."[120]

In many approaches to theology, the discussion of the Trinity, followed by a more specific discussion of the work of the Son, would be a sufficient theological framework to move on to topics of eschatology. Indeed, when Moltmann first devised his plan for his "systematic contributions to theology," this indeed was his plan, as he did not foresee writing a specific text concerning the Holy Spirit.[121] Yet, throughout his works there was a building force of pneumatological concern, expressed in his increasing concern to affirm his opposition against the *filioque*, to develop a Spirit Christology, and in other ways. This required, however, a more substantive understanding of the Spirit as a unique participant in the Trinity.

Toward the end of his life, Karl Barth suggested that pneumatology was the next, needed step for fruitful theological consideration. However, Barth worried that future scholars would seem to move on to the third article but never really move past the topic of humanity. "As if," wrote Barth, "pneumatology were anthropology!"[122] Thus, the idea of the Spirit in Christian theology

120. Moltmann, *Experiences in Theology*, 150, italics removed.
121. See Jürgen Moltmann, *God in Creation*, trans. Margaret Kohl (Minneapolis: Fortress Press, 1993), xvii.

should not be an internalized pietism nor is it an overoptimistic anthropology dressed in spiritualized language. Moltmann, Barth's "well-informed Theban," moves toward developing an understanding of the Holy Spirit without devolving the discussion toward anthropology. He gives the work of resurrection its "due weight" and seeks after a more holistic perspective on God's being and work in this world.[123] Barth started the turn away from idealism in making the significant move of pushing theology out of prioritizing anthropology through his magisterial considerations on the work of Christ.[124] Moltmann presses on in this move, emphasizing Christ but not limiting the work of God to the work of Christ. "Life in the Spirit," he writes, "is not absorbed by, or completely congruent with, the mere knowledge and acknowledgment of Christ."[125] A perspective that only looks at the cross leaves out the continuing reality of eschatology and in doing that does not progress to a fully Triune perspective.

This rising concern that just about takes over *The Way of Jesus Christ* suggests that the person of the Holy Spirit became increasingly vital for Moltmann's interests and indeed overall theological coherence. With the *Spirit of Life*, we find Moltmann's pneumatological concerns given free space for their own development, and in this text we, thus, find much of Moltmann's earlier proposals and contributions finding more developed resonance and integrity with a broader system of theology. This work of the Spirit is that which, ultimately, binds humanity together with God, orienting and renewing the people and all of creation in a certain way

122. Karl Barth, *The Theology of Schleiermacher: Lectures at Göttingen, Winter Semester of 1923–24*, ed. Dietrich Ritschl, trans. Geoffrey W. Bromiley (Grand Rapids: Eerdmans, 1982), 279.
123. Jürgen Moltmann, *The Spirit of Life*, trans. Margaret Kohl (Minneapolis: Fortress Press, 1992), 149.
124. Ibid., 150.
125. Ibid., 151.

and leading toward the eternal fellowship with God. As Moltmann notes, "The operations of God's Spirit precede the workings of Christ; and the New Testament tells us that they go beyond the workings of Christ."[126] The Spirit is an essential topic in "the context of life's quickening and its sanctification," and so Moltmann begins his study with the assumption that "the efficacy of Christ is not without the efficacy of the Spirit, which is its goal" and that "the efficacy of the Spirit is nevertheless distinguishable from the efficacy of Christ, and is not congruent with that or absorbed by it."[127] This efficacy is oriented toward life, a universal work that enables thriving and resists death and decay. Indeed, this brings us to the essence of Moltmann's overall theological schema as has been discussed so far in this text. It is in the Spirit that we find the emphasis toward life and against death being expressed in its most active and relevant form.

The definition he provides later in the text sums up Moltmann's pneumatology: *"The personhood of God the Holy Spirit is the loving, self-communicating, out-fanning and out-pouring presence of the eternal divine life of the triune God."*[128] In this condensed statement, we see the vital themes that constitute Moltmann's pneumatology, themes that emphasize experience, immanence and transcendence, community, cosmic breadth—all tied together with a very strong emphasis of the Spirit as a fully realized person in the Trinity.[129] The experience of the Spirit is the "awareness of God in, with and beneath the experience of life, which gives us assurance of God's fellowship, friendship and love."[130] This is historically experienced whenever Christ is made

---

126. Ibid., xi.
127. Ibid.
128. Ibid., 289. Italics in original.
129. Ibid., 12, where Moltmann writes, "The Holy Spirit has a wholly unique personhood, not only the form in which its experienced, but also in its relationships to the Father and the Son." This strong emphasis is what strongly distinguishes Moltmann's version of panentheism with other, more standard, definitions. See Laurence Wood, *Theology as History and Hermeneutics: A Post-Critical Conversation with Contemporary Theology* (Lexington, KY: Emeth, 2004), 212–13.

present within a context—when the eschatological anticipation of the new creation supersedes the determinative expectations. Such anticipations are "resonances of Christ, and a prelude to the kingdom of God."[131] The Spirit makes Christ present and the experience of Christ's presence is the experience of the Spirit. The Spirit gathers the past, the present, and the future in a holistic expectation of renewal, an expectation that draws the people of God into fellowship with God and transforms the contexts of the people of God, as the Spirit resonates broadly and deeply, in, with, and under each context.

This experience has an "outward reference" and an "inward reference," gaining meaning by our physical senses and the perception of change that occurs in the self.[132] This is not a form of self-transcendence, but an experience of God's transcendence becoming immanent among us.[133] "The experience of God's Spirit is not limited to the human subject's experience of the self," Moltmann writes.[134] As with the whole of his theology, the human subject is not the primary perspective for Moltmann. Rather, the radical theocentric orientation of his theology comes to bear in asserting a radical experience of God himself throughout every aspect of life.[135] The presence of the Spirit of God who is the Spirit of life imbues the presence of God with all that is living, including the self. The Spirit does not prioritize the experience as isolating or egocentric, but instead opens the person, and all of creation, to an awakening

130. Moltmann, *SL*, 17.

131. Ibid.

132. Ibid., 23.

133. Ibid., 144, where Moltmann emphasizes "the human experience of the Spirit and . . . the divine experience of the Spirit in this human experience of the self."

134. Ibid., 34. Rasmusson's charge that Moltmann engages in a theology of self-therapeutic idealism is strongly undermined here, as Moltmann makes especially clear in this text what has been present, but seemingly less clear for Rasmusson, in earlier texts. See Rasmusson, *The Church as Polis*, 104–8.

135. Moltmann, *SL*, 35. On the previous page, Moltmann writes, "It is therefore possible to experience God in, with and beneath each everyday experience of the world, if God is in all things and if all things are in God, so that God himself 'experiences' all things in his own way."

experience of God—whose presence it is that the Spirit brings to all contexts.[136] This experience of God is the transformative hope of each context. God truly is with us.

Because this is an experience of God and not an experience of self-realization or self-therapy, the experiences gather people into the narrative community of God's eschatological work. By participating in this work, one is "re-called and making present" the shared origin, providing a collective experience that is made up of the infinitely complex narratives of each participant.[137] Such shared experiences, then, orient a people within the community of God. In this community with the participating God, there is a renewal of the basic trust, with which people can fully commit themselves to life with expectation and with interest. They are no longer defined by despair or egocentrism. Instead, they trust others within this trust of God, an exocentric transformation that seeks out the meaning of God's work and actively affirms its realization.[138] This is the transformative discovery of the transcendent in each context, which is the discovery of the Spirit who imbues every context with the presence and hope of God. Such an understanding of the Spirit, then, insists on the development of a holistic pneumatology, one that, first, "must comprehend human being in their total being, soul and body, consciousness and the unconscious, person and sociality, society and social institutions."[139] With this, it must also broaden the expectation of community to include all of creation, every created creature and thing.[140]

---

136. Ibid., 25.
137. Ibid.
138. Ibid., 27. Cf. James E. Loder, *The Logic of the Spirit: Human Development in Theological Perspective* (San Francisco: Jossey-Bass, 1998), 215.
139. Moltmann, *SL*, 37.
140. Indeed, this insistence on a holistic pneumatology is reflected in the original German title: *Der Geist des Lebens: Eine ganzheitliche Pneumatologie.* The unfortunate English subtitle *A Universal Affirmation* not only ignores the original German subtitle, it points the text in a rather different

In light of the elements that derive from an understanding of God's *ruach* and *shekinah*, the messianic work of God in the power of the Spirit takes even more substantive shape.[141] This messianic work works from within the contexts, the experience of expectations being inspired and fulfilled, expecting a work of God that is the presence of God himself in re-creating a context. This is an expectation of God's work that is experienced in history and has cosmic dimensions.[142] Because the Spirit is the Spirit of all life, then, such a work of God actively substantiates the messianic expectations and creates a messianic people, a resurrection in their midst that bears a hope in the vivifying presence of the God for the whole of a context.

This story is not one of isolated heroes, avatars who can be the mouthpiece of God to the people. This is the story of "the whole people; and the whole people will itself be made a bearer of the Spirit."[143] The messianic people, then, become the bearers of the messianic expectations, in both word and in power, resonating the presence of God in "historical and everyday life."[144] The whole people of God become the prophetic people of God's Spirit, leading to the rebirth of all life and the rebirth of the community of all life, initiated in infinitely complex ways within infinitely complex contexts. This experience is, then, universal, total, enduring, and direct. The indwelling of the Spirit brings the community of God into the presence of the people, and raises the people into a renewal of life that completes God's mission in, with, and for this world.[145]

---

direction of emphasis. One wonders why the more accurate "a holistic pneumatology" was not used, given that this is both readily understood in English and more descriptive of Moltmann's specified goals. Not everything in the universe is, in fact, to be affirmed after all—as that which leads to death and decay should be specifically resisted.

141. See Moltmann *SL*, 42–51. Cf. Catherine Keller, "The Theology of Moltmann, Feminism, and the Future," in *The Future of Theology: Essays in Honor of Jürgen Moltmann*, ed. Miroslav Volf, Carmen Krieg, and Thomas Kucharz (Grand Rapids: Eerdmans, 1996), 144–53.

142. Moltmann, *SL*, 54.

143. Ibid., 55.

144. Ibid., 56.

Such a mission resonates in space and time with the mission of Christ, who experienced the Spirit in himself, and whose experience of the Spirit animated the community of his people.[146] This Spirit was given, then, to the disciples, and the whole community of believers, who then "bear the impress of Christ."[147] They recognize Jesus as Lord and enter into fellowship with Christ, finding salvation and enlivening power in this fellowship. As such, the community of Christ is "responsive to the word of the messianic gospel, and the resonance of that word in the hearts and lives of men and women."[148] This response is also a beginning of a resonating presence in which the identity of Christ extends deeper into the context, creating an eschatological upswell, as the community "grows in the sphere of the Holy Spirit into a charismatic community, where potentialities and capabilities are brought to life."[149] This is the awakening of the eschatological moment within a historical context, the bringing together of Christology and pneumatology in the experience of the Spirit, which is the origin and consummation of the kingdom of God.[150]

The experience of the Spirit has the positive dimension of awakening such possibilities, deepening community and providing a vitalization of transformative hope. This experience also has an apparent negative dimension, as what is deformed and destructive become increasingly apparent as binding chains, that which must be overcome rather than that which is simply how things are or must be. People recognize repression for what it is, whether as recipients or as perpetrators, as they experience of hope in the possibilities of

145. See ibid., 57.
146. Ibid., 65.
147. Ibid.
148. Ibid., 68.
149. Ibid., 69.
150. Ibid.

what God can do and is doing. This eschatological vision evokes deep groans and sighs, seeking out the positive transformation through the negation of the negative, calling forth the regenerating power of the Spirit to bring to completion that which is experienced in its beginning.[151]

Because the nature of the Spirit is anything but static and repetitious, there are manifold experiences of this continuing work of God. The vivifying works of the Spirit do contain certain similarities. There is a rapturous joy, which includes a strong affirmation of life.[152] There is a restoration of peace, a holistic stillness that includes both salvation and well-being.[153] All the experiences should lead toward a substantive discipleship of Jesus, and that involves more than an inner testimony of good feelings. It also leads to a renewal of our outward life and outward reaction to that which affirms life, and to our outward resistance against that which affirms death and chaos. "In faith," Moltmann writes, "we experience the peace of God, in hope we look ahead to a peaceful world, and in resistance to violence we confess God's peace."[154] Our heart expands in the work of the Holy Spirit, bringing us more hope, more experience of life itself, renewing us, broadening us, deepening us, constantly renewing us.

This process begins in this life, even now, but does not find completion quite yet. Faith and life grow as each person grows, each stage of life becoming enlivened and enlightened in particular ways by the always-fresh work of the Spirit. The Spirit perseveres in this work. Because pneumatology is not anthropology, this perseverance is not about human potential or human contribution, but rather concerns the faithfulness of God in bringing the work of life to completion. "Assurance of faith is the assurance of God's faithfulness,

151. See ibid., 75–77.
152. Ibid., 153.
153. Ibid., 154.
154. Ibid., 153.

and therefore the assurance of remaining in that divine faithfulness whatever happens."[155]

The Spirit, Moltmann asserts, is not the object of experience. Our goal is not to reach the Holy Spirit or to begin to have an increasing focus on the Holy Spirit. Rather, the Spirit is the "medium and space" for experience. The vivifying power of the Spirit enlivens us to live in increasingly renewed ways, reforming us to be more true to who God intends us to be. He writes, "God's Spirit is then closer to our inner being than we ourselves."[156] We look to Christ and see the work of Christ in the kingdom of God, but because the Spirit is so close, and is the power by which we can fully perceive and respond to the work of Christ, our focus can never rest on the Spirit. Rather, in the comfort and rebirth of the Spirit we see and live in the reality of the kingdom that brings increased intimacy, breaking down patterns of distance and resistance.[157] We enter into the community of Christ, liberated toward life into eternity.

What characterizes this new life? What is the experience of sanctification in this life? Sanctification is about a renewed experience of living, a holistic renewing that encompasses far more than the narrow, moralistic ideals so often implied by the word. Out of the work of the Spirit, we are enlivened into a context of love of life. He writes, "Our stirrings toward life are experienced by God, and we experience God's living energies. In the open air of the eternal Spirit, the new life unfurls. In the confidence of faith we plumb the depths of the Spirit, in love we explore its breadth, and in hope its open horizons. God's Spirit is our place for living."[158] Sanctification encompasses the whole of our experience and expression of life, in an interplay "between what is inward and what is outward."[159]

155. Ibid., 157.
156. Ibid.
157. Ibid., 159.
158. Ibid., 161.

Growth of faith contributes to a holistic field of experiencing and contributing to life, shaped by the source of life itself.[160] Moltmann suggests, with Wesley, we can see that holiness means "harmony with God, happiness a person's harmony with himself."[161] This reality includes both internal and exocentric renewal, that leads us into harmony with others, sharing with them in their joys and fighting with them against their oppressions. He writes that the "Christian testimony must be related to the sicknesses of the given society in a healing way."[162] The good news is truly, actually good news to specific settings and issues, always related to the time and context. The Spirit is not a set of idealized ethical guidelines, but the power of life with and for us leading us to new life.[163]

In the power of the Spirit, the participants with God are empowered to live this new life. The powers of darkness are broken by the power of the Spirit, and in the power of the Spirit God's people experience a new vitality. They are awakened, turned away from the abyss, and directed toward God's eschatological reality. All of life, in turn, begins to expand, increasing participation in this new life. New possibilities are seen, new spaces for action are created, and new freedoms to stretch creativity are discovered. "Life in the Spirit," Moltmann writes, "is a life in the 'broad place where there is no cramping.' So in the new life, God's people experience the Spirit as a 'broad place'—as the free space for our freedom, as the living space for our lives, as the horizon inviting us to discover life."[164] Moltmann

---

159. Ibid.
160. Ibid., 163.
161. Ibid., 165.
162. Ibid., 171.
163. Ibid.
164. Ibid., 178. Moltmann here writes, "We explore the depths of this space through the trust of the heart. We search out the length of this space through extravagant hope. We discover the breadth of this space through the torrents of love which we receive and give. God's Spirit encompasses us from all sides and wherever we are (Ps. 139). Christ's Spirit is our immanent power to live—God's Spirit is our transcendent space for living."

titled his autobiography with this in mind, seeing his own theological explorations as a participation in this "broad place." In this broad place, in this space in the Spirit, one encounters a truly holy life of exocentric freedom.

Moltmann makes a strong assertion for the uniqueness of the Spirit in the particularity of each person and situation. As it is the Spirit who enlivens the people to become who they truly are, the people cannot look to the Spirit to work in ways that are not inherent to each person's identity. Moltmann writes, "We must first of all discern *who* we are, *what* we are and *how* we are, at the point where we feel the touch of God on our lives."[165] The key, for him, is this question: "How is unity in diversity, and diversity in unity actually implemented in the community of believers?"[166] He begins his discussion with a brief look at the Scriptural perspectives on the charismata, and emphasizes again that the work of the Spirit is not separate to any part of our life, but rather in participating with the Spirit we become empowered in who we are for the work of the kingdom of God.[167]

These possibilities exist within the resonating rhythms of life. It is in the open spaces of life that a community of real freedom can thrive, "the differentiated community which liberates the individual members belonging to it."[168] The church, then, exists as this space of freedom, where the uniqueness is not as a social model but as

165. Ibid., 180.
166. Ibid., 181.
167. Ibid., 182. This includes our regular daily participation with God in our lives, which Moltmann, *SL*, 183 calls "everyday charismata of the lived life." There are, however, special gifts for the community, for the congregation, where the Spirit works in and among the participants leading to the kerygmatic, diaconal, and kybernetic charismata from which the church exhibits its purpose and mission. These are special gifts because they come into being as a community of Christ comes into being, reflecting a particular work of the Spirit in the midst of the community that cannot be rigidly separated from the everyday charismata, but do seem to have a special reality.
168. Ibid., 228.

a resonating presence of the Spirit working in and among the participants, creating a new expression of community and identity that itself is conveyed to ever-larger scales.[169] This is the experience of the fellowship of God who works within the smallest scales in order to re-create the larger. The redeeming work of Christ and the liberating experience of the Spirit give defining orientation for the community. The gospel is the promise of God and the people of the gospel are the people who express this promise in the way they live their lives, shaped in the free space so as to resonate this freedom in all spaces.

This then gives the church its two movements: that of gathering Christians into the church and that of sending out Christians into the world. This rhythm of inhaling and exhaling broadens the meaning of church beyond a Sunday service or building, including within it the whole context of the people—"in families, socially, and politically."[170] This transformative mission arises from a transformative participation. Christians become conformed to the Spirit, letting the Spirit orient their whole lives, acting with new responsibility and shaping their contexts in light of the Spirit's calling. "Christianity in the world is not there to say Amen to church meetings and events; it is there for something more and something different."[171] It is a transformative presence, a calling of the whole people of God, to be a community of equality and freedom, of discovery and resonance among the young and of the old, men and women—a community in space and in time, re-creating what it means to live together in the emphasis of God's prioritization of all of life. It is the free space where all can let go of insufficient forms

169. Ibid., 231.
170. Ibid., 234.
171. Ibid., 235.

of identity and take up a new way of living that highlights their particularity in the midst of a valuing community.[172]

This is the orientation of the kingdom of God, that enacts in particular spaces the messianic promise of God's work so as to be a messianic presence of God's work in a resonating way within every context.[173] This task is not to be the moral scold of the broader sinful world, to nag the world over its existential guilt. The church is an invitation. It is a movement of festal joy in the fellowship of the eternal God, throwing open the possibility for each person in all contexts to experience friendship with God, inviting people to be whole in the holistic work of God and experiencing this wholeness in renewing ways in communities of God's people in an increasing scope of reality.[174] The church, then, is the wide space of the Spirit existing in particular forms in particular contexts, awakening a new passion for life in the whole of the context, intensifying the love and the perceived possibilities, awakening a people to life itself and inviting them to participate in this new life even now.[175]

172. See ibid., 251–54.
173. See ibid., 247–48.
174. Ibid., 255–59.
175. See ibid., 267.

5

Practices of a Transforming History

In the first chapter, I began with a description of transformative churches and suggested these reflect in practice that which Moltmann has been emphasizing in his various theological works. In the previous three chapters, I focused on his major works and sought to highlight the ecclesiological themes that seem to run throughout his writings. The themes of history, anthropology, and trinity gather together these themes into a pattern of holistic transformation that orients as people and as a community in this world in light of God's work for this world. In this present chapter, I will highlight practices that relate to the themes of historical transformation. We are first transformed by the eschatological work of God and given a new perspective on history in light of God's encounter with us coming from the future. Our perceptions of the present become defined by the future instead of the past and this new perspective leads us to new patterns of life in our current contexts, as particular participants in the church in this world.

Transformative Eschatology

Just as this thematic study began with the study of the end in Moltmann's theology, *Coming of God*, so too does the first formal interaction with a transformative church practice.[1] "Merging ancient and contemporary spiritualties" does seem, on the surface, to relate more to topics of ecclesiology than a discussion of eschatology. However, it is precisely in how such an emphasis causes us to relate to God and time that we find the key orienting principle. Spirituality connects to all of life, whether our present culture wants to admit this or not. As such, our expression of spirituality is often an implicit expression of how we live our whole lives. The separation of the sacred from the secular in the modern world led to, in effect, a bifurcated spirituality in the church, and in each person, where going to church became a separated activity from being in the world, a purposeful moment of spiritual practice that could be contrasted with the rest of life. The rise of interest in spirituality over the decades, however, leads to another potential problem, in which the array of spiritualities provides a buffet of sorts, more supportive for one's chosen identity orientation and less formative or transformative.[2]

---

1. Cf. Jürgen Moltmann, *Ethics of Hope*, trans. Margaret Kohl (Minneapolis: Fortress Press, 2012), ch. 4, esp. pp. 38–41 and Peter Althouse, *Spirit of the Last Days: Pentecostal Eschatology in Conversation with Jürgen Moltmann* (New York: T&T Clark, 2003), ch. 3 for this phrase applied to Moltmann's own eschatology. See also Jürgen Moltmann's foreword in Althouse. He writes, "The more that Pentecostal theology is broadened into a kingdom of God theology, the closer it comes to that liberation theology that, through the work of Jon Sobrino and Gustavo Gutiérrez, is nowadays also embedded in a kingdom of God theology. In a comprehensive kingdom of God theology the healing of the sick and the liberation of the poor are effected together." While well outside the bounds of this present work, this quote suggests a key way in which transformative churches could be a fruitful conversation partner with Pentecostal churches.

2. Eddie Gibbs and Ryan K. Bolger, *Emerging Churches: Creating Christian Community in Postmodern Cultures* (Grand Rapids: Baker Academic, 2005), 218 write, "The pervasive practice of spirituality in Western culture marks the beginning of postmodernity, for as mentioned, modernity created secular space. Modernity separated spheres of reality into neat boxes. The so-called fact realms of the economic and the political were separate from the so-called value spheres of art, music, and religion."

The spiritual becomes a tool for secular success that broader culture defines.[3]

For those in transformative churches, there is an intentional move to navigate a different path than these two options provide. There is a pursuit of integration in spirituality, one that integrates time and space as it seeks to find resources throughout history that provide a holistic approach to worship. Such communities, Gibbs and Bolger write, "reach into the past for many of their spiritual practices. But they do not simply reach back for anything ancient. Instead, they select highly participative practices that integrate body and spirit."[4] This can be similar, certainly, to other postmodern expressions of spirituality that may combine a Buddhist or pagan spirituality as a boost to one's own progression in this world. The key issue is to avoid romanticizing such earlier spiritualities and to discern what is corrective for our era and what veered off track in past eras.[5] Such discernment can serve to resist the tendency for a "buffet spirituality," only supporting what is comfortable or aesthetically pleasing rather than actually formative. True formation involves the discipline of a coherent spirituality, not simply picking and choosing various elements.[6] Because of this, it is vital to commit to formative practices that are rooted in a Christian ethos, as well as practices that deepen discipline and challenge assumptions that are contrary to the kingdom of God.[7]

Because of the holistic intent, it is important to see such merging of spiritualities as going beyond a limited liturgy on a specific weekly service, and to see it creating rhythms for the community as the goal

3. This has much in common, as such, with many premodern spiritualities, in which the gods were not necessarily relational but functional.
4. Gibbs and Bolger, *Emerging Churches*, 220.
5. See ibid., 221, where they note the need for discernment.
6. For instance, the Rule of St. Benedict provides a holistic spirituality that is meant to be engaged as a whole.
7. See Gibbs and Bolger, *Emerging Churches*, 222.

throughout the week. These rhythms can help provide a continued orientation toward God and his mission in this world. "Christians need a renewed realization that God's mission can be engaged only as they are open to the leading of the Holy Spirit and recognize the need for his presence in their lives."[8] This intent to discover the Spirit's leading through the context of spirituality drives transformative churches to embrace patterns of worship that are grounded in tradition, as these practices have been broadly seen as providing substantive orientation toward God, as well as being less likely to conform to contemporary temptations of individuality, and other tendencies in our present era. By being discerning about the practices, these communities can gain from the strengths of the past while embedding them in the present. This allows both eras to contribute to the task of discernment—the past gauging the present and the present gauging the past—and communities to search out errors of assumptions in each era while embracing the wisdom that the Spirit provides throughout history.

Such an approach to worship puts aside the assumption that what is past is irrelevant and what is present is the pinnacle of human understanding. Seeking wisdom and formative practices in the past helps orient a person in God's eschatological history, seeing that God's work reaches to us from the future and so reaches beyond our time into our pasts, providing a source of great wisdom and guidance in any era. This approach, as such, pushes back against temptation toward idealism, understanding that our era has profound weaknesses as well, and that the determinative future may amplify those weaknesses or provide new ones if we are not continually reoriented within God's identity. This has led away from an emphasis on preaching or singing choruses as *the* expression of worship and

8. Ibid., 223.

toward more liturgical practices and indeed monastic models.[9] Gibbs and Bolger write that such churches "have shown a renewed interest in monastic spirituality, in which community is fostered through the practice of daily spiritual disciplines and mutual accountability."[10]

Spirituality is, then, a formative way of living that gathers insights from throughout the history of the church in order to provide a renewed orientation in this life that helps situate a person with God, instead of them being oriented by other identity-forming systems.[11] Such spirituality does not take a person out of this world. Indeed, such a spirituality should situate a person even more firmly in this world. The interest in spirituality by the broader culture is an impetus for transformative churches to embed a particularly Christian spirituality within their broader communities. Rather than bemoaning the trend toward vague spirituality, the goal is to affirm the search while orienting such a quest in light of the mission of God. The search is, after all, one of seeking the eschatological reality rather than the determinative experience. "They do this by living as 'spiritual' communities within their neighborhoods and among the networks they serve. They invite others to join them, welcoming them as people with contributions to offer."[12] The potential, again, is to use rhetoric of spirituality to substantiate one's own already-established identity. That is why many transformative churches include an element of spiritual direction from mature mentors. The context of spirituality insists on accountability so as to see past one's blind spots, and be the most effective resonance as possible within a neighborhood.

---

9. Celtic expressions are especially popular, combining as they do a tendency to mingle the physical with the spiritual rather than embracing a dualism that deemphasizes the physical. However, such "Celtic" practices tend to be modern reformulations rather than what really was some of the more extreme expressions of monastic life.

10. Gibbs and Bolger, *Emerging Churches*, 227.

11. See ibid., 230–31.

12. Ibid., 232.

An emphasis on spirituality in transformative churches is, in effect, much more than a postmodern trend. There really is a concern about "the extent to which lives are changed and gaining depth through the richness of encounters with God."[13] The exploration of God leads from the present into the past, and in this past and present one experiences the orientation of God's future, a future that is not defined by determinative or culturally mandated identities, but that is oriented around the God whose identity forms the basis of the world. This identity extends as mission into this world, and as participants orient themselves to this kingdom, they become empowered to live within this present as participants with God. This community then becomes "an anticipatory sign of the presence of Jesus" that is "commissioned and empowered by him and its life of obedience to his calling discovers his presence within and around in surprising and sustaining ways."[14] Spirituality that is eschatological in orientation is likewise not consumed with fear or concern about the future; it is a spirituality that is oriented around God's identity and presence. This is an eschatological interaction with this world in which we participate with God who is forming our identity in alignment with his identity.[15] This is a bond with God and others throughout time and space who have likewise joined in with this eschatological determination.

---

13. Ibid., 234.
14. Ibid.
15. Wolfhart Pannenberg, *Basic Questions in Theology: Collected Essays*, volume 2 (Minneapolis: Fortress Press, 1971), 248 writes, "Whoever has been gripped by God's future surely places himself, his trust, and his hope in it. But the ontological primacy of God's future over every presently existing form of human realization remains in force even here. For man will participate in the glory of God only in such a way that he will always have to leave behind again what he already is and what he finds as the given state of his world. Man participates with God not by flight from the world but by active transformation of the world which is the expression of the divine love, the power of its future over the present by which it is transformed in the direction of the glory of God."

Such a determination involves a way of transformative living that resonates this new life within specific contexts. Indeed, my third major conversation partner, Jon Huckins and his transformative church community in San Diego, have developed their six patterns as a path, noting that "we choose to walk through six postures of missional formation each year."[16] They frame this walk as the pilgrimage of a covenant community that, as Huckins notes, gives "intentionality to our practices while at the same time creating the context for us to employ our practices."[17] As a pilgrimage tends to progress from one point to the next in the journey, I will follow Huckins and his community in the order they provide.[18] This order provides a template of transformative living that takes seriously God's eschatological work in the specific setting of their community.

The first posture is that of "listening." While this may seem just the opposite of the previous section, it is indeed entirely in keeping with the main theme. Worship, in essence, is not something that God requires from us in order to sustain him. Rather, our need is to be in communion with God, to continually reorient and develop patterns of life that provide formative transformation, becoming more and more in tune with the work of the Spirit. This is, in essence, what the posture of "listening" is about as well. By listening we encounter others, and God, in a posture of openness to what they have to say, learning to receive and be shaped, rather than to assert or to dominate.[19] Huckins writes, "We desire to be attuned to God, to self, and to our neighborhood."[20] In effect, listening is analogous to retuning, listening for the chords of the context and the pitch of

16. Jon Huckins, *Thin Places: 6 Postures for Creating & Practicing Missional Community* (Kansas City: The House Studio, 2012), 27.
17. Ibid., 27–28.
18. Note by describing these as postures, they are not separated locations, but rather one can see them as liturgical expressions describing a particular stance along the missional pilgrimage.
19. See Huckins, *Thin Places*, 34.
20. Ibid., 28.

the Spirit in more precisely orienting one's own resonance within a setting.

Continuing this analogy, such retuning is less like a soloist—which is equivalent to individualism—and more like a symphony, in which a variety of different kinds of instruments are tuned together, in tune with one another and with the right overall pitch. This means that listening has, in transformative churches, a communal aspect that insists on the community walking together along this pilgrimage. By walking together, such a community grows closer together as they focus on the goal of aligning with God's work.[21] In this way, Huckins notes, they "are filled with hope, peace, conviction, and transformation."[22] This transformation has an eschatological nature, seeking to align with God so as to participate in his transformative work, a work that is oriented as his kingdom, determined by his identity, not by the past. By participating in this way with God, such a community becomes bearers of his resonance, reflecting within a community a new way to live for the community.[23]

This then carries with it an individual aspect, as the Spirit does not generalize but rather works in the complexity of particularities to build a renewed system of living. The task of individual transformation involves finding out who God desires a particular person to be. A mentor guides with discernment to help another person listen better to God, "creating a space" where questions are asked "that lead to realizing what the Spirit is already putting on our hearts."[24] This opening up to God in the context of community is about realigning oneself within the community to participate in the

21. See ibid., 36.
22. Ibid., 35.
23. Huckins, ibid., 36, writes, "When we commune with the creator, we allow his Spirit to transform and move freely through the life of our community as we continually put to death the ways of old, step fully into the mystery and conviction of life in Jesus, and live lives that reflect the transformation of Jesus' resurrection.
24. Ibid., 37.

eschatological renewing of God rather than other identity-forming systems. It is, in effect, by listening that one lets go and seeks to find integrity with God, an integrity that then, and only then, can lead to integrity with others in the focused community and integrity with the broader neighborhood.

This aspect of integrity within the overall context implies that transformative churches do not see themselves as bearers of the Spirit as much as they see themselves as participants with the Spirit, in alignment with Christ to join in with what the Spirit is already initiating. To listen in such a way means being present within diverse situations outside the narrow bounds of the church community.[25] God's eschatological history is a universal history, involving all contexts, and it is in the particular contexts that particular communities can see such universal work.

Implied in such work is the fact that participants with God are indeed advocates, not just models, of God's transformative work. They are advocates within the community for the broader community. "As advocates of the kingdom of God," Huckins writes, "we must put ourselves in contexts that allow us to listen to the myriad of stories that are being told."[26] Again, this posture of listening as advocates means that transformative churches are not seeking to impose their identity upon a context, but to align themselves with God's identity within that context, and helping others discover this identity in their own lives. Such advocacy of God's kingdom is participatory rather than representative.

The community is an advocate as a representative of the kingdom within the context, which listens to others and, in listening, learns how to participate in a transformative way. This pattern of listening

---

25. Huckins, ibid., 38, writes that "the listening posture requires our community to simply be present—both physically and emotionally—to the people, places, and issues that are the realities of our context."
26. Ibid., 39.

is not only for the needy neighborhoods, as such transformation is necessary in all contexts. Liberation is necessary in both the rich and the poor neighborhoods and those in between, albeit different kinds of liberations are necessary for different kinds of bondages, which requires listening to all the contexts for their particular issues and patterns of brokenness. "Without actively immersing ourselves in these stories, we simply become part of the problem."[27] There is a bigger story, as Huckins notes, and it is listening to this bigger story—first of God's universal work, then of God's particular work—that a Christian community becomes aligned with such a work and becomes participants with this transformative work in a way that orients itself with the identity of God.

Transformative Community

The pattern of "Living as Community" is one of the core three elements in emerging churches that Gibbs and Bolger noted in their text. All the churches they surveyed had this as a priority. The idea of community formation, is not, of course, one that is unique to either Christianity, emerging churches as they existed a decade ago, or transformative churches as they may exist now. The particular form of community is unique, as well as the underlying meaning substantiating such community. While it may not be a new expression as a value, it is, at the very least, a renewal of more substantive understanding of community than is common in most contemporary expressions of church. The emphasis on community in these transformative churches is one of created and sustained space where the kingdom of God can be actively pursued, shaping each person and the whole community together. By space, this is not

27. Ibid., 42.

implying a place, but rather a space for people to become who they are meant to be in Christ. It is the formation of "primarily a people," as Gibbs and Bolger note. These people are defined by Christ and seeking to live this out with each other, and in all parts of their lives.[28]

This transformative reality is possible through the power of the Holy Spirit as "the risen Christ now works by his Spirit, who operates through the community as well as beyond it, in the furtherance of his purposes in the wider world."[29] These purposes seek the overall work of God in this world. Rather than focused on the development of a church, the emphasis in transformative churches is on pursuing the work of the Spirit, and, in doing this, finding resonance with others in this pursuit. Thus, we can say that the Spirit works, and then the church is formed to work; first the Spirit works, then the Christian community must work.[30] "The kingdom gives rise to the community and not vice versa. The church is first the product of mission before it is an agent of mission."[31] This involves a change of allegiance, as well. In order to participate with the Spirit in this way, a person must align themselves with the identity of God rather than an alternate system of identity formation. Only in this way, and with a community of those likewise oriented, does a person truly resonate the life of Christ among others.[32]

28. Gibbs and Bolger, *Emerging Churches*, 90.
29. Ibid., 90.
30. Adapting Wesley's well known quote. See John Wesley, *Sermon* 85, III.2. Gibbs and Bolger, *Emerging Churches*, 91 write, "Consequently, to ask church questions without reference to the kingdom is fruitless. Emerging churches represent this viewpoint of kingdom before church. They are built on the premise that the mission God as entrusted to his church is concerned with actualizing the kingdom by being available to God and responsive to the leading of the Holy Spirit."
31. Gibbs and Bolger, *Emerging Churches*, 91.
32. I say "require" here more as an ontological insistence rather than some kind of enforced rule. However, this is one key way in which transformative churches are susceptible to error and, in my estimation, a good avenue for critiquing particular communities. Rather than critique them in terms of how they measure up to some standard template of church, critiques are necessary that gauge how well they are orienting wholly around Christ and God's overall work in this world—not establishing their identity around other ancillary or contradictory causes.

This emphasis on the kingdom as a priority means that the church itself is subject to critique and transformation. The priority is on the broader mission of God rather than prioritized practices that may have a basis in a different historic or geographic context. Ways of meeting and patterns of worship fall under a critical perspective. Transformative churches seek to discover a holistic understanding of life and learn how such a life is lived together. This tends to reflect more of a family-oriented model than a *polis*. "Church as family is primarily about relationships. It is not about meetings, events, or structures. Such rubric questions do not make sense when discussing relational issues."[33] With a relational understanding of community, the participants are more important than the practices, which then extends into the broader community as other people are also seen as priorities as particular people, rather than as targets or objects.

A danger, of course, with such a description is that families need not be transformative, and such communities that emphasize community as family or as friendship can easily devolve away from Spirit-oriented formation and into culture-oriented acceptance, maintaining the peace through nonconfrontation. This is why community formation has to be aligned with a Christ-centered orientation that provides a constant critique for practices and rhythms. Such a critique can especially be effective in such malleable approaches to Christian community, as there is a strong deemphasis on programs or any kind of regimentation.[34] Programs are often inefficient and often alienating, targeting some but leaving out others, and make it difficult to initiate new programs to address all the possible scenarios. The programs then themselves become the priority and people are assessed according to how well they fit, or how much they can volunteer for, the specified expressions

33. Gibbs and Bolger, *Emerging Churches*, 97–98.
34. See ibid., 103–4.

of church. Programs, then, can likewise become identity-forming systems embedded within a church, and can likewise become nonconfrontational and nontransformative expressions that exist for the sake of their own existence or as part of a tradition.[35]

The key issue is that community must not exist for its own sake but for the sake of accountability that leads to transformation into the likeness of Christ, for each person and for the community as whole. The goal is to listen for the Spirit and be led into practices that resonate the work of the Spirit for each person and for the community as a whole. A richness of relationship leads to Spirit-driven peace, a beloved community that expresses its love within—to each other—and outward, to those within its proximity. In essence, this redefines "quality of life" away from other standard answers—such as wealth, or sexual fulfillment, or security—and toward the more integrated and holistic, less egocentric, pattern of the Christ. This is an eternal dimension, which defines such eternity as entering into our present even now in the power of the Spirit. "Quality of life together here on earth," Gibbs and Bolger write, "points to the richness of relationships that can be fully realized only when the kingdom and the church coalesce with the return of Christ, but Christians must endeavor to embody that vision now."[36]

By embodying this vision as a community, participants become oriented within this Spirit-defined system and increasingly begin to reflect this in the whole of their lives, sharing a common mission with each other in the Spirit that reflects Christ in this world, in effect becoming incarnations of the Spirit as individuals and as a community.[37] Such people, then, are sharing life not only with each other, but being a model *to* the world—as if the church could

35. One wonders, for instance, how well the "Sunday School" model really leads to transformative realities for most church attendees, yet this is often maintained as the primary mode of Christian formation.
36. Gibbs and Bolger, *Emerging Churches*, 105.

somehow encompass all the elements of life that reflect life in this world. They are sharing the life of the Spirit with one another in the context of the world, which leads to sharing life with the whole of their context, becoming "a group of Christ followers who will act as change agents in the world."[38] This moves the idea of church from being a place people go to in order to find religion and into becoming a people who go where the people are to resonate the kingdom and the presence of Christ within established contextual structures. This is, to put it more simply, a matter of being like Christ in the midst of daily reality.

There is not a distinction made between "us" and "them" or any other kind of divisive differentiation. There is, to be sure, an acknowledgement of different identity-forming systems within specific contexts, but these systems are not inherent to the people themselves. Therefore, confronting the systems involves an attitude of inclusion rather than exclusion, inviting people to live in the new way of Christ in the midst of such alternative systems. Indeed this way of life in the midst of other approaches is the priority. Transformative churches "meet as a community to support their lives outside the community."[39] The community serves as a substantive place of resonance of Christ so as to provide tuning for the sake of living in the midst of other systems without being co-opted.

This is a creation of an intentional, relationally oriented, space that gives priority to a Spirit-driven identity, providing both a model and a mode for transformation. In providing such a space, new patterns of living emerge and are nurtured so as to become strengthened as a form of identity expression. These focused communities are not exclusive or sectarian but rather focused in their intent to form a

37. See Vladimir Lossky, *The Mystical Theology of the Eastern Church* (Crestwood, NY: St. Vladimir's Seminary Press, 1998), 173.
38. Gibbs and Bolger, *Emerging Churches*, 108.
39. Ibid., 109.

Christ-centered pattern of discipleship that can shape how they live the whole of their lives, thus becoming a source of resonance that can enter into a multiplicity of contexts with the resonance of the Spirit guiding and leading flexible approaches to ministry. "It is," as Gibbs and Bolger put it, "through living as a community that emerging churches practice the way of Jesus in all realms of culture."[40]

For the NieuCommunity in San Diego, Jon Huckins describes community formation in terms of two streams—inward and outward—that help orient them toward the *missio dei*.[41] Huckins understands this mission of God following Moltmann, as he begins his book with a quote from *Church in the Power of the Spirit*: "It is not the church that has a mission of salvation to fulfill in the world; it is the mission of the Son and the Spirit through the Father that includes the church."[42] A few pages later, he notes that as a church they are "acting as participants in the mission of God, which has been unfolding since the beginning of humanity's story."[43] The mission of the church, then, should contain the fullness of meaning that God's own mission provides, a mission that Christ and Spirit carry out in actively bringing this world back into communion with God. Those who participate in this mission become a "people choosing to extend, engage, and invite others into the story of God."[44] This, again, means that church is a people engaged in the mission of God; the mission of God is not defined in terms of the work of the church. This latter model prioritizes a preestablished definition of the church. With the former, the primary missionary in any context is God. God's work is the priority, with church communities aligning and

---

40. Ibid., 115.
41. Huckins, *Thin Places*, 19. Cf. Jürgen Moltmann, *The Spirit of Life*, trans. Margaret Kohl (Minneapolis: Fortress Press, 1992), 23.
42. Huckins, *Thin Places*, 15. He quotes Moltmann, *The Church in the Power of the Spirit*, trans. Margaret Kohl (Minneapolis: Fortress Press, 1993), 64.
43. Huckins, *Thin Places*, 17.
44. Ibid., 18.

orienting themselves within this pattern of identity and working in its complex particularity.

The two streams that Huckins notes are the monastic stream and the missional stream, which serve as the inward and outward elements of identity formation. In the monastic stream ("internal formation"), the emphasis is on communal and spiritual formation through a shared discipline of practices.[45] The kingdom deepens. In the missional stream ("external extension"), the story of Christ extends to others, to those who are living in other systems, and establishing their identity in insufficient ways.[46] The kingdom is shared. Huckins notes that in many faith communities, the emphasis is limited to Bible studies. He then asks, "Can the Bible be faithfully 'studied' if it isn't put into practice in the 'classroom' of our neighborhood, city, or world?"[47] Thus, there is need to integrate the deepening and the sharing, so that one feeds into the other. Such a "missional-monastic" emphasis, Huckins argues, allows a Christian community to express itself in ever-increasing maturity and influence. He writes that emphasizing the monastic-missional elements "creates a fertile soil to commune with God, live in deep community with others, and extend the good news of the kingdom in our local contexts."[48]

This kind of community reflects the life of Christ in three ways, which serve as three guiding values for their church. First, Huckins notes, "Jesus walked with God," a walk that prioritizes communion with the Father and is expressed in ways that illuminate such intimacy.[49] This intimate connection Huckins calls the value of

---

45. Ibid., 20.
46. Hugh Halter and Matt Smay, *The Tangible Kingdom* (San Francisco, CA: Jossey-Bass, 2008), 123, divide this into two further elements: "inviting in" and "living out." They then, in subsequent chapters, suggest four practices in each category that should be pursued by missional churches.
47. Huckins, *Thin Places*, 23.
48. Ibid., 24.

communion. Second, this walk was not exclusive but inviting, sharing with others so that they would share in the same intimacy. This generous intimacy is inherently inclusive, never isolating, with the very nature of the communion with God being relational. In restoring a relationship with the whole world, Jesus expressed relationships with particular people in a particular context. This gives both a deeper and a specific insight into the nature of the practices of God's kingdom with and among others. This is the value of "community."[50]

Third, Jesus did not limit his mission to his own life but made it part of his mission to help others to further the mission in their own lives, sharing and sending them with his mission as their mission. "Jesus commissions them to dive deep into their contexts as a sent people fueled by their communion with God and sustained by their commitment to one another in community."[51] The goal is to, as Huckins puts it, "enflesh" the good news in our own neighborhoods just as Jesus did. This is the value of "context." In all of these, there is an emphasis of pneumatological Christocentrism, an identity formed around Christ that is empowered and oriented by the Spirit. This integrates with God's identity and his mission in this world, as well as finding holistic integrity within each context as expression of Christ's mission to each context to bring every context back into relationship with the Father.

49. Ibid., 24–25.
50. Ibid., 25.
51. Ibid..

6

Practices of a Transforming Anthropology

Transformation in light of a new perspective on history allows us to see, as much as possible, the world as God views it, awakening us to possibilities even in the present. These possibilities lead us towards an engaged response to our own deficiencies and issues within our contexts. We are called towards a liberated and liberating anthropology. This transformation brings renewal as we participate with God's Spirit in becoming new people, living in a new way in, with, and for our contexts. This movement is the wayfaring journey towards an open fellowship with the Triune God, thus in this movement we rise upwards with the Spirit and resonate this movement in our relationships and encounters. This involves our being part of a new creation, resonating God's initial work, finding renewal in the context of Christ's work on the cross, and giving new exuberance to our hope in the fulfillment of God's promises.

Transformative Creativity

Redemptive activity in many churches—the idea of mission—is generally connected with preaching or works of service for those in need, or other more explicit expressions of obvious evangelism. The redemptive activity of God, however, ties into his identity as a whole, and with this is the reality that God is Creator. Jesus, as God, is about more than providing forgiveness for sins or providing the path to heaven. As God, he is also the Creator, and those who are called to be like him in their lives and contexts participate in this creativity as part of the process of redemption. "Part of that redemptive activity," write Gibbs and Bolger, "involves participating with the Creator in seeing entire realms of reality come to life. When Christians participate in this way, they share in the creativity of the Creator."[1] This is the transformative priority of creating as creative beings.

A theology of hope is, in essence, a theology of imagination, and such an imaginative hope expresses itself in creative ways within the community and context, creativity that can take many forms. This creativity in created beings is a participation with God, a resonance with God in accordance with his identity, as his identity orients our identity. Because he is not isolated in his identity but exists in triunity, so too do such creative acts within a Christian community involve the whole community.[2] "Creativity without full participation has minimal value for the worshiping community."[3] Thus, transformative churches seek to create space for creativity to flourish, a creativity that is not limited to ecclesial environments but is

---

1. Eddie Gibbs and Ryan K. Bolger, *Emerging Churches: Creating Christian Community in Postmodern Cultures* (Grand Rapids: Baker Academic, 2005), 173–74.
2. Cf. David S. Cunningham, *These Three Are One: The Practice of Trinitarian Theology* (Malden, MA: Blackwell, 1998), ch. 4.
3. Gibbs and Bolger, *Emerging Churches*, 174.

embedded within the whole of a community's context, which as such helps to enable creativity for that whole context.[4]

This creativity is an enlivening creativity that bonds us to our contexts and communities, awakening in the community a newfound love for what God has done and is doing. God's identity as Creator characterizes redemption itself, and participating in this redemption involves first discovering, then enacting, creativity. This creative exploration involves everyone. "Creativity without full participation has minimal value for the worshipping community."[5] This broad creativity pushes against the concept of a limited participation, with only a few encouraged to exercise their gifts, and such gifts being valorized as epitomizing the creativity of the community as a whole—with the others only given the role of responding. By encouraging and enabling the broad expression of creativity, creativity expands in scope, making and filling space. In many cases, space is redeemed. "One way they play a redemptive role is through creating beauty from what was considered ugly, thereby making sacred what was once profane."[6] At the core of this is the realization that all of life is worth salvation, bringing creativity to bear as way of reverence for the context and affirmation of its possibilities.

This pattern insists on a participatory structure in a community, where people go well beyond observing and receiving, and learn how to express the creativity that the Spirit works within them—a creativity that is life giving even as the Spirit is the Spirit of Life, and is sanctifying even as the Spirit is the Holy Spirit.[7] In this way, the

4. See ibid., 186. Here Gibbs and Bolger write, "Emerging Churches are more concerned with developing indigenous forms of worship that take context seriously."
5. Ibid., 174.
6. Ibid. It is important to note the terminology here. The sacred is opposed to the "profane" not to the supposedly secular. It is the "profane" that offers an alternate identity structure and is inherently opposed to God's identity. It should also be noted that "ugly" is both an aesthetic and theological category, but not one that provides estimation of ultimate value. What is ugly can, and should be, redeemed. What is beautiful can, and often is, misused in a profane way.
7. See ibid., 175–77.

expression of creativity within a community is not about egotistic identity, but about exocentric participation, learning with and among others, becoming open to freedom through the space provided by the beloved community, and in this freedom learning how to free others to find their creativity.[8] Creativity that is squelched is a squelching of the Spirit, as it is the Spirit who is forming people into a particular identity, and the process of this formation is always a creative transformation. "In Spirit-filled worship, people celebrate the diversity of God's gifts, gratefully acknowledge the gifts he has given to others, and discover their own gifts that can be offered on the altar as a gift to God and used in the body of Christ to enrich worship."[9] The spiritual gifts are, in essence, Spirit-driven transformation, which is embodied in each person in a unique way, and this unique way is an essential part of what they and the community need in order to find fullness.[10]

The danger of such an emphasis is that creativity itself can become an alternative identity system for its own sake.[11] This is not only happens in expressions of clear profanity but also in expressions, like preaching or music, that may be generally worthwhile liturgical practices. Creativity can lapse into egocentricity when it is establishing one's own self as important within a community. Gibbs and Bolger write, "For creativity to be truly worshipful, it must point

8. This exocentric approach can be itself understood as a proleptic movement in the life of believers in a church, moving beyond the distorted and often ego-centered relations that seek to establish community through means that are destructive to the identities of others. A renewed human identity established in Christ does not require authoritarianism or coercion or unity through uniformity. Instead, such a proleptic exocentricity reflects in the present the fullness of God's reconciliation in bringing unity through diversity. See Wolfhart Pannenberg, *Anthropology in Theological Perspective*, 529-532.

9. Gibbs and Bolger, *Emerging Churches*, 176. Cf. ibid., 178, where the lists of gifts in Scripture are discussed. They write, "The gifts listed are simply offered as examples of the many ways in which the ascended Lord continues to operate through his Spirit to accomplish his mission on earth. Furthermore, the context in which gifts are expressed is not restricted to ministering to the needs of church members."

10. See ibid., 189.

11. See ibid., 184.

beyond the persona and the giftedness of the individual or the team of artists to the one who has enabled them to exercise their creativity."[12] When the creativity points to the individual rather than pointing to Jesus it can become dangerous. The Spirit, after all, is always pointing toward Jesus.[13] When creativity is about egocentricity—establishing one's own identity—it is generally coupled with forms of jealousy or covetousness, fearful of the creativity of others. Such results indicate a lack of the Spirit's work in the creative act or even the pursuit of spirits other than the Holy Spirit.

This then leads to divisive interactions, which may hide in religious- or spiritual-sounding language. God-driven creativity, in contrast, affirms and gives space for the creativity of others, celebrating it with an attitude of joy and playfulness. Such playfulness also guards against taking oneself too seriously or letting the creative fervor go beyond the sustenance of the Spirit, and into one's own limited capacity, often leading to feelings of exhaustion or dullness. "An emphasis on playfulness provides a safeguard against artists taking themselves too seriously and against downplaying the contribution of others."[14] It is here that Moltmann's emphasis on orthopathy becomes especially valuable.[15]

Creativity is the avenue through which hope is expressed. By enabling creativity, one enables the imagination of each participant, and imagines the possibilities in every context. "Such a view is rooted in the theological conviction that every person is creative in one way or another for the simple reason that every person is the outcome of a Creator God, in whose image all have been made."[16] This

---

12. Ibid., 179.
13. Cf. Vladimir Lossky, *The Mystical Theology of the Eastern Church* (Crestwood, NY: St. Vladimir's Seminary Press, 1998), 159–60.
14. Gibbs and Bolger, *Emerging Churches*, 182.
15. Cf. Jürgen Moltmann, *Theology and Joy*, trans. Reinhard Ulrich (Bristol: SCM, 1977), 82. See also Jürgen Moltmann, interview with the author, May 19, 2011, beginning at 53:00.
16. Gibbs and Bolger, *Emerging Churches*, 190.

imagination that centers on possibilities rather than on determinative or negating identity fosters a hope for what God is doing, orienting a context toward the work of the Spirit that is enabling that context to resonate Christ rather than other alterative identity systems. Transformative churches thus "make space for imagination to thrive," and as such "participat[e] in God's works of beauty, making all things holy."[17] This creativity emphasizes participation from all because it emphasizes the creativity of the Creator God who is working in and through all, calling the whole world back into relationship with Father, Son, and Holy Spirit.

The creativity of the Spirit is empowering and affirming, redeeming each person and each context from destructive and profane expressions, into resonating with the fullness of life. This is an enlivening field of force, a resonating presence of God that allows people to see the world around them in a new way, as they discover the world as it was created and as God is redeeming it into becoming a new expression of his splendor.[18] This creativity is an expression of worship by the beloved community, within and for the whole context, embedding this creativity within the structures of that context. It creates a self-similar fractal of beauty within the context, one that affirms all that which leads to life and breaks down that which leads to death.[19]

One cannot be an outsider and know what lies within. For the community that is faithful to the work of Christ to resonate within a context and discover the beauty that is within the context, they must enter into the context. This involves learning and listening,

---

17. Ibid., 189.
18. Cf. Michael Welker, *God the Spirit*, trans. John Hoffmeyer (Minneapolis: Fortress Press, 1994), 22.
19. Gibbs and Bolger, *Emerging Churches*, 190 write, "Worship is part of the witness of the faith community to the wider community that God restores alienated humanity and in the process bestows beauty and creative energy."

discovering how and where the Spirit is particularly working. This involves being free to participate in whatever way the Spirit creatively leads them to enter into this work. This practice of discovery and participation in a context is what Huckins calls the posture of "submerging." By submerging, a person and a community gain a sense of the true reality of a place, no longer dependent on generalizations or mischaracterizations. They learn the context while in the context.

It is easy to judge and discern from afar, as there is often no way to accurately gauge the veracity of such judgments, yet such judgments can still serve as the basis for proposed action. Such actions would be, then, themselves malformed and mistaken, leading to deficient responses to hypothetical situations. A theology of participation that takes the Spirit seriously engages in the particularity of a context, developing a creativity that arises from the ecology. "Ultimately," Huckins writes, "it is only in submerging that we can get a clear picture of the landscape God is using to redeem us and to help us discover our role in it all."[20] This is a participation with the Creator God who loves what he has made and is seeking to redeem it, as its exists in infinite complexity. His people, too, must enter into this complexity, learning to appreciate what God appreciates, to love who God loves, to resonate with God's work as it is happening in the multiplicity of stories that exist in a given context.

By submerging into a context, transformative churches are choosing to be participants with God. The God who created is also the God who himself entered into this creation, incarnating within a very specific setting so as to accomplish his will in the midst of a very particular story. Those who participate with such a God likewise embed themselves in the narrative that is continuing

20. Jon Huckins, *Thin Places: 6 Postures for Creating & Practicing Missional Community* (Kansas City: The House Studio, 2012), 60.

to unfold, oftentimes speaking into such contexts with a depth of insight and wisdom that comes from becoming in tune with both the context and God's work in it. They deepen the context by bringing creative imagination to its history, culture, and current reality. "We become residents," Huckins writes, "who are engaged in the deeper realities of our cities and neighborhoods as we find ourselves in the places other may never have seen, experienced, or even know existed." He then adds, "We find ourselves exactly where Jesus wants us."[21] This involves being wholly in a place, committed to it, affirming it as a place loved by God, spreading reverence for what is enlivening in that place and resonating the enlivening power of the Spirit through creative engagement.

Huckins eschews the term *attractional* as being opposite to missional. People who are loving and affirming, who work to invest themselves in a context, should be attractive to those in the context. Very few things inspire love like being loved first, and people respond to acts of loving community. A submerging church contrasts with an "extractional" model, which pulls people away from a context or culture, leaving that culture and context without a resonance of a faithful community and leaving the faithful community without a context in which to discover the Spirit's broader work. A "submerging" posture refuses to concede the world to alternative identity systems, and expresses a love for the world by participating in the world, and in doing so working to draw others into the liberating freedom that comes with participation with God, a liberating freedom that redeems the context, not rejects it. Huckins writes, "When we submerge rather than trying to find ways to draw people into another world, we take it upon ourselves to draw close to our neighbors in contexts that are normative to them."[22] In drawing close,

21. Ibid., 49.

the mission is no longer about trying to solve problems as much as it is about resonating the imaginative creativity of God in a way that often surprises both those inside and outside the transformative churches, bringing resolution and redemption to the life that is a work of the Spirit.

As such, the point of submerging is not to be the knights in shining armor who save the day for the downcast villagers, but instead to be participants with God in contexts where God is already working, participating with those who are already there by creating spaces where the Spirit can resonate deeply and broadly.[23] It is about participating together so that God's identity can be the answer, where people see and experience his love. Submerging is, then, a posture of humility, an exocentric way of living that emphasizes the possibilities in others. It involves looking for God's work in people who are outsiders to many churches.[24] Submerging is also a posture of patience. As it is the Spirit's work, a community cannot force transformation or initiate redemption on their own. By submerging, a community is committed to resonating the work of the Spirit in their midst in creative ways, ways that sometimes do not bear very much visible response. Huckins notes that just as Jesus waited thirty years for his ministry to become public, so too with transformative churches, "what may feel like wasted time is quickly redeemed by the Spirit when we linger and submerge with intentionality."[25]

This is a creative intentionality. It resonates the work of the Creator God in creating this world, submerging so that by being in

22. Ibid., 50. Such a posture also insists that those submerging likewise leave behind alternative forms of identity formation. See also ibid., 53. Here Huckins writes, "As followers of Jesus, we accept the vocation to be mediators between God and humanity. We must put to death . . . former identities and agendas and be brought to life . . . for the sake of the contexts in which we finds ourselves."
23. See ibid., 59–60.
24. Ibid., 59.
25. Ibid., 52–53.

tune with God people discover the contexts as God sees them. This creativity celebrates the ecology of a place by helping it to discover its own unique contributions, redeeming the creative passions already present, and providing avenues of participation so that the contexts themselves become alive anew.[26] The posture of submerging is both active and humble, entering into the context as a participant with God's mission, embedding a liberating community of Spirit-resonating men and women in the midst of a neighborhood so that the work of the Spirit in that neighborhood can resonate even more deeply and broadly.

Transformative Welcoming

Part of identity formation in alternative systems is a distinction between who is included and who is excluded, the exclusion happening because alternative identity systems are not substantive enough to maintain their structure without creating boundaries. They are susceptible to dissolution precisely because they are inherently unstable and noneternal. This is also true for philosophical systems—orienting philosophies that often serve as a proxy for religious devotion, providing the same sense of self in light of an often utterly incomprehensible existence. Modernity, as mentioned earlier, can thus be defined as orienting a culture into opposition against reality itself, imposing our potential upon the world to shape it into what suits us best as individuals.[27] The model of Jesus in the

---

26. See ibid., 60–61.

27. Gibbs and Bolger, *Emerging Churches*, 119 write, "Postmodernity represents, on the other hand, a time when plurality is accepted and order and control are relinquished. Within culture today, both modernity and postmodernity exists side by side. Risking oversimplification, modernity is evidence in those areas in culture and society where control, homogeneity, and universals reign, whereas the areas that express freedom, difference, and plurality are postmodern." This is indeed an oversimplification, but one that does seem to especially reflect the expressions of churches. It must be noted that with this "freedom, difference, and plurality" come new problems, as there

PRACTICES OF A TRANSFORMING ANTHROPOLOGY

Scriptures, however, shows the willingness of God to seek out those who are estranged from him, willingness to come into our world so that he can bring the world back into relationship with himself. The incarnation is a transformative submerging, one that enters into a context in order to welcome people, inviting them as beloved participants into a new way of living that, in their context, reflects the fullness of life that is oriented around Christ in the power of the Spirit in accordance with the Father. God's identity as God is secure in his eternal triunity, and in this security God can welcome others without fear of dissolution or being co-opted.

This is precisely why those communities that seek to orient their personal and communal structures around the mission of God also must go beyond merely meeting in a place. Their passive involvement often substantiates the structures of identity formation that exist in that place, or on the other side, insisting foreign, preestablished patterns of being must be adopted by the context.[28] Thus, part of a spirituality that is oriented around the mission of God in a place insists on welcoming those in that place, including those who are often excluded. "A truly missional church," Gibbs and Bolger write, "integrates worship with welcome. . . . They demonstrate welcome by identifying with people of all walks of life in their contexts."[29] Again, this is not about establishing a building where people can be invited into it, as much as it is a willingness to be among people who would not see themselves as included within a

---

is a significant wariness to critique others, not wanting to appear judgmental. This can become so thorough that the church community loses any prophetic voice within a culture, merely baptizing it with spiritual pursuits, while unwilling to offend even those who are deserving of offense. The model of Jesus as accepting others must be balanced with the model of Jesus who was not wary about affirming what is right and denouncing what is actually wrong.

28. Such as happened in many cases by missionaries going to previously exotic lands like Hawaii or elsewhere—where being "Christian" often meant adopting the patterns of American or European culture.

29. Gibbs and Bolger, *Emerging Churches*, 119.

Christian community—and who would not respond to invitations to attend a church service—people whose identity is elsewhere.

There is an evangelistic element—especially in terms of witnessing to the holistic transformation of Christ to those who inquire—but just like the ministry of Jesus, there is more to the welcoming than speaking words about salvation. "Worship and welcome find expression in witness, both verbal and acts of kindness and sacrificial service, and in the pursuit of peace and justice."[30] This is, in effect, an expression of exocentric hospitality, extending a welcome to those outside of the narrow bounds of Christian community in order to share with them the extension of life found in such a community. Sharing a meal together is a regular expression, one that contains a multiplicity of meaning shared across subcultures, bringing diverse people together in a moment of trust and openness.[31]

---

30. Ibid.

31. Although it is outside the bounds of this current study, seeing the meal fellowship as a way of welcoming the stranger and affirming the bonds of a community at the same time is a worthwhile expression of the Eucharist, one that may have more in common with the early *Agape* feasts of the early church and less in common with the heavily liturgical, and often divisive and alienating, practices that have developed over the last many centuries. Such a communitarian view of the Lord's Supper is likely the best way to understand how transformative churches celebrate this practice. See, for instance, Steve Sommers, "Church as Subculture" (PhD diss., Fuller Theological Seminary, 2001), ch. 6. Sommers, 209 notes the particular elements that fit within a postmodern milieu. He writes, "To counter the mistrust of grand narratives, one must consider again the core message of the Lord's Supper. In this ritual meal, we make space for the other, even others who are our enemies. According to Thiselton, we must realize that at the heart of the celebration is the idea of gift which demands nothing in return. This understanding of gift contradicts any notion of the validity of manipulative power or domination that corresponds to a 'church' concept of ecclesiality versus the subcultural model. This gift which comes from God is the very love of God. Only love that genuinely gives itself to the other in the interests of the other is capable of dissolving 'the acids of suspicion and deception.'" He goes on to note that such a gift without demand is primarily oriented toward the outsider. He writes, 209–210, "The gift without demand refers to the relationship of the community to those still outside the community of faith and those who are yet unreconciled within the community itself. Communities whose identity is formed by habituation to the Lord's Supper are committed communities—communions of committed persons whose service to neighbor is the test of the authenticity of Eucharistic life." For a more direct interaction with transformative churches. see Janine Paden Morgan, "Emerging Eucharist: Formative Ritualizing in British Emerging Churches" (PhD diss., Fuller Theological Seminary, 2008).

The model of Jesus is one of welcoming the outsider, going to and in the midst of the excluded, inviting them into fellowship with God. This is an invitation to an eternal communion, the grandest scale of all. In representing life oriented around Christ, in the pursuit of modeling the kingdom of God, communities committed to such a kingdom reflect a self-similar impulse at the smaller scale of a particular neighborhood. As such, "if they are to be faithful to the way of Jesus" they "must welcome the outsider."[32] This involves the creation of physical and relational space where distrust and disillusionment can break down so that healing can begin. Such outsiders, to be sure, are often outsiders for a reason, whether because of forms of societal disapproval or because of antipathy to the identity of God.[33]

By being a safe and welcoming community, people learn how to lower defensive boundaries and resist asserting an alternative identity in contrast to others. This involves both a continued commitment to Christ, along with an openness to other perspectives and experiences that may reveal more of an individual, more of the community, and different aspects of the work of the Holy Spirit. In being both focused and open, a welcoming community allows those who are outside of Christ to learn how to listen and discover who they really are in light of the Spirit's work, becoming whole in Christ by being free to be who they are without a need to protect themselves from identity dissolution.

This approach to welcoming tends to embrace what can be called an "embodied apologetic."[34] Roughly, this is similar to the common

---

32. Gibbs and Bolger, *Emerging Churches*, 121.

33. It is important to note that the term *outsider* is not limited to those who are obviously rejected by society, cast out or stigmatized as being lesser. Even the wealthy and seemingly successful can often experience the alienation of self or society, often masking such alienation even more in individualized pursuits of apparent success or by establishing themselves even further within alternate identity systems such as may be created by wealth or power.

narrative-writing advice to "show, not tell." Instead of relying on rhetoric or verbal arguments, living out this life with Christ amidst others best exemplifies the apologetic for a life with Christ. Such expression validates the message with lives that reflect this message in practices, and includes others in the context so that they likewise experience the resonance of a life oriented toward Christ. "One cannot," Gibbs and Bolger write, "understand the truths of Christianity as an outside observer. One needs first to experience the embodied truth of the community."[35] Life lived according to the Spirit is not, after all, merely a set of practices for their own sakes. It is an expressed identity that values unity and diversity, which requires not only observation but also interpretive experiences that convey holistic meaning, thus sharing the identity of Christ by inviting others to experience the meaning of this identity in practice, making it an aesthetic reality rather than a logical determination of alternative truth claims.

The latter are insufficient partially because of the postmodern tendency to accept the paradox of seeing multiple truths, as well as the experienced reality that identity formation is often untrustworthy as an immediate argument. The path of wealth and power, after all, provides a much more substantive identity in theory—providing for one's physical comforts and control over one's own life. The experienced alienation of such identity paths, however, contrasts with the fullness experienced in a committed community that is oriented around Christ. Modern apologetics tends to emphasize orthodoxy, which is helpful but insufficient for people's experienced realities. Forms of response that only "presume to have definitive answers to every barrier to belief" can actually be both alienating and egocentric,

---

34. Gibbs and Bolger, *Emerging Churches*, 125. See also Tim Morey, *Embodying Our Faith: Becoming a Living, Sharing, Practicing Church* (Downers Grove, IL: IVP, 2009), ch. 1. Morey makes an embodied apologetic the central approach of his ecclesiology.
35. Gibbs and Bolger, *Emerging Churches*, 125.

as the goal may often be less about leading someone into relationship with Christ and more about being "right"—thus asserting one's own ego against others.[36] An embodied apologetic that welcomes the stranger, including them for who they are in their particularity and interacting with them as real people, becomes a more thorough apologetic in its christocentric humility and greater responsiveness to the work of the Holy Spirit in a particular situation.[37]

At the root of authentic welcoming is its own christocentric identity formation—becoming servants to the community—and that involves becoming a cruciform community. Much evangelism has more of a sales sensibility about it, getting people in the door in order to get the convert, expanding the church in numbers, and deploying those numbers for more sales opportunities. In such an approach, there can indeed be elements of hospitality, but these are often thinly veiled moments with clear ulterior motives—not unlike hosting a party where a salesperson can opine about the usefulness of Tupperware or a beauty product. Instead of welcoming, these can become alienating as people begin to distrust the motives of those who only want to sell a product.

A truly welcoming community is one that does not offer a product, it offers itself as a community for the sake of the broader community, a servant to the context. Such a community is willing to sacrifice and suffer for the sake of others, resonating the work of Christ by being Christlike among their neighbors, looking to enhance and help rather than drain and take, committed to real people as people, not as targets or objects. The goal is to help change lives, to confront false forms of identity formation by the resonance of an identity that is formed in and expressive of Christ, a life that breaks down the barriers of enemies and competitors. The messianic people seek to include other

36. Ibid., 126.
37. See ibid., 126–27. This more fully reflects orthopathy and orthopraxy in addition to orthodoxy.

people in a holistic community, where they are free to become who they truly are, as who they are aligns with the one who created them to be.

This is a humble apologetic and also a highly public apologetic.[38] In a rhetorical apologetic, outsiders deliver words to the context then withdraw back into isolated enclaves. A lived apologetic, however, is effective only inasmuch as it brings the transformative reality of the Spirit into diverse situations, living out the identity of Christ precisely where other insufficient identity systems seek to hold sway. This living out the life of Christ in the midst of a context is a community endeavor that seeks to include others in the life of a Christ-oriented identity, again not by insisting on losing one's identity but by coming alive in the light of the Spirit's freedom. This requires a welcoming community to welcome strangers as themselves bearers of Christ and the Spirit, bringing with them a particular story and a particular identity that Christ is himself wanting to enliven. Welcoming the stranger thus involves learning about Jesus by being with those who Jesus is with—the outsiders.

The purposes of a transformative church community are oriented toward the kingdom rather than self-focused, as seeking the work of the Spirit outside the narrow bounds acknowledges the fact that the Spirit was in the context long before the church itself became established. Instead of excluding and conforming to a narrow perspective, a truly missional community participates in the mission of God by seeking out this mission with and among others, including and welcoming so that a multiplicity of stories can be empowered in the life of the Spirit to resonate the fullness of Christ in every context. The agenda, then, becomes about breaking down established boundaries, including others, seeking those who are left out, discovering the fullness of Christ by being with those who Christ is

38. See ibid., 130–31.

with. As this is done, the kingdom of God becomes a transformative identity for the people and for the whole of the context, resonating a new peace and hope in an imaginative creativity.

It is only through listening to a context and submerging into the midst of it that Jon Huckins and his church community in San Diego feel it is possible to invite others to participate with them "with softer hearts and more intimate understanding."[39] This idea of intimacy is particularly important as it reveals a quest for a living relationship, being open to the other and letting the other enter into the vulnerability of one's own space, while being willing to enter into the other's space. This is also a posture of storytelling, a continuing narrative of the story of God contributing to the stories of the committed participants. This continuing narrative, then, invites others to share and include their own stories. By inviting others in such a way, a community learns even more about the inviting God, deepening this story of God by participating in it, and through this discovering the depths of such a God and intimacy with him.

Jesus modeled such an invitation, and so the community that is seeking to model itself after Jesus must likewise model this kind of invitation. In this way, the example of Jesus continues to spread through the power of the Spirit into the lives of those who experience such openness, breaking down the barriers that alternative identity systems erect and resulting in lives that are being transformed Christward. Huckins notes the example of Patrick of Ireland, who had been submerged involuntarily into Irish culture when he was captured as a slave, and then there, in his humility, learned to listen to others and especially to God. When he listened to the voice of the Irish in his dream, he followed the lead of the Spirit to enter back into the context of Ireland, illuminating for them and with them the love

39. Huckins, *Thin Places*, 66.

of God—a transformative love that confronted what was evil while embracing who they truly were.[40] Huckins writes, "He understood that most people need to belong before they believe. They need to be listened to and understood because when people sense that someone really understands them, they begin to believe that maybe God can understand them too."[41]

Using the language of invitation in less than inviting ways is not uncommon, such as the Tupperware style parties mentioned earlier, where an ulterior motive increasingly causes suspicion against people whose only motive is to gain sales. The invitation as Huckins means it is not about marketing. On the other side, Huckins notes, this invitation is likewise not equivalent to absolute inclusion (which Huckins calls "radical hospitality"). Such absolute inclusion requires substantive commitment. Their community is committed together in light of their commitment to and with Christ, an apprenticeship that is aware of the variety of identity-forming systems that may seek to co-opt such commitments. Such commitments involve submitting "all aspects of your life to Jesus and to your community of faith and to collectively practice the way of Jesus."[42] With this center, the community can then be open to practice practical hospitality (helping those in need) and inviting people to begin sharing the life that is being resonated within the committed community. "We invite people," Huckins writes, "into a radical reorienting of life in the way of Jesus that is submitted to the reign of God as it is manifest in his advancing kingdom."[43] This is an invitation into a new way of living expressed in the context of a community, a relational reality that expresses God's redemption and restoration in words and in practice.

40. See R. P. C. Hanson, *The Life and Writings of the Historical Saint Patrick* (New York: Seabury, 1983).
41. Huckins, *Thin Places*, 71.
42. Ibid., 72.
43. Ibid.

Jesus was, as Huckins notes, the Messiah and as such, the promised savior who spoke words of truth.[44] However, he was not the Messiah that people expected, coming in glory or exerting political power. He expressed his power in his participation with those who yearned for substantive salvation, and it was around Jesus that they found the acceptance and meaning and, indeed, salvation that allowed them to participate as whole people once again. "It was not," Huckins writes, "an invitation that was to be contained within the Jewish communities, but one that would transcend and transform people of all races, religions, and regions."[45] It was an invitation contained in the approach of the cross, an invitation that extended to the forsaken and the outsiders and the suffering in the midst of forsakenness and outsiders and suffering. This invitation extended itself outside the preestablished bounds of the people of God, inviting the outsiders to be insiders, gentiles joined with the Jewish believers.

This extension of the people of God continued as the members of the church were committed to each other and to prayer, while also showing such commitment in the midst of their contexts, wherever this was. They "made themselves available to the community through intentional presence and engagement."[46] This orientation is open to

44. Ibid., 76.
45. Ibid., 77.
46. Ibid. Huckins goes on to write, "They were willing to step out of their assumed traditions and follow the Spirit's leading and receive renewed revelation that would greatly advance the kingdom of God." Here we see a significant distinction from Hauerwas's approach. Even though Hauerwas is often very popular among transformative churches, his effective sectarianism that has the church be a model *to* the world, rather than a people *within* the world, is not followed by transformative churches. Indeed, one may argue that Hauerwas is, essentially, promoting a Pharisee-style relationship with the world, illustrating a commitment to God that serves as an example to others. See, for example, Stanley Hauerwas and William H. Willimon, *Resident Aliens: Life in the Christian Colony* (Nashville: Abingdon, 1989), 46. They write that Christian testimony should be "an alternative polis, a countercultural social structure called church." This also reflects more of the American fundamentalist style, which dissociated from political and social involvement. Hauerwas and his supporters protest the sectarian label, but tend to twist the common meaning of sectarian into a more specialized charge in order to avoid what is often seen as more of a negative appellation. See for instance, Arne Rasmusson, *The Church as Polis: From Political Theology to Theological Politics as Exemplified by Jürgen Moltmann*

the Spirit's continued invitation to be a people and to embrace all the people the Spirit is seeking, participating with the mission of God as the Spirit is orienting it within a context, rather than relying on sales techniques or artificial relationships in order to build the church through human management. The invitation, then, is not to a meeting or event, but to experience a system of life that is oriented around and in Christ, where the Spirit resonates freedom and renewal. This is effectively a space—not a place—of discovery that can exist in a variety of ways and formats and moments.[47] It is a space where people feel both accepted and motivated to discover more about this reorienting life with Christ.

Huckins notes a woman named LaDonna who was invited into the space of the community: "Although much of what we did was foreign to LaDonna, being surrounded by people who cared so deeply for her and her family while they worshiped the God who so clearly informed the lives they were living created a space for her to feel her own connection with God."[48]

This invitation, then, is the beginning of discovering the acceptance that a person has in Christ and the beginning of the transformation that is enabled by Christ in the power of the Spirit, a transformation that orients them anew within their context. This is an invitation to help redeem their history and their context, not to ignore it or dismiss it. As they participate in the inviting community, the resonance of the Spirit's work within this community transforms them as well, reshaping their identity away from insufficient systems

---

and Stanley Hauerwas (Notre Dame: University of Notre Dame Press, 1995), ch. 11, where he engages in a somewhat tortured exegesis of the root *sect* in order to make his case. The more common meaning of sectarian is a people who set themselves apart—which is precisely what Hauerwas is arguing for—so that the church within itself is a model *to* the society rather than a mission *within* a society.

47. Though Moltmann's favored phrase "A broad place where there is no cramping" is also certainly apt.

48. Huckins, *Thin Places*, 79.

and toward the fulfillment and fullness that can only come in Christ. There should be no other agenda than seeking to help each person find their own fullness in Christ. This is an invitation to rest—to a banquet in which people feast together in celebration of life together.[49] This is a perichoretic invitation, in which lives begin to intertwine and speak into each other, an expression of the kingdom that exists in specific contexts, with specific people, culminating in the infinite complexity of God's kingdom, which invites all those particularities into eternal communion with him.

Transformative Hope

How we live expresses the hope we have. A life filled with hope experiences life in a renewing way and a life filled with hope responds to other lives in a renewing way. It is through this hope in God that a person and a community become free to help others discover this hope for themselves. Real hope can never be egocentric, as it is the promises of the God of hope that establishes such hope. God calls his people out of deficient forms of identity and into a new life—a life expressed with generosity. Gibbs and Bolger write, "At the core of the gospel is God's generosity embodied in the concept of grace."[50] So too do those who are committed to him and empowered by the Spirit to be his people express such hope within a context through a generous grace. This is especially important in our present culture, where competition and monetization are such ingrained elements in just about all facets of life. Such responses are reflections of fear rather than hope.

49. Ibid., 81. Here Huckins writes that it is "the invitation to shared life that has been unfolding through the everyday experiences of daily life." He adds that further, it is "no longer about our invitation to them; it was about their invitation to us. We were given the gifts of deep friendship, shared life, and communal transformation."
50. Gibbs and Bolger, *Emerging Churches*, 137.

Competition and monetization express themselves through a consumerist identity, where one seeks to gather all that is possible and orients life toward what can bring the greatest gain, establishing themselves, oftentimes, as isolated bulwarks in competition with other resource gatherers.[51] A person can express such an identity in many different ways, often including ways that have helped shape the contemporary ecclesial landscape. Because "the economic sphere permeates all other spheres to the extent that virtually all parts of a society are touched by economic concerns," there is a prophetic role in shifting the orientation away from consuming—which is establishing hope in oneself—and toward the forms of hope that exhibit a confidence in God's identity.[52] This is true for individuals as well as for churches, often exhibited in mutually supporting competing claims that shape practices toward an almost antagonistic struggle for dominance.[53]

This reflects more of the marketing ethos than a christocentric ethos, wherein marketing seeks to attract customers to their product—tailoring their marketing for what would sell the product, while consumers are both wary of and attracted to such marketing.[54] "The underlying assumption is that customers are never satisfied

---

51. See, for instance, Ayalla Ruvio, Eli Somer, and Aric Rindfleisch, "When Bad Gets Worse: the Amplifying Effect of Materialism on Traumatic stress and Maladaptive Consumption," *Journal of the Academy of Marketing Science*, 42 (2014): 1–12. The authors researched trends in Israeli society and noticed that when fear of death or disaster increased, people increased their purchasing. They argue, in marketing terms, for stores to take advantage of this by making higher cost items more visible during times of perceived danger. This points to how a fear of death underlies much consumerist motivation rather than greed for its own sake. Thus, hope may serve as a more precise counter to consumerism than guilt or other responses.

52. Gibbs and Bolger, *Emerging Churches*, 136.

53. Of course, no one would argue this struggle is portrayed as such, or even acknowledged as such.

54. Indeed, given the research mentioned in n51 above, this would point to an implicit marketing motivation for a fear-inducing eschatology, one that emphasizes judgment and hellfire, thus leading people to be more willing to give to the church what they had. When consumer society has many more options and less trust in the teaching of the church, this methodology is no longer effective as a marketing technique and never was quite effective as good theology.

---

and are liable to take their business elsewhere. Satisfaction is an elusive target, constantly moving and taking on new forms."[55] Such approach to life in general and church in particular creates a fine balance of mutual antagonism in which each side expresses a desire for the other, but only insofar as the other meets their felt requirements. When Jesus is the product, then he is a commodity among all the others, tested for usefulness in any given situation and either discarded altogether or relegated to a separate sphere of perceived efficacy.[56]

For transformative churches, however, Jesus is not a commodity. When Paul notes in Philippians that "to live is Christ," he is pointing toward an expressed identity, not what we take but who we become. A community expresses this hope by seeing people as particular people, not as objects or targets or commodities. In doing this, they resist allowing "anonymous consumers to continue consuming."[57] This is a major issue, especially in industrialized countries. The effect of consumerism is not freedom but a new form of slavery in which identity is formed by addiction to goods and services.[58] This usually expresses itself through oppressing, orienting people in competition and envy, defining the kind of liberation that is needed in such societies. Transformative churches "believe that people need to be delivered from their covetousness and selfishness so that they can be liberated for a life of service and generosity."[59] Compulsory means

55. Gibbs and Bolger, *Emerging Churches*, 137.
56. For Evangelicals, such a sphere is often limited to issues of existential guilt.
57. Gibbs and Bolger, *Emerging Churches*, 138. Gibbs and Bolger here use the phrase "do not allow," which not only is too strong and suggests a form of authoritarianism, but it is also not particularly true. The distinction is the commitment away from a consuming lifestyle, but as with all of life, there are mistakes and exceptions, often occurring in ways that are justified by particular communities and not perceived as consumeristic. One need only consider the predominance of Apple products in all their varied contemporary culturally impressive splendor.
58. Echoing Romans 7.
59. Gibbs and Bolger, *Emerging Churches*, 139.

generally do not accomplished such liberation, with the compulsion often inverting the power structure rather than changing the system. In contrast, a community must learn to express life so that consumers become givers. This expression is one of hope, hope in something greater than itself and more thoroughly life sustaining than what can be consumed.[60]

Instead of competing for resources or attention, instead of interacting with people in terms of what they can provide, a christocentric hospitality "means reaching out to one's neighbors, first to meet their immediate needs and then to address their deeper, long term needs."[61] This embodied spirituality takes seriously the fact that we are a physical people whose reality involves our physical and spiritual needs overlapping in complex ways. This expression of the kingdom is worldly inasmuch as the Creator God is involved in this world. The work of the Spirit enables the kingdom to be experienced even now in this world.[62] Social action, then, cannot be separated from Christian spirituality, which seeks to embody the kingdom rather than to preach an escapist revivalism.

This is, essentially, an ethos of hope in God's promises of redemption, and results in interacting within a community with an eye toward such redemptive moments, seeing the possibilities rather than abandoning the neighborhood as Godforsaken.[63] In light of the forsaken one who was resurrected, there is no person or place wholly

60. I am reminded of Eph. 5:18, extending the quote to suggest we should avoid getting satiated with any kind of product—many of which are often much more addictive, and more insidious, in our day and age than wine. The emphasis on avoiding alcohol has long been, historically, accompanied by the outright encouragement of other kinds of greed and identity distorting practices.

61. Gibbs and Bolger, *Emerging Churches*, 140.

62. This means the goal is not to take people away from their life, or point to a hope that is only in the future or only outside of their present experiences, but to bring hope within present lives and circumstances. See ibid., 152. Gibbs and Bolger here highlight one leader, Mark Scandrette, who "notes that teachers, lawyers, and others are all under God's reign." The goal then is not "to pull people away from their life but to push them farther into it": farther into it so as to discover the fullness of God's work in their present context and callings.

forsaken by God, and so to be engaged with God is to be engaged in this world in the ways that reflect God's own grace and generosity to, especially, the "least of these."[64] In helping others, "they see this as a spiritual practice, not a social service. They look to serve others as part of a holistic way of life."[65]

This emphasis on holistic generosity as an expression of the hope that is found in Jesus affects evangelistic strategies as well, where the goal is not as much to discover targets to evangelize but to get to know particular people, and by loving them in practice exhibiting the good news of the gospel.[66] This is an exhibition of hope for them and with them, hope that is expressed in the establishment of an alternative kingdom within the midst of a community, a kingdom that is, essentially, an alternative identity system oriented around the identity and promises of God. "The kingdom is a specific response to a specific context."[67] It is an ecological hope, one might say, that expresses hope in action within the complexity of a location, rather than providing a generalized message to anonymous people. It is also ecological in the sense that evangelism in many cases involves less reaping of the harvest and more rejuvenating the soil. Countries in the industrialized West, after all, do not lack access to churches, but

63. See Gibbs and Bolger, *Emerging Churches*, 152. Here Gibbs and Bolger write, "It would be a serious mistake to interpret the foregoing conversations as simply a return to the liberal, social gospel of the 1920s. Emerging churches are committed to Jesus and to making him known."
64. See ibid., 142. Gibbs and Bolger here note that such churches "in the context of their lives, take care of the marginalized." This generally means avoiding establishing formal programs, though often does mean getting involved in community programs that offer help to the needy—such as Habitat for Humanity.
65. Ibid., 144.
66. See ibid., 145. The wrongly attributed quote of St. Francis was often used early in the emerging church movement. "Preach the Gospel at all times. Use words if necessary." This has changed over the years as the reactionary tendency has become more balanced. Dan Kimball, on Facebook, http://www.facebook.com/DanKimball, July 19 writes, "I also stopped using this quote because I learned how St. Francis DID use a lot of words and did teach/preach in addition to actions. And more importantly, I think I over-reacted to some degree when I first used this quote—and fully believe now that we must preach the gospel WITH words and have it backed up by action."
67. See Gibbs and Bolger, *Emerging Churches*, 147.

often—and increasingly—lack a sense of relevancy of those churches. We are a burned-over culture where people often are rejecting their perception of Jesus—and rightly so in many cases—rather than rejecting the truth and grace of Jesus.[68]

One key way to express generosity is by particular service with and among the poor. "If God is with the poor, then Christians should give high priority to giving to the poor."[69] It is important to note that such giving cannot only be directed "to," but should be with and among, because otherwise it devolves into yet another transactional relationship. Gibbs and Bolger note this, adding that transformative churches do not help from a distance, but "work in and among, not from the other side of a divide. They minster out of a relationship, for compassion signifies feeling with, not simply for, another person."[70] This leads to a further development of holistic generosity rather than a generosity that is limited by preestablished perception of needs.

When one lives with and among others, the complexity of their lives take shape and so a complexity of generosity develops, indeed a mutuality of generosity develops, as all people have needs of one kind or another, some of which are financial, some emotional, some in ways that might be unexpected. There is, with this, "a renewed emphasis on all of life." A life of generosity is shaped in community by a holistic pattern of interactions. People give space to each other, and open up to each other so there is a mutually supporting context

68. See ibid., 147–49. Gibbs and Bolger, 150, quote church leader Dave Sutton who says, "The church has no voice. I work with the most vulnerable people and families. As I work with them, the people begin to think the church is relevant. And what if that begins to happen on a larger scale? The message of the church, the gospel, can then be heard. It is very much about working slowly, doing achievable activities, supporting what is going on. And that is what is attractive—when we see the needs of the community being met." Cf. Jürgen Moltmann, *Religion, Revolution, and the Future*, trans. M. Douglas Meeks (New York: Scribner, 1969), ch. 6. Moltmann here shows his early insight into the particular problems and transformative solutions for the Western church, suggesting four key areas in which such Christians are in need of liberation.

69. Gibbs and Bolger, *Emerging Churches*, 149.

70. Ibid.

of provision—an exocentric emphasis where one does not have to fight to gain but is free to live in light of the generosity of others—a generosity that is mirrored in one's own life. Theologically, we might see this as developing a perichoretic life that established on mutual *kenosis*, elements that reflect Trinitarian community itself.[71]

People also express hope in the life of a particular context by contending for this context. In a way, this is the counterpart to generosity. Generosity helps make up for what is lost and missing, while contending for a person or a context is actively seeking to help the person or context overcome old barriers and discover new possibilities. It is only through the imaginative creativity of a hope in Christ, empowered by the Spirit, that such contending becomes a substantive expression of the kingdom in the life of a community. Indeed, contending is an important part of hope, and an important corollary to generosity, precisely because it is activating hope rather than responding to crises, which can easily become discouraging or overwhelming, especially in those places that need the resonance of the Spirit the most. In discussing his committed community's posture of "contending," Jon Huckins writes that "while simply ignoring those who are in need is a temptation and far too culturally acceptable, our role as God's people is to step into these stories and contend for those who are broken, hurting, and alone."[72] This contending is part of who we are as participants with God. He adds, "We are to be the manifestation of the good news brought about with the arrival of God's kingdom."[73]

This is indeed, an expression of the body of Christ, incarnating Christ in the power of the Spirit, within a variety of contexts. This

---

71. At least in Moltmann's conception of the Trinity. See Patrick Oden, "Liberating Holiness for the Oppressed and Oppressors," in *A Future for Holiness: Pentecostal Explorations*, ed. Lee Roy Martin (Cleveland, TN: CPT, 2013), 205–24.

72. Huckins, *Thin Places*, 86.

73. Ibid.

posture of contending is exocentric in practice but includes self-awareness and a willingness to put aside the tendency to compete against others for one's own gain. As with all the practices, such a posture is transformative for the individual, for the committed church community, and for the context—orienting responses to this world in a way that resonates the values of Christ and his kingdom.[74] This includes confronting what is unjust, praying for and among the community, and drawing others into the sphere of the Spirit's resonating influence so that they can find a new freedom from their determinative history in the movement of the Spirit's eschatological activity.[75]

This posture of contending is an expression of Christ's continued work, as it was Christ who contended for his context, and then for all contexts, contending against forms of oppression, deceit, illness, and much more, contending against the ultimate enemy, that of death. In contending for their neighbors, the community reflects the image of Christ as the community is contending together. This posture creates an expectation of hope, where specific instances give rise to specific problems, orienting the committed community within God's kingdom. This kingdom is not a generalized understanding of God but extends actively throughout this world in infinite complexity. Huckins writes that he is "convinced that the very act of joining God's heart of global justice actually gives us courage to stay in the game in our own context and keep following after Jesus."[76] They seek to join with those who Christ seeks to join with.

74. See ibid., 88. Here Huckins writes of the questions that living in community prompts him to ask: "Am I riding the bus with the people in my life who I have been called to love and serve? Am I willing to set aside an excessive lifestyle which can only be sustained by a certain income in order to be fully available and present to meet the needs of my community and neighborhood?"

75. See ibid., 88 as well as the whole chapter for examples of what this means in their particular context.

76. Ibid.

This contending as a community includes contending for both the committed community and for the wider community that forms their overall context. Huckins notes that one problem with other intentional communities he has heard about is the fact that they became so focused on contending for the broader context that they lost a focus on the need to contend within. They forgot to confront the kinds of problems and issues that arise within the committed community and because of the commitments of that community. Huckins and his intentional community seek to avoid the idealism that characterizes unsustainable Christian communities by being willing to contend for the community by confronting and resolving issues as they arise.[77] At the core of this commitment to contend for the community is the idea of covenant, which following the model of Exod. 19:8, is "rooted in the belief that this commitment would be beneficial to the parties involved as well as to the surrounding community." It was an exocentric covenant rather than a competitive or adversarial one.

Huckins notes three elements of this covenant as it is portrayed in the exodus narrative, and which bear upon the present covenant community's own commitments.[78] First, the covenant shaped Israel's sense of identity, especially as God worked in delivering them from bondage and then as he walked with them through the trials of the wilderness. The presence of God was with them in the tabernacle as well as in the charge to be God's people in the midst of the world, "being a community on mission for the good of the nations."[79] God was faithful and contended for his people, but the people struggled to reciprocate this faithfulness. Even still, there were always people

77. See ibid., 91.
78. Ibid., 94–96.
79. Ibid., 94.

willing to contend for God, and in doing so they were models for the rest of their community.

The second element of covenant was invitation. In effect, this relates to the posture discussed in the previous section, where an invitation was into becoming part of this new people of God, with specific implications for those who were part of this covenant commitment.[80] The choice to enter into community is a choice to enter into contending for the community, being willing to shape one's own life as oriented toward God, and being willing to contend for more harmonious relationships with others in the community. This leads into the third element, that of vocation, in which the covenant community "was to be marked not by power and prestige, but by faithful submission to the God who was faithful and present."[81] As this covenant community contended for adherence to these elements, they were an "alternative community that reflected the good news by living radically different from the world around them yet remaining radically engaged and inviting."[82]

Contending for a community, whether for the covenant community or the broader community, does not imply one has the power to fix everything or that one has all the answers. Indeed, oftentimes, as Huckins notes, the most effective community-building contending involves brokenness.[83] This orientation toward Jesus then helps people orient toward other people, experiencing the openness that one's own brokenness needs and the communion that comes from refusing to accept such brokenness as definition or all encompassing, turning instead to participate with and for others. This

---

80. I am reminded here especially of the story of Rahab in Joshua 2 and her salvation and inclusion in Joshua 6. Her testimony in chapter 2 is especially notable as a testimony of faith in God's identity, a testimony that can be contrasted with much of the grumbling of the already-included people up to this point.

81. Huckins, *Thin Places*, 96.

82. Ibid.

83. Ibid., 108–9.

deep community then, in its brokenness and commitment shaped by hope, enables honesty, being open to being helped as well as helping. This honesty in a covenant community builds trust so that competition and egocentricity need not drive one's identity formation. As one is free to be whole, and experiences the transformation of hope and trust in the midst of a covenant community, people become missional. As Huckins notes, "Our other-centeredness takes us beyond this community."[84] By becoming in the covenant community who they are to be within the broader context of this world, this "exodus" church contends for their community against the polarizing and autonomy-emphasizing elements of identity that defines so much of Western culture.[85]

84. Ibid., 109.
85. Cf. Jürgen Moltmann, *Theology of Hope* , trans. James W. Leitch (Minneapolis: Fortress Press, 1993), ch. 5.

7

Practices of a Transforming Trinitarianism

The goal of transformation is not the fulfillment of the human self as a determining subject. In highlighting the anthropological elements of transformation, it is important to see these are initiated and oriented towards God's self, his triunity, a unity of persons who exist in eternal relationality. The mode of transformation involves our particular selves in our particular contexts, with the shape of this transformation finding fulfillment in the presence and personalities of the triune God. God who creates, creates in line with his own being, and it is this being that provides the substance of our own identities. In light of this, a truly Christian transformation involves practices that reflect the Father, Son, and Holy Spirit as persons and as a unity. Such practices, then, orient us to live in light of God's own reality, conforming to the Kingdom that is his presence and rule, in light of the way initiated by Christ, and through the constantly renewing power of the Holy Spirit.

1.2 Transformative Trinitarianism

Gibbs and Bolger open their eighth chapter by writing, "The Gospel makes possible full participation with God in the redemption of the world."[1] This full participation is a living relationship in which God draws us into participation with his work as we find a renewed orientation in his identity. This is a sharing of life with him, a joining with him in the perichoretic mutuality, and as we do so our actions and identity within this world become aligned with his kingdom and resonate his presence wherever we go. It is a witness of words and it is an ontological testimony of our being amid this world that participates in the redemption of our contexts as the Spirit uses and leads us toward redemptive acts that prepare and transform our locations. This is, essentially, a living out of Trinitarian theology as a formative reality for our lives and our communities. This perichoretic community expresses itself with God and with this world. There are two practices of transformative churches that especially emphasize this particular Trinitarian ontology, both of which are in the Gibbs and Bolger text. In what follows, I will look first at the practice of "Participating as Producers" and then "Leading as a Body."

When inviting people into the kingdom, Jesus invited the insiders and the outsiders, those with clear gifts of service and those with questionable pasts, pasts that suggested a variety of ways they were not able to offer very much to their context. In the power of the Spirit, however, the work of the kingdom is not what we bring to the table, but rather whose table we sit at, so that, in joining with this communion, both insiders and outsiders are empowered for participation.[2] Gibbs and Bolger write, "Once seated at the table

1. Eddie Gibbs and Ryan K. Bolger, *Emerging Churches: Creating Christian Community in Postmodern Cultures* (Grand Rapids: Baker Academic, 2005), 155.
2. Cf. David S. Cunningham, *These Three Are One: The Practice of Trinitarian Theology* (Malden, MA: Blackwell, 1998), ch. 5.

over which the Lord presides, the participants together represent the reality of the universal priesthood, a kingdom of priests, in which all have equal say."[3] The Spirit who empowers resonates the life of God into the life of the community, and this resonating life reflects the mutuality of God's own experience of eternal communion. In other words, the Spirit forms as the Spirit is. God forms the community that reflects God's experience of community.[4]

Because God invites people into community rather than creating a transactional kind of relationship that reflects an exchange of service for worship, so too does a particularly Christian community formed by the Spirit move away from a consumeristic approach to church or life.[5] The actual practice of a community of equal participants is part of the transformative work of the Spirit. A continuing development of community expresses sanctification, not simply something that people can do out of their own power or ideas. The determination to move toward such expressions of community, however, is part of the Spirit's resonance among a people and among a context.[6] "Emerging churches," Gibbs and Bolger write, "are determined to move from a consumer to a producer form of church."[7] Attending such a community insists on participation, as it is in participation that one joins the resonance of the Spirit. One might say there are no wallflowers at this dance. Resonating with the Spirit means participating with the Spirit and participating with the Spirit means participating in the life of a Spirit-resonating community, receiving as one gives, and giving as one receives—not transactionally but

---

3. Gibbs and Bolger, *Emerging Churches*, 156.

4. See ibid., 157. Here Gibbs and Bolger write, "Seeing the kingdom at work through egalitarian ways of being was not simply a theory for the early church—it was an observable social reality."

5. We can see an interesting example of the contrasting approaches to religion can be seen in Acts 14:8-20. Cf. Ovid, *Metamorphoses* 8:611-727.

6. It is here that an interesting study can be pursued that looks at the transformative churches and the early Pentecostals—whose emphasis on the gift of tongues was often accompanied by a countercultural pattern of community, especially in terms of racial diversity.

7. Gibbs and Bolger, *Emerging Churches*, 159.

relationally, and often counterculturally against our mode of passively receiving entertainment.[8]

Worship is, by nature, participatory, as we are particular people who are called into particular relationship with a relational God—whose Spirit provides particular gifts to each person so they can participate in a particular way in a community, giving each community a particular expression of the fullness of God's resonance in this world.[9] "Christians," Gibbs and Bolger write, "need to be enfolded into the worship experience through the gifting of those who lead, but each person has gifts to extend and to enrich that worship experience."[10] The formative elements of a participatory worship lead into an active, rather than passive, interactivity of spiritual community, the result of which is the proactive spirituality of those who are in such church communities. They become ontologically formed into producers within the church setting and they thus are such people in the whole of their lives. "Christians are worshipers not one day in seven but seven days a week."[11] The formative act of worship, then, orients how someone worships throughout their lives—passive worship creates passive Christians and participatory worship forms participatory Christians, so that being involved with Christ throughout their week is not one of volition but of ontology.

There is no wall between sacred and secular in our relationship with God or in our relationship with others. Worship thus reflects

---

8. Of course, this passive reception is changing as technology has enabled an expectation of interactivity that moves away from the lecture or showmanship or musical performance model, where people in an audience are expected to receive while the professional provides the content. Indeed, here we can see the movie industry as reflecting the older model while video games represent the participatory culture that is developing. On understanding the cultural aspects, and ontological implications, see Jane McGonigal, *Reality Is Broken: Why Games Make Us Better and How They Can Change the World* (New York: Penguin, 2011).

9. See Gibbs and Bolger, *Emerging Churches*, 162–65.

10. Ibid., 159.

11. Ibid., 160.

and forms who people are, with created artificial divisions becoming formative to the kind of person someone is in their life. Thus, to suggest that the church itself is a model *to* the world is to create a people who are bifurcated into living two kinds of realities, an existence that is ontologically confusing and unsustainable. In light of God's integrity as Creator and our integrity with him, the economic church is the immanent church and the immanent church is the economic church. We communicate to the world who we actually are, and who we actually are is shaped in the context of who God is, a formation that is oriented within a covenant community so that the people of this covenant can be such people throughout the whole of a unified life.[12] Kester Brewin notes that transformative church leaders "are looking for the time when people begin to take responsibility for presenting worship to God which has integrity for who they are, involves their own struggles and gifts, and shows some personal investment in communion with their creator."[13] In essence, this responsibility is the expressed affirmation of each person as a particular participant, affirming their life as a unique life and pushing against the dehumanizing, and death-oriented, systems that seek to deny a person's vitality in church or anywhere.

Transformative churches involve people in the planning and expression of their focused worship meetings to encourage a transformation that propels people to continue such participation and involvement in worship throughout each moment of their life, learning how to think creatively in resonating good news to all their overlapping contexts. "Members, in the exercise of their gifts in their life settings, become good news as they function in the way in

---

12. This works the other way around as well, in that the church expresses who it is, so that if it is, in itself, oriented around someone or something other than God, its expressions in this world will likewise be insufficient. Thus, orthopraxy and orthopathy become an insights into the substantive, rather than rhetorical, orthodoxy.

13. Quoted in Gibbs and Bolger, *Emerging Churches*, 160.

which the ascended Christ has equipped them in accordance with his purpose."[14] Full participation as part of a covenant community that forms people in a particular way to be a particular kind of Spirit-resonating people in the broader world, with their participation in the church extending as the church's service to and with the world.[15]

This is an identity that is formed around the identity of God, and inasmuch as it is so formed, it reflects this identity for and with this world, even as Christ was this identity for and with this world. The resonating incarnation of the kingdom-oriented people in their context becomes a transformative reality for this context—a presence of life, of healing, of renewal, a resonance of hope. This empowered formation is formative within and outside of the covenant community, transcendent in its formative identity and immanent in its physical participation. Indeed, Gibbs and Bolger write that these churches "embrace both the transcendence and the immanence of God."[16] This is the expression of God's identity with and for this world. All of our participation with and for this world expresses this, as individuals, as a covenant community and as people within contexts where there are competing systems of identity formation. Thus, the formative practice of these churches seeks to avoid the tendency to be disconnected or remote from the world that can happen when emphasizing God's transcendence in isolation. It also seeks to avoid the tendency to so overemphasize God's immanence that he becomes an always-affirming buddy, valorizing our contexts for how they already are.

The transcendent God only challenges, becoming an unapproachable Other, distant, remote, and life-negating in its

14. Ibid., 169. I do quibble a little bit with the emphasis on the ascended Christ as the equipper. This is more properly the role of the Spirit; though of course, it becomes dangerous to draw too fine a line between the Spirit's and Christ's work.
15. Ibid.
16. Ibid., 170.

splendor. The immanent God only comforts and supports, never challenges, becoming a far too approachable compatriot, who reflects our image, and as such becomes life negating by, essentially, sustaining alternate forms of identity formation rather than calling people into a transformative identity system. "It is," Gibbs and Bolger write, "in the dynamic tension between the immanence and the transcendence of God that people encounter the holy, the *mysterium tremendum* that both attracts and causes people to withdraw in awe-inspired, reverential fear."[17] This is an ecclesiology of *transcendent immanence,* which becomes the counterpart to the Spirit's immanent transcendence, a reflection of the life-sustaining participation of God in this world that is resonating in the life of the people of God in this world.[18]

For participation to be truly free, and for a community to be truly equal in a way that everyone's resonance of the Spirit is taken seriously as a worthwhile contribution to the community—thus allowing for formative space to develop further such resonance—there must be forms of leadership that give space to such participation. As we are made in the image of God, and God exists as Trinity, then when we emphasize the reality that as participants with the Spirit each individual in a covenant community not only can, but also must, participate in the worshiping life of the community that extends into the context as a whole, we are also emphasizing leadership that itself is modeled after the Trinitarian identity of God. Leadership that is authoritarian in expression inherently deemphasizes the Spirit for the sake of a more binarian structure. Here a different pattern takes shape. The Father transmits authority to Christ to the apostles, and then to us through the authority passed down through

17. Ibid.
18. Note that both concepts are necessary together, and express the work of the Spirit moving from God to us and us to God. See Figure 1.2 in chapter 1.

generations and acknowledged in ordination.[19] However, our access to the Father is through Christ through the Spirit, each of whom mutually emphasize each other. The church, then, as a priesthood of all believers is where we gather through the Spirit through Christ in covenant with the Father. As Gibbs and Bolger put it, "The church should resemble God's beauty as it displays a peaceable community through the nonhierarchy of the priesthood of all believers."[20]

A participatory people engage with God in participatory fellowship.[21] Instead of a leader giving identity to a group of followers, as happens in many churches, leadership must be about the creation of space and the formation of a context of faith where participation and freedom and safety can thrive, so that in such a space people become more fully who the Spirit has created them to be. In this becoming, they resonate the same new life in all their contexts—creating space for others to find their way to Christ. Transformative churches, "in their attempts to resemble the kingdom, avoid all types of control in their leadership formation."[22] Certainly, some forms of leadership are necessary—even being a gift the church is given by the Spirit. Some forms of control often are less about creating a context for people to thrive and more about conforming people to a preestablished model assumed by the leader—a form of control that establishes the leader as the identity-forming system in many cases.[23] Inasmuch as such control stifles and

19. Gibbs and Bolger, *Emerging Churches*, 192 see this expressed in modern churches as an expression of the modern God, where authority is "based on power, control, and submission to authority."
20. Ibid. In using the term *peaceable*, Gibbs and Bolger echo a term utilized especially by Hauerwas. Moltmann would, of course, quibble with this phrase, arguing that the church is a peacemaking, not merely a peaceable, community. See Jürgen Moltmann, interview with the author, Tübingen, Germany, May 17, 2011, 25:05. It is active, not passive; involved not contained.
21. Gibbs and Bolger, *Emerging Churches*, 200 write, "A single leader produces a truncated form of Christianity, one that does not offer the richness of all gifts shared."
22. Gibbs and Bolger, *Emerging Churches*, 192.
23. See ibid., 193.

limits the development of people according to their life in the Spirit, such control is oriented toward death.[24]

Leadership, thus, has the very distinct potential of being either enlivening and inspiring or discouraging and depressing. Even if such control is intended with good motives, such motives move away from the example established by a social model of the Trinity and impose an artificial boundary upon the community. "For emerging churches, the key challenge is to dismantle all systems of control and to reconstruct a corporate culture according to the patterns of the kingdom."[25] This may be a difficult task, yet the difficulty is not itself a reason to reject it as a goal, even a sign, of a church increasingly reflecting the values of God's kingdom—and the patterns of work of his Spirit—instead of models of power that may be more immediately successful in maintaining order. Not only is this necessary in terms of practices, it is also an aspect of the whole vision of the church—for the church to reflect the vision of the Spirit for the context, one person cannot be deemed the only bearer of such vision in the church.[26]

Leadership as it exists in transformative churches tends to be oriented according to a more free-flowing system of positioning, in which leaders are the people exhibiting Spirit-oriented leadership gifts within the community. Such leadership is not about wanting to lead—which is often an expression of an identity requiring outside validation—but about simply being someone who does lead. Often, but not always, this includes the founder of the community, a position many would call an apostle.[27] When people gather, some emerge as leaders, and so the task is to recognize such gifts while

24. Ibid., 197.
25. Ibid., 194.
26. Ibid., 196. See also ibid., 203–7.
27. For use of this term in transformative churches, see especially Alan Hirsch, Tim Catchim, and Mike Breen, *The Permanent Revolution: Apostolic Imagination and Practice for the 21st Century Church* (San Francisco: Jossey-Bass, 2012). Hirsch here and elsewhere is a strong proponent of using Eph. 4:1-16 as *the* key framework for ecclesiology.

orienting it within a community that emphasizes all gifts. "Leadership based on gifting requires people to give place to others. This means they acknowledge their own limitations as well as the gifting and the leadership authority and potential of others."[28] Indeed, being gifted in a particular area implies a leadership potential for that area, so that while leadership in general is a gift, almost everyone is called to be a leader in their own specific ways.[29]

Leadership also becomes evident through a passion for the context and the commitment for developing kingdom-oriented practices. The hardest working and the most active in such tasks tend to lead, as they have invested the most into such contexts, and often such passion is a result of the Spirit's motivation.[30] However, while passion is an indicator, there is still a necessity to determine leadership as a community, with the quiet and less active also able to contribute in key ways. The tendency to manipulate and create power structures based on who works the most must be continually addressed so as to maintain a balance, not only for the community but also for the people who want to work.[31] The practice of the Sabbath becomes a very helpful discipline, as also is the task of community discernment.[32] Discernment can take place in a number of ways, but one key way to discern Spirit-led leadership is to look at the record of such leadership. Instead of emphasizing a role, one that is based on having worked in

---

28. Gibbs and Bolger, *Emerging Churches*, 199.

29. Ibid. Gibbs and Bolger here write, "Once gifts are discovered, the individuals with those gifts can be expected to lead in certain areas." The analogy of noncommissioned officers in the military may be useful here.

30. This is not always the case, as a discernment is needed in order to reveal Spirit-imbued passion versus passion that arises from feelings of inadequacy or a need to prove oneself—elements that suggest a misaligned identity.

31. See Gibbs and Bolger, *Emerging Churches*, 201–2.

32. While not strictly a transformative church in the present framework, the Society of Friends (Quakers) have long promoted community discernment and are, in many ways, a substantive historical precursor to contemporary transformative churches. See Lon Fendall, Jan Wood, and Bruce Bishop, *Practicing Discernment Together: Finding God's Way Forward in Decision Making* (Newberg, OR: Barclay, 2007).

churches or being credentialed to work in churches, transformative churches emphasize leadership that exhibits successes—success in the areas that are valued by such churches.[33]

The most important element of transformative church leadership is that it "is invested from below, rather than imposed from above."[34] The participants in the church recognize leadership and continue to affirm it by a shared vision of participation. The goal is not to tell people what to do, but to help create and maintain a context where people are free to do what the Spirit is leading them to do—a place of restoration, creative imagination, exploration, and becoming. Jon Huckins notes, "Leaving room for the Spirit to initiate these encounters of divine imagination for our lives, we embrace a leadership structure that is built from the bottom up rather than the top down."[35] Those who lead, then, lead most fully by helping others find their own freedom to be leaders—to become alive in the Spirit and express more fully their identity that finds substantiation in God. The consensus helps shape the direction and vision of the church, while leaders help create and maintain the context that allows this vision to blossom.[36]

Access to God is not accomplished through the leader—instead, access to God is seen as part of the Spirit's work in creating each person anew, and in this enlivening process, the leaders help each participant discover how best to discern this enlivening work and how best to discern areas of life that lead away from Christ and his kingdom. The space is made for the Spirit, which creates a dangerous space of sorts, one that takes a risk that the Spirit may actually lead

33. See Brandon Hatmaker, *Barefoot Church: Serving the Least in a Consumer Culture* (Grand Rapids: Zondervan, 2011), 163–73. While he uses different terms, Hatmaker's criteria for success can be loosely connected to the themes of orthodoxy, orthopraxy, and orthopathy.
34. Gibbs and Bolger, *Emerging Churches*, 205.
35. Jon Huckins, *Thin Places: 6 Postures for Creating & Practicing Missional Community* (Kansas City: The House Studio, 2012), 127.
36. See Gibbs and Bolger, *Emerging Churches*, 211–13.

particular people and the community in ways that are initially new or uncomfortable to the leaders. Again, the goal is not to steer the church, but to help maintain the context of the church as a space for people to develop their gifts and identity. This is important not only to avoid substituting one's own identity for the work of the Spirit in the community, creating a controlling environment that maintains order through submission. It is also important because controlling leaders create passive followers and develop churches in which a small number of people do most of the work.[37] In contrast to this, Gibbs and Bolger note that leaders "must create a space for others to do the work."[38] By creating space for the involvement of everyone, leaders help everyone invest in the mission of God in that context, participating in the work that God is empowering the people to accomplish in their varied contexts.[39]

Jesus exemplified this model of leadership.[40] His ministry expressed wisdom and works of power, expressions that revealed the depth of his connection with God, and, as such, a credible witness for the kingdom that others should follow. The kingdom is the priority for transformative churches, and so leaders must submit to this kingdom and express their leadership by helping people in their communities discover more fully God's work in that context. Such help is a visible expression of servanthood. A true leader in such a community pushes against forms of deficient identity formation, helps to interrupt stifling power structures, gives voice to the voiceless and strength

37. See ibid., 210. Here Gibbs and Bolger write, "Gift-based ministry does not flourish in a controlling environment. This is evidenced when controlling pastors preach sermons and lead seminars on spiritual gifts, but all their teaching fails to translate into getting more people involved in a wider variety of ministries. Creating awareness without creating space simply leads to mounting frustration followed by apathy."

38. Ibid., 210. See also Jürgen Moltmann, "The Church in the Power of the Spirit," in *The Holy Spirit in the World Today*, ed. Jane Williams (London: Alpha International, 2011), 16–18.

39. Cf. Cunningham, *These Three Are One*, ch. 9. He calls this emphasis the Trinitarian practice of "persuading."

40. See Gibbs and Bolger, *Emerging Churches*, 215.

to the powerless, and helps those who do not know how to walk along the way to find their legs and begin to dance on the path that is leading to the kingdom.[41] Leaders also are servants by helping individuals find connection in the community, and participants to find deeper connection with each other and in the community.[42] In all of this, the goal of leadership is to help each person become in full who they are called to be in the whole of their lives. As this is accomplished, such people become leaders in helping others along the way, forming a resonating network of transformation that expands into the space of every context, resonating the life of the kingdom deeply and broadly.

Transformative Identity

In prioritizing the mission of God, transformative churches seek to prioritize the particular emphases and manner of such a mission—a mission that the person of Jesus embodies.[43] This mission is one of incarnation and involvement, becoming embedded in this world so as to bring salvation to this world, dying forsaken and rising again in the power of the Spirit. This priority then relativizes every other element of church life, and as such identifying with Jesus—with the whole of his life and mission—is the first core element discussed by Gibbs and Bolger.[44] It is the center from which everything else develops, the constant that forms other expressions of being and meaning.[45]

---

41. Ibid.
42. Ibid.
43. Cf. Jürgen Moltmann, *The Future of Creation*, trans. Margaret Kohl (Philadelphia: Fortress Press, 1979), 106–9.
44. See Gibbs and Bolger, *Emerging Churches*, 59–61.
45. For an interesting study of Christ as the constant—analogous to Einstein's theory of relativity—see Jim Geiger, *Christianity and the Outsider* (Eugene, OR: Resource, 2012).

The whole of his life and mission includes his teaching, his practices, as well as his death and resurrection, all of which are a single expression of a focused mission of God in this world—a mission of hope that shows us the way to and in this life of hope. "It is this kingdom hope," Gibbs and Bolger write, "that inspires emerging church leaders as they seek to realize that promise within their communities, striving for them to become servants and signs of that kingdom as they live God's future, which is both already here and remains to come."[46] This goal is vulnerable, of course, to interpretations about the life and teaching of Jesus—as well as interpretations of the overall *missio dei*—so this pattern is both especially important and especially in need of constant theological assessment.[47]

Incarnation is the most general model of the mission of God as seen in the life of Jesus, in which God comes into this world and goes out among the people. So too the emphasis in transformative churches is about being in the world and going out into the world, a continuing incarnation of the body of Christ that seeks out those in need of good news.[48] Instead of putting time and resources into an increasingly professional service that can attract an audience, the emphasis becomes equipping each participant so that they can

46. Gibbs and Bolger, *Emerging Churches*, 47–48.
47. See ibid., 49. Here Gibbs and Bolger note that these churches rely "heavily on the New Testament scholarship of N.T. Wright and to a lesser extent the work of Mennonite scholar John Howard Yoder and missiologists David Bosch and Lesslie Newbigin, among others, for [their] understanding of Jesus, the gospel the kingdom, and the *missio Dei*." See Jeremy Begbie, "The Shape of Things to Come? Wright Amidst Emerging Ecclesiologies," in *Jesus, Paul and the People of God*, ed. Nicholas Perrin and Richard Hays (Downers Grove, IL: IVP Academic, 2011), 183–208. Begbie notes five reasons why Wright appeals to transformative churches and five themes in Wright that seem to be ignored. To this list can and should be added the work of New Testament scholar Scot McKnight, whose intentional connection with the transformative church movement has provided "in-house" New Testament scholarship of sorts, through his books and his very popular blog Jesus Creed, http://www.patheos.com/blogs/jesuscreed.
48. This is meant in its most literal sense, rather than as a euphemism for giving an reductionist evangelistic message. See Gibbs and Bolger, *Emerging Churches*, 56.

resonate the life of Christ in diverse settings, with this resonating field of force being "centrifugal" rather than "centripetal."[49] The covenant community is a resonating community that flows with the Spirit's flow in this world, being among people in many contexts so as to give specificity to the Spirit's work—not unlike the events in Acts where the disciples were, seemingly, always just barely catching up with the Spirit's work.[50]

This emphasis on incarnation also brings with it an emphasis of church as relationship rather than church as a place or event. "By emphasizing relationships, emerging church thinkers are advocating not inwardly focused huddles but rather multiple circles of relationships lived out in the wider community."[51] This moves the focus of the mission to include both those who are already committed to the covenant community as well as those outside the covenant community, many of whom might otherwise dismiss any connection with Christian community. The mission, then, likewise continually challenges the multiplicity of other identity-forming systems, which provides impetus for more thorough and consistent contextual theologies that can address questions and impart discernment in the midst of such challenges. Evangelism in such a model becomes, in essence, a task of discernment.[52] God's active participation in this world insists on our active participation with this world. The work of redemption was a work of God's pursuit of his creation, bringing life and hope into what was destined for death and despair.

By going into the infinitely complex contexts, those who are participants with God in this mission bring with them the renewed

---

49. Ibid., 50.
50. Cf. Acts 8:26–40; Acts 10.
51. Gibbs and Bolger, *Emerging Churches*, 52.
52. We can see the story of the woman at the well in John 4:1–42 as a good model of such evangelism, which carried with it both a message of God and a deep insight into her particular context.

identity of God that affirms life and hope. They help others discover God's vivifying work in their own life—calling them to be more of who they truly are and as such being a message of freedom among those who are lost. This comprehensive mission encompasses all of life inasmuch as our identity is likewise holistic in orientation and affects all aspects of our interactions with each other and this world. It brings people into the identity of God, pointing toward restoration and redemption and leading to a new way of living in this world. God's mission, then, requires people to express this new pattern of life within the world he is redeeming.[53]

By identifying with Jesus, those in a covenant community are reorienting their own lives. This involves, first, becoming people who reflect the kingdom of God rather than other identity-forming systems. This is, in effect, the essence of holiness—a term not often associated with transformative churches. The expression of the kingdom that is holiness is a witness to the power of God and a witness to the presence of the kingdom that is already among us, a transformative reality in which the incarnation of Christ continues through his people. In letting go of other forms of identity, participants in this mission take on their own cross so as to discover the resurrection of Christ in their lives and contexts. The invitation, healing, and restoration of the kingdom are "both the pathway to the cross and the pathway Christians walk throughout their lives with the cross as those who have died to self with Christ in order that they might live in his grace and power."[54] The "kingdom is present wherever Jesus is present," and Jesus is present wherever his people are present, resonating the work of the Spirit in the pursuit of the kingdom of God.[55] This kingdom is about how to live in

---

53. See Gibbs and Bolger, *Emerging Churches*, 53.
54. Ibid., 54.
55. Ibid.

this present, oriented by the eschatological reality of God that breaks into our contexts, thus questions about heaven or hell or other future events become themselves relativized. Identifying with Jesus means, for these transformative churches, learning how to express the fullness of life and combat the emptiness of death in their current lives and contexts; it is "about being increasingly alive to God in the world."[56]

This embrace of life brings with it an openness to others, as an identity that is secure in Jesus is able to enter into other systems without experiencing the despair or dissolution that insufficient identity-forming systems bring. The perceived enemy in such situations is not the particular people but the alternate systems themselves, which creates a contextual expression of the mission of God to live within particular contexts, in contrast to such systems but not to the people caught up in them. This insists on a community that can continually reorient covenant participants toward Christ's expression of identity in that context, without which a person would far too easily become co-opted into one of the contextually dominant alternate systems. That is why transformative churches must be holistic in their expression. Life itself is holistic and so challenges and opportunities come from every direction, all of which must align themselves in light of Christ's identity. This is a sanctifying expression of the work of the Holy Spirit, who implements the kingdom in the covenant community and in the context as a whole, empowering each participant to "live like Jesus, to lean into the kingdom, to serve, and to forgive."[57] It is only through such power—the power of life itself—that the covenant community and each person in it can truly be in their particular culture and offer a redemptive presence for and within it, a redemptive presence that

56. Ibid., 55.
57. Ibid., 59.

expresses the life and teaching of Jesus as a continuing reality—words and practices of good news—in each context.

With the vast array of alternate identity-forming systems and persistent destructive powers of death in a context, it is no easy task to first discover and then implement what it means to initiate kingdom-oriented life within that context. While the Gospels give us a guide to who Jesus was within his first-century context, there is not an exact correlation to our context. Seeking to participate in God's kingdom as a participant with Christ in the power of the Spirit involves more than simply following an established template. In our present contexts, we encounter issues, cultures, values, and other elements that form identity—many of which Jesus did not address or even experience during his time of ministry. In seeking what it means to express his identity in the midst our contexts, then, we require a pneumatologically oriented imagination—a discernment that not only can distinguish the righteous from the unrighteous but can also orient our actions, practices, and participation in general in ways that will help further the reality of the kingdom of God in our context. Such an imagination serves as the fifth posture for Jon Huckins and his covenant community in San Diego.

Imagination is about seeing the world in a new way, not contained by the determinative realities but awakened to begin seeing the possibilities, the sort of possibilities enabled by the kingdom of God. We begin to see old patterns and systems for what they are, and this invigorates us to a newness of life, even in the same context as before. Jesus himself did not ask the same questions as others or give the same answers, but instead he approached the world in a vitally new way, awakening others to what he saw as he expressed his empowered imagination in a myriad of different ways. Huckins writes, "Divine imagination transcends the constructs that swallow us and frees us to live into a new story that is marked by kingdom anticipation, advancement, and hope."[58] Such imaginative living seeks to maintain the status quo or maintain a defensive posture against the rest of the world. Instead, a posture of imaginations "will set us free to live in the way God designed his creation to thrive and support his restoration project."[59] Because it is God's design, such imagination leads us toward the reality that Jesus expressed, and away from succumbing to the insufficient expressions that may currently hold sway in a context.

A posture of imagination is a creative embrace of God's kingdom. It is about seeing the potentials in a community and in such discovering the path for practical answers to substantive longings. As a practical expression of God's empowering presence, imagination is the first step toward embodying the kingdom, reflecting Christ ever more thoroughly in specific and holistic ways. This is not idealism, which often misinterprets the potential for change and how such change can occur. Instead, it is embracing the hope that God provides, seeing Christ as a model for our mission and taking steps to engage this mission in our specific contexts.[60] "It is," Huckins writes, "taking on the eyes through which we are created to see all along."[61] Imagination as formed by God is seeing the world through God's perspective.

This is countercultural inasmuch as such perspective is oriented toward God rather than oriented by other identity-establishing systems. Such systems may involve a form of imagination, but just as deficient forms of identity cannot bear the weight of eternal hope,

---

58. Huckins, *Thin Places*, 115.
59. Ibid.
60. This is a constructive way of understanding Moltmann's own theological method, which is sometimes critiqued for supposed idealism and an overemphasis on human potentiality. The emphasis for Moltmann—as mentioned in earlier—is on God's power, not human potential. Humanity has potential only inasmuch as God enables this, and it is precisely the stated mission of God to enable such potential—an enabling we call salvation and sanctification.
61. Huckins, *Thin Places*, 116.

so too do such systems lack the ability to provide a thoroughgoing hope in present transformation. Putting hope into such systems often results in incremental change and, often, alienation for many within the context. A transformative community that is oriented by God's imagination offers the hope for redeeming the whole of a context, offering a shared story of redemption and renewal for all. Living out this imagination in practice then helps foster the reception of God's perspective in the context. Expressed imagination awakens the imagination of others, who then provide their own expression of resonating imagination that gives insights into more potentialities and possibilities, resonating farther and deeper and wider as people become awakened to this imaginative mission of God.[62]

This imaginative life is "no longer only about waiting for an expected deliverer in the future; it is about entering the kingdom life and restoration in Jesus in the here and now."[63] When a person aligns with God, a person experiences the world in a new way, a way that may contrast other expressions, but is not inherently contrasting a context. The people who live in this hope live out God's hope for the world. This reality then shapes how we act and how we respond, often in ways that are confusing to people still operating within other identity systems—just as Jesus confused people. That which is impossible according to other identity-forming systems becomes possible in light of the fullness of God's work.[64]

Huckins calls living out God's hope a way of orienting toward the "true north" of God's identity, the identity that is expressed by the kingdom of God. "In our missional community," he writes,

62. See ibid., 123.
63. Ibid., 119. On p. 136, Huckins writes, "As we act as a safe harbor for apprentices of Jesus to dream, explore, and experiment, we see that God's imagination is captivating the minds and hearts if his people all over the globe."
64. See ibid., 120. Here Huckins writes, "When God's people are open to the divine imagination, the things that we formally thought could never happen become reality."

"we seek to tap into God's divine imagination for our community by navigating toward true north while discerning how each of us uniquely contributes to this communal movement."[65] The emphasis here is not on being "Christlike" (though this is an element of it). The posture of imagination focuses on the kingdom because this is the way of Jesus. Imagination in the Spirit leads us to where he is, and where he wants us to be, rather than where he was, and we cannot be. This involves more than a relationship with Jesus, which can express itself in passive ways. The posture of imagination orients toward the true north of God's kingdom as that is the way that Jesus was and is pointing, and that is the way to partner with Jesus—and the Spirit—in enabling the reality of God's kingdom to become present in our contexts.[66]

This posture insists on a community that shares the same imagination, a community that shares the life of Jesus and is committed to learning together what this means to be incarnated in their shared context. In this present experience of life, the multiplicity of other identity systems compete for our attention and devotion—often without our conscious awareness of such. The path away from the kingdom is usually not grand or obvious. It is a slow turning, a stepping aside followed by another step. In the same way, steps along the way of Jesus are often subtle, so that we may doubt decisions or actions that, at first, we felt were part of the imaginative steering of the Spirit. For such moments, an orienting community provides caution and encouragement. Such a community also provides the space to discover how to listen to the Spirit, learning what it means to takes tentative steps, at first, which is important for one to gain confidence in more drastic expressions. The individual

---

65. Ibid., 121. Cf. Alan J. Roxburgh, "The Missional Church," *Theology Matters* 10, no. 4 (2004): 5. Roxburgh makes special note of Paulo Friere here.
66. See Huckins, *Thin Places*, 122.

imagines in the context of the imagining community and the community imagines in the presence of the imagining individuals, both requiring the other in order to express the infinite complexity of God's orienting reality. Such imagination enables freedom and such freedom enables imagination for each person to live in their context in the way of Jesus in the particular manner that the Spirit is uniquely inspiring within them.

This then leads to every missional community expressing their own uniqueness in this world as they respond to their contexts in the manner that their particular participants imagine. No two missional communities are alike—there is no cookie-cutter model, other than the way of Jesus that brings unity through diversity. The imagining church is the liberating church as it seeks out the possibilities and potential of each person in every context. It does not shape individuals to fit into a finite system or conform to an organization, seeing people as objects to fill the space of an already-established entity. Instead, as Huckins puts it, the "church is an embodied people who are living on mission, in community, and seeking the guidance of the divine imagination of a God who is ceaselessly working to restore all creation to himself."[67] In the church, people learn with imagination how to be who they are supposed to be in the world, a world that God so loved that he sent his only Son, who shows us the way and walks with us as his people pursue it.

Transformative Space

There are two broad ways in which the Spirit radicalizes our understanding of the church, which moves the discussion away from the stalwart model of the church as a city and toward a model of

---

67. Ibid., 127.

a missionary people in the midst of the world.[68] Gibbs and Bolger emphasize one of these—that of *transforming secular space*—while Jon Huckins emphasizes another—that of *entrusting God's work to God's people*. For Gibbs and Bolger, the insight that the kingdom of God enters into contexts and cultures leads to the particular emphasis of sacralization by transformative churches, which is about, as they say, one thing: "The destruction of the sacred/secular split of modernity."[69] This is, essentially, an ecological emphasis, one that does not contrast soul with body, the world with the church, the spiritual with the physical—but rather invests in a Moltmannian expression of postmodernism that emphasizes the sacredness of all of life. "The postmodern (or non-modern) is about the sacredness of all of life. For emerging churches it means to give all of life over to God in worship, to recognize the work of God in formerly unspiritual things or activities."[70] Indeed, this is so definitive for transformative churches that Gibbs and Bolger include it as one of the three core elements that define such churches.

With this, it is understood that the work of the Spirit, and thus the nature of the church, is holistic and nonlinear in expression. As the Spirit of life, the Spirit is connected to that which is life, and, as all of life is connected to the Spirit, there are not places where the Spirit cannot be. "All can be made holy. All can be given to God in worship. All modern dualisms can be overcome."[71] In recognizing that all space is God's space, the church does not concede space to that which is not God, but seeks to be participants in the redemption of all space, which is not to impose some kind

---

68. Gibbs and Bolger, *Emerging Churches*, 65 write, "By now it should be clear that in discussing the emerging church we are not simply talking about a different style of church adapted to a particular age range. Rather, we are talking about a radically different ecclesiology that reflects the church's call to mission in a post-Christendom and postmodern context."
69. Ibid., 66.
70. Ibid.
71. Ibid., 67.

of theocracy—making everything secular into the governance of the church—but to recognize that everything is already under the governance of God, and so to seek to discover and illuminate the work of God throughout each context. Indeed, this is the reverse of much of what modernity sought to do, which was to limit religion to a narrow boundary of expression, and then proceed to invest even those expressions with secular identity-forming systems—thus creating churches that mirror the kinds of systems found throughout any context. Churches express consumerism, or sectarianism, or predictable political partisanship.

This holistic understanding of God's work, and the work of the church in pursuing it, thus also insists on a nonlinear approach to ministry—as a ministry that is holistic expects to see the Spirit's work in every direction. This nonlinearity allows for multiple narratives, and releasing control over requiring a single initiating narrative to define one's stance with God or with the church. "There is more than one way to do things, more than one thing going on at a time, and more than one message coming across."[72] Not only does a nonlinear approach place the emphasis on the creativity of God's own work in this world—it also deemphasizes forms of leadership that exercise control by maintaining a strict pattern of liturgy or programmatic ministries.[73] This also creates an inherent flexibility in regard to theology—which while affirmed, is not packaged as a set of propositions that must be logically affirmed one after the other. The nonlinearity of contextual ministry understands that "God communicates with humanity, not primarily through the form of

72. Ibid., 68.
73. See ibid., 70. Here Gibbs and Bolger write, "We are not at liberty to treat [the story of God] as a paint-by-numbers canvas or to paint over what has been given either because we do not like it or because we insists on details being included out of our own imaginings or under the claim of new revelations." This, of course, provides both an opportunity and a challenge for new approaches to church.

propositions but through a story illustrated by parables, riddles, sayings, and folk songs."[74] This story "is still unfolding" and so transformative churches see their identity as being a participant with the continual telling of this story—as it exists in particular contexts—which requires a continual openness to seeing God work in surprising ways, and being flexible enough in ecclesiality to respond and adapt to such ways.

In contrast, many churches followed modernity's insistence that religion is a solely private affair, part of a personal religious life but not a part of public relevance. Churches then were isolated in suspicion toward broader life (the "world") and the "world" became suspicious about churches. A church that is suspicious toward life is a church that is suspicious to those who are living, placing the church likewise as being marginal and irrelevant to the experience of living—relegating it to the topic of ephemeral spirituality. When society, however, revives an interest in the spiritual, such divisions continue, and a church seen as irrelevant to society continues to be seen as irrelevant. "The end result of this increasing isolation is that a spiritual culture now surrounds a secular church. At the sunset of modernity, the church refuses to create a holistic spirituality for its people and fights to stay at the margins of society as a spiritual chaplain."[75] In refusing to accept this bifurcation of religion and the rest of life, transformative churches are, essentially affirming and embracing life—an embrace that seeks what is truly life giving and life sustaining and, as such, pushing against structures, strongholds, or forms of deficient identity that lead away from life as it is meant to be lived. The work of God is seen as embedded within this world as the source of life itself, and so participation with God insists on participation with the life that he is enabling and redeeming.

74. Ibid.
75. Ibid., 72.

This is, likewise, a refusal to accept the boundaries of religious expression that became especially notable in the early twentieth century, that of social activism (immanent religion) versus evangelism (transcendent religion), each of which tended to align with a whole set of approaches to Scripture, spirituality, other religions, and just about every other topic. The result is a conservative church that did not know what to do with the present world and a liberal church that did not know what to do with an eschatological world. In contrast—and confusing to many critics who still associate particular positions with the whole package—transformative churches "refuse the false choice of secular modernity, voting with neither the conservatives nor the liberals. They recognize God's deep work in material reality while at the same time embracing the invisible reality of God."[76] There is a commitment to both God's immanence and his transcendence, and in this commitment such churches express a transcendence through their immanence and are oriented in their immanence by their transcendence. As Gibbs and Bolger put it, "By immersing themselves in all forms of media, emerging churches retrieve God's immanence while maintaining a commitment to God's transcendence, thereby creating a rich and beautiful worship environment."[77] And as the "worship environment" is not limited to a particular service or location, but extends into the broader context, these churches seek to bring such an orientation to the context as a whole, resonating the immanence with transcendence, helping others to discover the work of God among the apparently mundane or commonplace.

This is, then, a highly contextual expression of worship, as what is transcendent is enmeshed in what is immanent, immanence itself necessitating the particularity and specificity of a context. This

76. Ibid., 73.
77. Ibid., 74.

involves responding to a context in the specific ways that fits the context itself. Instead of being negative or reactionary, transformative churches seek to engage the context as insiders, helping the context itself, and thus all within it, to blossom into the fullness of its possibilities, staying "true to both their faith *and* their culture."[78] This is Christianity as it exists in a particular ecosystem, refusing to accept fragmentation and offering a renewed sense of integrity that helps the context discover a wholeness—finding integrity with its past and its present and its future.[79] This requires an intentional way of living, intentional not only about maintaining a life of faith amidst other identity-forming systems but also intentional in being even more present in its particular context—which may often be ignored as a topic of consideration even by long-time residents, for whom it is just where they are at. Yet, where each person is at, whether they acknowledge it or not, is a part of a person's identity and context of being—both physically and spiritually.

With this, then, the contextual intent is oriented toward discovering what is truly integral to a context, not just a trendy or outside influence. Like with particular people, particular contexts have their own identity and personality—often a confluence of good and bad, expressed in a myriad of ways. Transformative churches seek to know a context as well as it can be known, knowing it so well that the covenant can speak into the life of the context and be accepted within the context as real contributors. "These churches do not use cultural expressions because they are trendy but because they are rooted in people's lives, and this is the only way to be honest before God."[80] This intentional understanding requires persistent observation, interaction, and spiritual discernment—all of which we

78. Ibid., 75.
79. See ibid., 78.
80. Ibid., 77.

see modeled in the ministry of Jesus. Thus, incarnating the transcendent within the immanent requires a commitment to integrity with the context, intentionality about discovering the context, and discernment about God's work within the context—all of which help a covenant community be in the community who the community needs and resonates with.

Such investment as particular individuals and as a community points toward a formative model of evangelism that is a holistic way of life, not just words separated from context and generalized so that it does not matter who the listeners are or where they come from or what they have experienced. It is a becoming, not a speaking, expressing the work of the Spirit through being transformed by the Spirit, so that the work of the Spirit can be incarnated in the person, among the covenant community, and into the context. It is indeed evangelism, as the goal is to resonate the work of Christ so that others are drawn into this resonance—this field of force—of the Spirit, becoming themselves oriented within God's identity, thus becoming their own domain of resonance for their various networks. It is, to put it simply, "about living like Jesus in postmodern cultures through one's relationships."[81] This is an embodied evangelism that is an embodied apologetic that is an embodied transcendence that is an embodied expression of the fullness of the work of God in a specific context for a specific context. In this, the news about God is experienced and transformative, truly good news for the context—and as such breaking down previously held assumptions and helping to project the transformative power of God within each particular setting.

The process of embedding a transcendent reality within an immanent context is one of illumination, seeing reality for what it is and, in this, making the truly worthwhile stand in contrast to the

81. Ibid., 80.

wrong and misguided. Such a process for a person, or community, or context is not always easy, or welcomed. The whole problem with alternative identity systems is that they are forming identities, and our identities are who we think ourselves to be and orient us in how we act for ourselves and among others. This is why a person who is being illuminated by the Spirit, and seeks this illumination, needs a safe space in order to become who they are called to be—a space where there is encouragement to walk along the way and there are fellow travelers accompanying the journey. Such a community of people are becoming together who they are called to be in their lives and in a specific context, which itself is—as a context and as a space filled with many people—called to redemption in the light of God's immanent transcendence. As people resonate with this work of the Spirit they are both lifted up toward Christ and situated even more in their place—becoming incarnations of God's reality with, for, and among a particular location. This is a work of transcendent immanence, participating with the Spirit in the redemption of a context, helping it to realize what it was called to be and helping those within it learning who to be.

This is, to be sure, a profound work, a work that we see most fully realized in the work of Jesus, whose incarnation resonated within his particular context, and then as people were transformed, began to resonate in many other contexts, reaching all around the world. These pockets of resonance carry on this mission of the Father, which is the mission of Christ, which is the mission of the Spirit, gathering all of space and time into the resonance of God's redemption and relationship. Put in such terms, it seems incredible that such a mission would be entrusted to people—all of whom are not yet fully who they are called to be themselves and yet are, in the midst of their own becoming, called to participate with God in the liberating work of the church. We are being formed as we are being sent. "It is," as Jon

Huckins puts it, "the only way to fully step into a vocation of Jesus apprenticeship. It is emulating our rabbi."[82] Part of this emulation, then, is the posture of entrusting.

Just as Adam was intended as a mediator and to represent God's identity to creation and to steward it in submission to God, so too Jesus came among us, in part, to serve as a model and a mediator—for creation in general and for misguided humanity in particular.[83] This role of mediator and representation was passed on by Jesus to his disciples, not staying among them but leaving, and in this leaving, allowing the Spirit to enter into the life of the church with new power and authority. This is not necessarily something the disciples would have chosen on their own, as Jesus was, without a doubt, much more trustworthy in such a mission than they were. Indeed, one might say that entrusting such people—then and now—to such a task is dangerous. Yet, this is the work of God, calling others to be who they were made to be in the midst of the mission each were called to participate in: being sent into this world for the sake of this world. This is a community task, as it is as persons within a community that we begin to represent God to this world. "God's mission wasn't designed to advance with a set of sent individuals. It was designed to advance through a faithful people living as advocates of the *missio Dei*."[84]

By seeing this work of the covenant community as a posture entrusted by God to us, with us, we take this work much more seriously—as we realized both the danger of such a mission and realize the depth of trust that God is showing us. As this is a holistic mission, then, it involves "seeing every experience, conversation, and interaction as an opportunity to participate with God in his

82. Huckins, *Thin Places*, 133.
83. Ibid.
84. Ibid., 135.

restoration project."[85] God entrusts us as his sent people, and as such people we entrust each moment with the resonance of the Spirit, not discounting or dismissing anything as being outside the resonance of God's Spirit.[86] And as God entrusts his people, his people entrust themselves and those around them to the work of God, letting go of that which distorts or binds, and investing in that which renews and enlivens, acts of liberating that include letting go and moving into a new way of living.

This new way of living is participating in the infinitely complex story God is weaving through our history. "We believe that the only way to be a people of peace is through entrusting ourselves and all of these relationships to the story God is telling all around us."[87] Showing this trust is a display of *kenosis*, a *kenosis* of the Spirit who chooses to work in and through the covenant community, and in the general context; a *kenosis* of the covenant community who hold all things loosely so as to submit most fully to the will of God, choosing to be formed in his identity rather than imposing an identity upon others and upon the context. This is a mutual *kenosis* in which God entrusts us to trust him with entrusting us with his mission, a mission that seeks to gather all into his presence. This is the way of peace and the promise of hope. This is a way of liberation, being liberated out of deficient systems of identity and being liberated into God's story.

This act of entrusting is God's continued work of creation, and our participation in this posture of entrusting leads us to provide space where others can be formed into the likeness of God. This is itself a letting go, letting go of control over God's story so that others discover their own part in this story as the Spirit works in their lives.

---

85. Ibid.
86. See ibid., 143. Here Huckins writes, "Being a sent people means that we view what in the past may have seemed mundane or normal as a potential opportunity for God's kingdom to be made real, for heaven and earth to be only thinly separated."
87. Ibid., 136.

"We entrust ourselves to the Spirit's movement in each of our lives because we believe God's kingdom expands through multiplication rather than accumulation."[88] This multiplication happens through the intentional practice of being among the context, so that all manner of intentional and unintentional moments can lead to the fruition of more people aligning themselves with God. The resonance of the Spirit involves entrusting the Spirit with the mission, and entrusting one's own presence as a way of resonating this mission. This is the vocational mandate of the whole people of God, to simply live as the people of God amidst their contexts, not serving as a model *to* others but as a resonance *among* others, reaching well beyond the narrow bounds of the covenant community and reaching into all the various elements of life that make up the broader community. "It is being fully present in these places and fully expectant that the Spirit is at work that we experience heaven crashing into earth—a thin place."[89] It is by doing this, that each person increasingly experiences the perichoretic experience that resonates eternity—the fullness of being—in their present, bringing the not yet that much closer to becoming the already.

88. Ibid., 138.
89. Ibid., 144.

8

Conclusion

Around the year 200, Tertullian wrote a passionate defense of the Christian faith, and in this he presented a very interesting picture of the church in Carthage of his time. He makes note of their weekly gatherings, the support they give one another, their unity and dedication. He goes on to write, "We are in our congregations just what we are when separated from each other; we are as a community what we are as individuals; we injure nobody, we trouble nobody."[1] There is a unity to identity; an example that is set in the church is the example set throughout the life of these Christians. The community reflects the life of the individuals and individuals reflect the identity of the community. Whether together or apart, they are who they are,

---

1. Tertullian, *Apology*, 39 (in *The Ante-Nicene Fathers*, vol. 3, ed. Alan Menzies (repr. Peabody, MA: Hendrickson, 1994)). He goes on to write, "So we sojourn with you in the world, abjuring neither forum, nor shambles, nor bath, nor booth, nor workshop, nor inn, nor weekly market, nor any other places of commerce. We sail with you, and fight with you, and till the ground with you; and in like manner we unite with you in your traffickings—even in the various arts we make public property of our works for your benefit. How it is we seem useless in your ordinary business, living with you and by you as we do, I am not able to understand " (ibid., 42).

representatives of Christ. And they are far from sectarian. Indeed, part of Tertullian's defense of Christians is that they are particularly good citizens, at least in terms of what would actually bring a boon to the society. They were part of it, enmeshed within it, transformed and transforming by their participation.

They were a model to the world inasmuch as they were participants within it, an expression of a way of life in the midst of a culture, a way of life that was both participatory and distinct. Their confession of Christ provided a dynamic orientation of this way that could adapt to different questions, situations, and conflicts. Theology was about a particular God and about how this God worked among his people in order to form them into a new kind of people, not isolated from the world but embedded within it.[2] In this new way of living in the midst of the world, the church was a testimony in, with, and for this world. The church was a place where the people of God gathered, learning and teaching, shaping their lives with one another in ways that reverberated with how they lived the whole of their lives. They, it seems, became in the church who they were to be in the world, a community and a people who reflected the work and identity of Christ in all of life.

This is, I argue, also the goal of what I am calling transformative churches in the present era. This goal of transformation is, at its essence, the goal of liberation. For those in situations of oppression, freedom arrives by a change in the situation or context of oppression; palpable problems need palpable answers. These needs may also involve a change of the internal person, but the key element of

---

2. Richard Niebuhr thus mischaracterizes Tertullian's position in his famous *Christ and Culture* (New York: Harper, 1951). He uses elements of Tertullian's theology, but misses the fact that for Tertullian the starting point was Christ, not culture, and culture could be approached in a very participatory way depending on the particular aspect of the culture. His was a very dynamic and nuanced approach, something missing from many modern approaches to such topics, which try to fit everything into a more manageable framework.

a liberation of the oppressed is that they are relieved from such experiences of oppression—a promise of Christ for freedom that takes the present experiences of history into account. If, as Moltmann argues, liberation must happen from both sides, that the oppressed and the oppressor both need liberation, then there must be a corresponding theology that addresses the particular issues of both sides. It is only in such contexts that such a theology can be developed and honed.

In the industrialized West, the context is one of oppressing. Whether we are in positions of power or wealth is not as much the issue as the overall context of our society—a society that emphasizes competition, dominance, individualism, and in general exemplifies gaining at the expense of others. We want to feel better, stronger, faster, more righteous, more intelligent, wealthier, more influential than the other person. We form our society around such idealization of competition, and our churches themselves express the same kind of value. In such competitive and isolating poses, however, we are tending toward death and disintegration rather than hope and integration with God's holistic work in creation, a work exemplified in the incarnation—the Son among us.

We are not like Jesus, however, either in our private or our public lives. We are oriented around our particular forms of corruption and disintegration, moving away from our calling to live in Christ as we seek to establish our identity in insufficient and ultimately futile ways. There must be a change, but this change is extremely difficult because the need for change itself is often not recognized. In the context where oppressing is the ever-present temptation, the task is a difficult one, for we are experiencing much present bounty and are promised more if we only establish ourselves the way others are doing. Thus, for the oppressors—those who are experiencing the bounty and richness of a particular society—the issue is not so much a change of context as much as a need for the transformation of the person into being a new kind of person, able to let go and put aside that which can be gained through domination. The way of Jesus Christ points toward a different way of living this life, and it is only through being transformed that we become the people who we are called to be, a people who represent in our contexts who Christ calls all people to be—people who reflect life and hope rather than death and fear. Liberation is, in essence, transformation—the particular task of liberation in a particular culture calling for different emphases of this transformation.

Our present experience of Christ, then, as individuals and as a community, insists on a process in which we who were destined for death become oriented by life. "We are here to be transformed," Arthur Danto writes.[3] Even more than this, in being transformed, we become transformative people, living in a new way so as to invite others into such a transformed life and participate in the transformation of each context so as to exemplify the patterns of God's holistic mission in each such context. How does such transformation take place and what does it entail? Since God orients this transformation, such transformation is not a simplistic ideal with a simple checklist of tasks. All of life is involved—and all of life involves the whole of who we are, where we are, where we have been, where we are going, and who we are with.

This is a comprehensive task that calls for a comprehensive transformation—a rebirth. This is a rebirth of ourselves, our communities, our contexts, and the whole cosmos. It is with this in mind, then, that it becomes essential to assess this task in a comprehensive way, not placing forms of knowledge or experience in separated spheres of discussion, but seeing the need to reintegrate

---

3. Arthur C. Danto, *The Abuse of Beauty* (Chicago: Open Court, 2003), 131.

the systematic and the practical, the theoretical with the pragmatic, the analysis with the experiences.

The Substance of a New Ecclesiality

Because this is a comprehensive task, it is well outside the bounds of any single work to provide a comprehensive discussion. In this present work, my goal was certainly much more limited. I sought to coordinate a discussion between Jürgen Moltmann and transformative churches, showing how they share a broad range of emphases even as each expresses these in distinct ways with distinct approaches based on their own particular expertise. Moltmann's theological emphases are well suited to such a discussion, as they insist on the place of experiences in theological discussions and likewise insist that theology has a transformative role to play in who we are, how we live as a church community, and how we are to be involved in our broader contexts. Those in the transformative churches have been influenced by such theological priorities and have applied these to particular situations, learning from missiologists and from their own contexts, emphasizing the need to be participants in these contexts, informed by them and involved with them—integrating the church within these contexts so as to be a resonating presence from within.

Moltmann offers theological proposals for understanding transformation, and the transformative churches suggest practices that express such transformation. Together, then, they can provide a substantive starting place for understanding the church as a transformative community, one that participates in holistic liberation. They are each pointing toward such a model of embedded Christian community, and thus offer a starting place for a comprehensive liberation of the oppressor. Yet, because they are operating in such distinct spheres of knowledge, it was necessary first to show their affinity and how they are oriented in very similar directions, despite the differences in form and style. That was the immediate task of this present work, to place Moltmann and transformative churches in conversation so as to show they are speaking within a common goal.

This goal is integration with God and with God's work in this world, an integration that has three general categories of orientation, all of which are concerned with the pursuit of whole life in contrast to death. These categories are the historical, the anthropological, and the Trinitarian. It is with these general categories in mind that this present work took shape. More specifically, Moltmann's proposed hermeneutical framework as written in *Experiences in Theology* informed each of these categories. He specifically applied this framework to his approach to Scripture. However, I propose this also forms a substantive model for how we should interpret his theological approach as a whole and how we should orient our overall understanding of transformation.

In the first chapter, I introduced the key participants in this present conversation. I brought together the somewhat divergent streams of what have been variously called emerging, missional, neo-monastic, or Fresh Expressions as being expressions of what I termed *transformative churches*. Each are expressing a model of ecclesiality that share common priorities and are distinct from most traditional ecclesiologies. They emphasize an embedded, nondivisive approach to Christian ministry, one that entails both an inward and outward mode of transformation, refusing to see God's work as being limited to, or even primarily expressed within, the context of a narrow church community. They shape their communities with a more open approach to leadership, community, and participation in general.

I chose two main representative texts within this movement, one that has long served as a definitive guide and the second that serves as a very recent expression of a current transformative community. These texts provide a helpful framework for discussing the broader transformative church emphases. In my brief discussion of Moltmann, I sought to note specifically those elements of his theology and method that are the most relevant to this present discussion. Having established their place and role in this present conversation, I developed the rest of this present work in light of the framework Moltmann proposed in *Experiences in Theology*, a framework that emphasizes the furthering of life and the opposition to death—the key element in a transformative life that expresses holistic liberation.

Transforming History

The second chapter emphasizes the first two elements of this framework, and I categorize these elements as being reflective of transformation in historical perspective, as they help orient the overall discussion in terms of the future, past, and present, situating our identity as individuals and as a community in light of God's work in each of these instances of time.

Moltmann begins his framework with this guideline: "What furthers life is whatever ministers to the integrity of human life in people and communities."[4] Integrity is about identity, who we are and how we live in this world, responding to this world in a way that is in tune with its whole reality. Such integrity can be attempted through diverse approaches, but only that which corresponds to God can bring true and lasting integrity with ourselves, with each other, and with this world—as it is only by being wholly aligned with our Creator that we can be and act as fitting our true selves. God's overall

4. Jürgen Moltmann, *Experiences in Theology*, trans. Margaret Kohl (Minneapolis: Fortress Press, 2000), 149.

identity and purposes substantiates integrity, an orientation that we see most fully in light of God's future, and an eschatological reality in which this future defines the past. Thus, eschatology ministers to the integrity of human life, giving us hope and guidance for who we are to be in light of God's holistic work. Moltmann's *The Coming of God* is his most fully developed eschatological work and thus provides this key orienting function.

In this text, Moltmann emphasizes that the determinative flow of phenomenal history is not the defining reality for this world or our experiences of it. Yet, such experiences certainly seem definitive, as our present is seemingly an amalgamation of previous experiences. The eschatological work of God, however, does not submit to such determination and it is in this eschatological work that Christian theology asserts is the actual defining reality of the cosmos and our experiences within it. The promise of God involves the transformation of the present and the past in orientation with the future, God's future that breaks into our present as a new beginning, an advent. In these transformative moments, the determinative insistence of the past is broken and what has come to pass is reinterpreted and reoriented in light of God's thoroughgoing participation, and through the work of those who are aligned with such an eschatological reality.

Such people who seek to live in light of God's eschatological reality in the midst of a phenomenal world participate in this promise of transformation. The past is not dismissed, certainly, as those who are becoming eschatologically informed can see God bringing what is new in past, earlier works, breaking the power of a determinative flow, and thus bringing hope even to our present that this God of promise and fulfillment is still at work. The present is itself a place of confrontation between the determination of phenomenal and transcendental history. This place of confrontation undermines idealization of human achievement thus far and places the present within the context of God's transcendent history. Here, the present is understood as full of possibilities, but also full of principalities and powers that offer alternative identities for this world.[5] The future is thus not a culmination of the past flowing into the present and thus defining what is to be expected. Rather the eschatological hope of the future is precisely that what seems to be determined is never, in fact, actually decisive.

Yet while this may be true, the reality of our present experiences thrusts determinative phenomenal history upon us, leading even otherwise faithful people of God to understand God's work only in light of phenomenal patterns of historical cause and effect. With this, then, Christian eschatology has tended to either dismiss phenomenal history, and with it the physical world, or dismiss God's eschatological priority—resulting in forms of triumphant millenarianism or the seemingly more humble process theology. In contrast, a messianic people oriented by the messianic person of Christ are living in the advent of God's promise, oriented by transcendental history and expressing this through new patterns of phenomenal life.

The substantive expression of transformative worship is central in the process of continual reorientation toward God's holistic priorities, and as God's work is transcendent in scope, rather than phenomenal, such worship cannot express any kind of epochal priority—either an era in the past or the present—as somehow containing the fullness of human understanding about God and God's work. Eschatological worship involves attuning to the rhythm of God's work throughout history, resonating with those in the present and in the past, orienting

---

5. See Patrick Oden, "Spirits in History," in *Interdisciplinary and Religio-Cultural Discourses on a Spirit-Filled World: Loosing the Spirits*, eds. Veli-Matti Kärkkäinen, Kirsteen Kim, & Amos Yong (New York: Palgrave MacMillan, 2013), 71–84.

toward God's future to live in increasingly eschatological ways. Worship that is transformative takes us out of our determinative flow and generational constrictions, transforming as it is informing who we are in the context of God's work throughout time and space. Our identity, thus, begins to prioritize God's transcendent determination rather than phenomenal determination, leading us to live in messianic ways within our present contexts.

This context includes all of creation, for all of creation groans toward this fulfillment and completion. Kevin Corcoran writes that "we human beings have been made from the mud and dirt—God-blessed, God-loved, and God-embraced mud and dirt—and made for life in an equally earthy environment."[6] God's kingdom includes this whole world inasmuch as "God's reconciling, redemptive, and restorative activity takes place within the natural, material world. This is the theater of God's redemptive activity, the theater of God's kingdom."[7] This is the theater and we are a participating audience. Our first role is to follow the guide and lead of the director, orienting the process and transforming the people continually so as to bring the most out of each moment and lead each context into its fulfillment—its experience with eternity in which it becomes in full that which may only presently be expressed in part.

This continual orientation insists on formative spirituality that does not prioritize one era but involves the whole of the Spirit's testimony in, with, and through the church. This continual orientation, likewise, listens for the Spirit's work outside the church, in the context, in the people, in each particular and complex way for the signs of God's particular, present work. In this way, eschatology is not an otherworldly topic or extraneous to a transformative church's

6. Kevin Corcoran, "Thy Kingdom Come," in *Church in the Present Tense: A Candid Look at What's Emerging*, by Jason Clarke et al. (Grand Rapids: Brazos, 2011), 67.
7. Ibid.

work, but indeed absolutely essential as the primary understanding of reality in general and God's own transformative work in bringing the whole of this reality back into communion with Father, Son, and Spirit.

The transformative practice of merging ancient and contemporary spiritualities allows participants with God's mission to transcend their own era, finding a rhythm with God in ways that refuse to see a particular time as definitive, allowing each era to speak into the present and give us insight into who we are to be in light of our future with God. This accordingly involves a substantive listening—to the past and to the present and to God's promises for our future, as a people who wait for God, who listen for God's work, and take seriously how this work is being shaped around us. As Ignatius wrote, "Understand the times. Wait expectantly for him who is above time: the Eternal, the Invisible, who for our sake became visible; the Intangible, the Unsuffering, who for our sake suffered, who for our sake endured in every way."[8] We must listen and learn from our contexts and from God's context.

While formative in many respects, these practices are not necessarily sufficient, given the importance of this topic. Becoming people who are eschatologically formed requires a substantive and more explicit re-embrace of eschatology as a guiding doctrine, which would only then find more depth and breadth in a variety of expressions. These present practices are key, however, in beginning the process of an implicit formative eschatology that helps orient integrity with God in time and space. Further work must develop such understanding even further, and, with this, develop

8. Ignatius, *Letter to Polycarp*, 3.2, from Michael W. Holmes, ed. *The Apostolic Fathers: Greek Texts and English Translations*, updated ed. (Grand Rapids: Baker Academic, 1999). Cf. Jürgen Moltmann, "What is Christian Theology," *Theological Review* 29, no 1 (2008): 34. He writes, "Christian theology is theology of the wandering people of God through the times."

coordinating practices that are more fully an "anticipation ethics of the future."[9]

How can our present experiences express this integrity? That question leads into Moltmann's second guideline: "What furthers life is whatever ministers to the integration of individual life into the life of the community, and the life of the human community into the warp and weft of all living things on earth."[10] We are to be integrated with God in light of his overall work and, in this, we are integrated as particular people into the life of the community. This work of integration is, at its core, the mission of the church, which calls all people to God, becoming a messianic people who resonate the messianic mission together. Thus, Moltmann's primary work on ecclesiology, *The Church in the Power of the Spirit*, becomes a key orienting text. The task of the church in light of the full guideline is one of integration together so as to integrate into the world, a participatory fellowship in, with, and for this world.

Jesus was born as a human, the Messiah, whose life enfleshed the mission of God in this world. In encountering the world in this way, Jesus intentionally put aside the kind of authority and power people expected of God or the Messiah. Born among humanity, he ministered among humanity, gathering disciples and forming a community of those who were increasingly oriented toward his teaching and his mission. This community, then, was empowered in the Spirit at Pentecost to express this mission in its immediate context and in increasingly broader contexts, becoming a sending community that reached from Jerusalem to around the world. This community was the method of the mission that God instituted, empowered to be a people who enacted and who preached a message of new freedom, a liberation that called all peoples out of insufficient

9. Jürgen Moltmann, *Ethics of Hope*, trans. Margaret Kohl (Minneapolis: Fortress press, 2012), 38.
10. Moltmann, *Experiences in Theology*, 149.

forms of identity and out of modes of living that provoked competition and isolation. The community of Christ asserts the substantive peace of Christ in contrast to the peace that idols of power or sin offer.

Instead of imposing this mission from the top, Jesus instituted this mission from within, then called his people to continue to orient themselves within this mission in whatever context they were in. The Spirit was given to the whole gathered community, as a community, for the community, continuing the method of this messianic mission, which offered hope and renewal to those who were outside the hope and promise of the alternative forms of power. Inasmuch as it continues to contextualize this mission, then, the church participates in the mission of Christ himself, each particular person a vital contributor, each particular context a necessary step. In its complexity of many particular participants, the church expresses the work of the Spirit in equally complex ways. There is no general church structure within which people are included that is the church apart from the people, there is only the particular work of the Spirit in particular people who in their gathering join together as the body of Christ, resonating the mission of God in each setting.

This mission is communal, expressed together by particular people with a shared orientation, integrated into the whole mission of God by the work of the Spirit who both gathers and empowers. In this gathering and expression, these people become messianic representatives, resonating a new way of life in the midst of each context, not separated from these as though the mission of Christ were one of distance and aloofness—a model away from the world—but rather representatives of a new way of living among the peoples, resonating a transformative life in, with, and among each context. This resonance has both an inward and outward stream, calling each person within the community toward a transformed life that resonates within both streams.

Both the inward and outward streams are necessary for full transformation, continually reorienting each person to be in tune with the mission of God and continually orienting this mission in particular ways within each context. These inward and outward streams confront the compulsion of sin, providing both an inner and exocentric expression of holiness. With these inward and outward streams expressed in communal life, the church can never be isolated or seen as a model to the world, in contrast to the world. Instead, the church is a nondivisive differentiated community that participates in the messianic mission as Christ himself expressed the messianic mission, ministering outside the confines of the narrow community.

The messianic community must likewise be transformative, inwardly and outwardly, among such people, to truly participate with the incarnated Messiah. This is transformative liberation, not only for the poor and outcast, but also for the wealthy and powerful, as becoming integrated within a messianic community provokes the liberation of the self in whatever way such liberation is required; some by being included and celebrated, others by letting go and making space. In this way, we can see the inward and outward stream analogous to the process of *perichoresis* and *kenosis*, in which the body of Christ inhales and exhales—gathering together and emptying, pouring in and pouring out—in mutual participation.[11]

Who we are in Christ determines who we are in our lives, and who we are in our lives reflects back onto the kind of Christ we actually, not just rhetorically, believe in. It is only in understanding our being that we can conceive of how this relates to our present contexts, with their particular hopes and particular challenges. Eschatology

11. See Patrick Oden, "Liberating Holiness for the Oppressed and Oppressors," in *A Future For Holiness: Pentecostal Explorations*, ed. Lee Roy Martin (Cleveland, TN: CPT, 2013), 205–24.

points to who we are in light of God's identity and meaning, while ecclesiology points to who we are to be in this world as part of God's messianic mission, oriented by Christ, empowered by the Spirit. This is a historical expression of God's mission, oriented by God's perspective and involvement within history. It is only as such that we can find integrity with God, his people, his world, and all of his creation.

From our perspective, this is an ontology of the future. However, just as eschatology is not itself a future event, but a transcendent reality that awakens our present to the possibilities contained in God's fullness and intent in creation, so too would labeling this an ontology of the future be a misnomer. Instead of limiting this to our perspective, it is helpful to consider God's perspective. In this way, I suggest we should consider this overall approach to be an ontology of *transcendent immanence*, in which we find our true being as we participate with God's transcendent identity in the context of our present.[12] This is a fellowship ontology, where our identity is not lost in others but in which we become full in the relational presence of others, a messianic community that orients us with integrity to all things. This is also a historical ontology wherein we are defined by history, just not by phenomenal history. We are defined by God's eschatological—his transcendent—works in history.

The transformative practice of living in community is the expression of this value—which is not an idealistic community but one that takes seriously the possibilities and contradictions inherent in realizing this in reality. With this, then, there is the accompanying emphasis on the two streams of mission—the inward and outward, the monastic and the missionary—that emphasizes a holistic

---

12. *Immanent transcendence* is a key phrase in Moltmann's concept of the Holy Spirit. The Spirit of life relates also to our being, but is oriented from below, and raises us into communion with God. This different starting point is why I turned this phrase around in regard to human identity. See figure 1.2 in chapter 1.

transformation for such a community. This is a historical expression of transformation as it situates us wholly into our specific context—in this present and in our place, participating in the stream of the Spirit's work in our specific moment of history. Indeed, of all the attempts at integration between Moltmann and transformative churches, this topic provides the most natural connections, as Jones's published dissertation makes evident.

In the third chapter, the emphasis turns to looking at transformation in anthropological perspective. What does God's reality imply for who we are and who we are to become? How do we encounter ourselves, others, and the whole of this life in ways that are in keeping with the kind of historical integrity mentioned in the previous chapter? Moltmann's third guideline orients the answer by emphasizing a reverence for life. He writes, "What furthers life is whatever spreads reverence for life and the affirmation of life through love for life."[13] This reverence and affirmation is given substantiation by understanding God's work in creation, his creative work in creating life itself and calling it good. With this in mind, it makes sense that Moltmann's primary work on creation theology, *God in Creation*, is extremely helpful. This helps establish our integrity with this world in light of God's foundational work, showing us who we are to be in light of who we were created to be in the context of all that was created.

God created. In creating this cosmos—all there is—he declared it to be good. He created humanity to be participants in this creation and participants with him, reflecting his image in the midst of what had been made, a reflection that was intended to resonate the self-same creativity, love, and community that God expresses in eternal triunity. In creating this world, God invested himself in it, as a

13. Moltmann, *Experiences in Theology*, 149.

creative expression of his own divine liberty, forming out of nothing that which could resonate life back to him, in a space he made within himself for other particularities to exist. In light of the turn toward sin and death, this world no longer resonates the fullness of God's intended order but experiences the suffering and frustrations of disoriented life, bound in a common destiny toward death and decay. God, however, does not abandon that which he created, but invests himself in the redemption of the world, calling the whole of the cosmos back into renewal and redemption from the body of death, calling those who would be his people into a common destiny with this redeemed world that longs for liberty. As people participate with God in this movement—this messianic mission of redemption—they enter into the depths of a broken world with a message and promise of hope, responding to the longing for liberty with a redemptive presence that resonates the presence of God in each context.

A new thing is possible in each and every context. Determinative history does not have the final say. Decay is not inevitable. Neither will decay right itself, independently from God's work. God has invested in his redemption through the Son, through the Spirit, and through the people who participate together as the church. With this participation, there is an active way of liberating intervention that is both a message of hope and an expression of it in particular and diverse ways. This liberating intervention leads each context toward real and thorough freedom, carrying forward the identity of the Creator in each context, working toward sustaining that which carries hope and re-creating that which is oriented away from God's eternal identity.

Things are not as they seem, no matter how dark or dismal they may appear. What tends toward death can be made new and alive. Where there seems to be no hope, there can be a new hope, a promise of *recreatio ex nihilo*. There is a promise and there an empowering presence that participates in, through and for this world, a power that speaks new life into each moment and person and place. Such new life insists on an imagination that is oriented, and constantly re-oriented, in light of God's redemptive identity.

Just as God made space for his creation, so too must God's people continually make space for God's re-creation, giving space for others to express their Spirit-empowered creativity, changing from passive participants to imaginative creators, investing anew in each context so that each context resonates the multiplicity of infinitely complex creative works, calling this world back into what is good. For this creative imagination to take root, the people of God must deeply invest in each context. They must submerge in its hopes and its struggles, incarnating the continued presence of the Spirit in always particular ways, resonating the transformative power from within the midst—just as Jesus brought transformation and renewal to the depths of suffering and death on the cross. In submerging into a context, in participating with a creative imagination, creating new space and investing in transformative works, the future of Jesus' work on the cross becomes the future of Christ's continued work in each context.

These transformative practices are, inherently, a celebration of the life we are experiencing in each moment, an affirmation of what is living and what brings life. To be sure, these practices suffer a clear limitation. They are primarily egocentric and anthropocentric, focusing on *our* role in contribution and suggesting a priority of the human culture in fully understanding a context. A more thoroughgoing set of transformative practices in line with Moltmann's theology of creation would entail more classically ecological involvement, emphasizing a participation with the surrounding nature in particular and with environmental concerns in general. Such transformative emphases would help turn the egocentric tendency toward a more adequate exocentric and theocentric transformation that emphasizes life in a broader sense, by caring for what God cares for.

The reality of this world also involves significant encounters with death and suffering, with expressions of darkness and despair that enter into our souls. Our deficient attempts to define ourselves express such death, and we experience death as others try to define themselves over and against us. The wages of sin is death, and death abounds in every context and time. To be whole people, then, we must acknowledge such reality—one that goes beyond our situation. We need redemption and we need renewal, for we are estranged from each other, from God, and from life itself. Thus, transformation in anthropological perspective requires a way to bring renewal to this estrangement. Moltmann's fourth guideline orients the need for such transformation. He writes, "What furthers life is whatever heals broken relationships and liberates life that has been oppressed."[14] This is the way of the cross, an expression of God in bringing restoration to a ruined people, inviting those who were strangers to him back into a relationship, suffering among those who suffer, participating in despair so as to bring the hope of transformation to even the most Godforsaken experiences.

Moltmann's *The Crucified God* helps orients such a perspective, giving theological guidance to how God sought to heal broken relationships and bring liberation into oppressed life. God fixes that which is broken by investing his very self within the brokenness. While the cross certainly is not a neglected element of Christian theology, a theology of the cross has traditionally emphasized certain elements, most of which have the discussion moving quite quickly to prioritize the cross as an existential resolution of our personal guilt.[15]

14. Ibid., 149.
15. For example, see Stanley J. Grenz, *Theology for the Community of God* (Grand Rapids: Eerdmans, 2000), ch. 12. I use this example because Grenz is specifically interested in how theology shapes

It was a sacrifice for our sins, an expression of Christ's mission in bringing us back into communion with God.

Rather than emphasizing the particularities of this specific kind of death, the emphasis becomes oriented around the questions of what it means for our individualized anthropological situation—thus we have questions of the cross turning quickly to the topics of atonement theories and doctrines of reconciliation. The issue of the cross becomes yet another egocentric endeavor—Christ died even for *me*. There are two significant elements of the cross, however, worth emphasizing, inasmuch as they are key orientations that Jesus himself seems to have emphasized. These elements are especially vital in understanding the transformative mission of a messianic people. The cross is also telling us about an event within God himself, and the cross is oriented toward others, with this orientation serving as a guide for our own perspectives as we consider the cross as a specific work.

At the core of the particular event of the cross are the elements of confrontation and forsakenness. The cross confronts oppression and insufficient forms of identity that drive such oppression. The cross likewise involves the experience of being forsaken, by the principalities and powers of this world and by God himself. The defining event of Christian theology forces us to look inward and outward, orienting such a theology both vertically and horizontally. It gives us insight into who God is in triunity, and it gives insight into how God works in bringing this world back into relationship with himself. The reality and particularity of the cross insists that we can never see this mission as emphasizing a multiplicity of individual instances of salvation that solely concerns each person's private relationship with God.

the community, and yet very quickly passes through the life, touching briefly on the cross, before moving more thoroughly to discussions of the atonement.

The event of the cross, then, not only tells us what God did but also where God can be found, with the answer that he can be found among the suffering, broken, forsaken, and outcast. Where was God during the holocaust? He was in the concentration camps. He was there and in being there brings with him the future of hope and promise, declaring that the determinative end of such a place is not the final end at all. In such places of forsakenness, Jesus brings his future and invites those who are with him in such forsakenness to join him in such a future. Thus, we find the *missio dei* oriented around the despised, abandoned, and oppressed, with God himself entering into solidarity with such as these. This takes the confrontation of the cross deeper and further, providing hope to the lost and also, in the same movement, undermining assumptions of power, control and honor. We experience identity with God through identifying with the identity of Jesus on the cross. He who is a brother in brokenness and expulsion expressed his identity in obedience to the Father, suffering the determinative consequences of confronting the forces of this world and suffering the even more radical experience of death—utter forsakenness in regard to God.

In asserting his identity in this way, this defines the path of messianic identification. The cross is the place where we let go of attempts to formulate an answer to our own existential identity, forsaking attempts to define ourselves over and against others in an attempt to substantiate our own sense of meaning and purpose. In identifying with the forsaken Christ, we become open to those Jesus is open to, with such openness to others being the very definition of our substantiation by God in salvation—God is open to us and re-creates us to be open and inviting to others.[16] In this, we are

16. See, for example, Matt. 6:12.

identifying not only with Jesus on the cross but also the whole history that this event—and that of the resurrection—represents.

As this man on the cross is the face of the God who sustains our own identity, we cannot join with such a man, and such a God, while still asserting forms of identity that finite systems have created, nor can we assert the sorts of valuation and judgment that such systems exert. Instead of rejecting those whom such systems reject, if we are to be messianic people in a messianic community, we must welcome those who are strangers to us, those who are forsaken or outsiders—and we must invite such people into the true and deeper peace that the cross initiates. This cross confronts false and temporary forms of peace that are enabled by creating distinctions between peoples, classes, races, or other categories. In doing such, this testimony is always public and embodies a politics, one that seeks out the outsider and invites in the outcast.

The cross is a choice—a choice to join with Jesus or to join with those who crucified Jesus. It is precisely how we welcome those who Jesus welcomes and defy the judgments of alternative identity systems that we live out in our practices that we declare in our worship. Welcoming and inviting become liturgical practices expressing the inviting and welcoming God who calls us to be participants with all the others in a new expression of human identity, one that seeks integration and wholeness with all of God's works. In identifying with the forsaken, in including and welcoming, we identify with the Jesus who experiences the depths of suffering and despair and forsakenness. In joining with such as these, we then share the future of Jesus and those with whom he brings his promise of whole and eternal life.

The cross, however, involves much more than welcoming and inviting the broken. While these transformative practices express an element of the work of Jesus, these are likely the least satisfying of the connections in this present work. The cross also involves sacrifice and confrontation. It involves a stronger awareness of both structural and personal sin, with an element of judgment that implies the need for such a sacrifice by God for God. By limiting the practices to what was discussed, a deficient theology of the cross could very well be assumed, and as such there must be accompanying transformative practices that are informed by a more holistic and thorough staurology.

With healing and liberation comes hope. Hope is an orientation for the possibilities of a new way of life, one that transforms our perspective of the present in light of what we see as God's promises for the future. This is a call to begin to live in a new way with and for others, a way characterized by the promises of God rather than the denouncements of the past. Moltmann's fifth guideline emphasizes this transformative task. He writes, "What furthers life is whatever leads to the new beginning of life in hope."[17] His text, *A Theology of Hope*, of course, provides a substantive guide for how hope orients this new beginning of life. Such a new beginning must be much more than a perspective. The task is one of expressed transformation, and it is through the transformative practice of generosity that people express the values and hopes they actually have, not hoarding that which they may be owed or feel they need but being open with their lives and possessions so as to provide for the needs of others. This mutuality of generosity expresses the hope that is in God, giving clear expression to where we find our identity and our future.

The God who promises tells us where he was and, more importantly, where he will be. In seeking this God, we do not stay in the past but seek his fulfillment on the way in history. We recognize him through his faithfulness in that past but do not limit this identity

17. Moltmann, *Experiences in Theology*, 149.

to what has been already done but through what is still promised, as it is this promise that defines his present calling in our own context. However, it is precisely in the past fulfillments that we can trust that the God of the past is also the God of the present. God remains God and so the past becomes a testimony to our future. Lessing may have struggled with this ditch, but God commits his identity to the fact that history is a revelation of the God who was and is and is to come. An eschatology from anthropological perspective understands the process of God's work and asks, then, what this means for those of us whose lives are still oriented within a seemingly determinative and certainly phenomenal history. Above all, it means we should hope.

Hope, if it is truly hope, initiates movement, and where we put our hope expresses what kind of movement this is. There are two substantive expressions of a particular hope in this particular God who promises a particular redemption that help characterize a truly transformative church, one that is itself instantiated by the promising and fulfilling God. If we hope in God, rather than other forms of insufficient identity, then we can live this life with a divine perspective on the value of our time, possessions, and priorities.

This life of hope is about becoming a messianic people—as individuals gathered as a community. Hope that is a risk, a trajectory, and a mission involves our active participation with others and for others. We let go our isolating demands and prioritize our values while at the same time contending for others to realize their possibilities, working in the midst of a context so that people experience liberation and in experiencing this liberation can likewise become people of hope and promise. Our life of hope initiates movement in the lives of others, working for them and working against structures or dependencies or modes of false identification that seek to undermine people in a context. We are, in effect, saved from depending on insufficient forms of identity by letting these things go, a form of *kenosis* in our own lives.

It is in our hope in God that we become, in essence, freedom fighters—not in the sense of typical zealots but in the mode of God's messengers of fullness and peace—seeking out others and seeking out the best in and for others. Indeed, we contend for others. We who have been opened up by our *kenotic* move of generosity are able to experience the countermovement of *perichoresis*—contending with and for others in a mutual celebration of life. We are filled with their generosity and share together the fruits of a context being actively redeemed by the fulfilling promise of a God who gives us an actualizing hope. We, in our life of hope, are saved from false forms of identity and saved into a community of celebratory mutuality—which is not a narrow or restricted community but seeks the inclusion of the whole of a context, as the hope of God extends to all that he seeks out, which is all things.

Approaching eschatology from an anthropological perspective provides a number of easily identifiable practices, as hope is one that suggests a wide variety of transformative expressions. The key element is not to allow such practices to devolve into an overrealized eschatology or an idealistic assumption that human systems will provide the necessary solutions to perceived injustices. Of all the transformative practices, these are the most likely to become subtly influenced by deficient approaches and then oriented toward insufficient forms of identity, a danger which insists on the continual need to re-orient such practices in line with the transcendent eschatology mentioned earlier.

In the fourth chapter, I followed Moltmann's guidelines in emphasizing the identity of God as Trinity. The Trinitarian identity of God defines our understanding of reality and life in general. This chapter thus emphasizes transformation in Trinitarian perspective, describing how each person provides a particular element to the overall transformative process.

Father

Moltmann's sixth guideline begins this chapter: "What furthers life is whatever ministers to God's covenant with life, and whatever breaks the covenant of death."[18] God's covenant with life and his resistance to death essentially defines the whole mission of God in, with, and for this world, oriented by God's identity as Trinity and expressed through the realization of his kingdom in the instances of our experiences, a transformative reality that expresses the will of the Father in its accomplishment. *The Trinity and the Kingdom* helps provide a substantive orientation to this understanding of God, his will and his way.

Moltmann establishes two general starting points for an understanding of the Trinity that radically affects the subsequent understanding of ecclesiality, and the whole interaction of God and God's people in this world. First, the Trinity is a social trinity—oriented in relationship—and, second, the Trinity should not begin with an emphasis on oneness or unity but with an emphasis on the three persons who form a triunity. These starting points emphasize the priority of interrelationality as the basis of unity and emphasize the distinction between particular persons as mutually determining the others. In this trinitarian ontology, we find our own substantive identity forming as particular persons and as a particular community.

God's identity itself is not vulnerable to loss, but his identity as love in relationship is vulnerable to pain and passion, with such

18. Ibid., 149–50.

vulnerability the consequence of being open to this world in creative interaction, responsive to our responses. God's identity determines our identity and our identity is ontologically one of being relational beings, expressing love, vulnerable to each other. This is not, however, something to be guarded against, nor are we as people or as a community called to express our identity as the people of God in terms of a defensive posture, protective stances, or isolated reflection. Love insists on participation, not only with those who are amenable, but also and especially with those who may bring us pain. As God expresses love in relationship, the people of God express their freedom of identity in an expression of friendship, being vulnerable and open in an invitation toward mutuality—inviting others to find their freedom in the context of God's holistic and inviting identity.

If we begin with the idea of the identity of God being one of love in relationship, then we see the image of God in self-similar patterns of expressed love. The nature of love resists a homogeneous unity. Love is the communication of the good with such communication presupposing self-differentiation. Love does not impose but invites reciprocation, involving a disclosure of true being to another and encouraging such disclosure in response. This pattern of love avoids domination and so authority itself reflects the love of the Father to the Son, a necessary and participatory love.

The expression of love as seen in creation involves self-limitation—giving space for the other in order to facilitate that other to thrive, grow, and respond. Thus, images of leadership likewise are oriented around participatory love, creation, and facilitation of space so that all can participate and grow and respond in love in a multiplicity of ways. The freedom and fellowship of such a loving interrelationship thus never imposes domination or passivity. Instead, such love initiates deliverance and liberation from whatever form of contextual bondage may be limiting each person's reciprocal participation or understanding of their identity as one made to be in eternal communion with God himself and all of creation.

The church participates in the mission of God, a mission that points toward the kingdom of God. The kingdom is not the church, nor is the church the full expression of the kingdom. In other words, the church is not an alternative *polis*, but rather the church is a representative people—a beloved community that expresses within the world that which the world is called to be—embedding the mission within the context, inviting others into a relational unity based on love. The role of leadership is to discern this work of the Spirit and to maintain the posture of inviting openness and participation—resisting structures and forms of alienation or domination. The way of the church is to be a people who are filled with God's love. This love enlivens and awakens such life in others, creating space and giving space to others. Each person participates in a free mutuality that seeks a transformative expression of life in the midst of each context, resonating the life of God to each person and every context. They participate together, producing spiritual fruit in diverse ways, among diverse people, expressing unity through the infinite complexity of God's kingdom in the fullness of his all-encompassing love.

God's people express their hope in ways that are oriented by God's identity and his kingdom. The transformative practice of participating as producers thus expresses the call of all God's people to join in with this work, each in their own way. With this, leadership is a way of constructing a context where this participation can thrive. By leading as a body, the whole of the people of God can express the manner in which God himself invests in this world, as a community of fellowship rather than a hierarchical expression of domination. While both leading and participation easily integrate together with a social Trinitarian theology, the difficulty lies not in these as topics but as lived experiences. The emphasis on participation and shared leadership are good in theory but continue to need honing in practices—as these are also likely the biggest pitfalls in transformative churches, and often lead to dissolution of such communities.

Jesus

Becoming a people who reflect these priorities is beyond our own efforts and beyond our own understanding. We need renewal, redemption, and substantive orientation for how we are to live the life we are called to live. This was the substantive ministry of Christ, whose life and work brings renewal and re-orientation to all of life, and brings the salvation that is the only hope of life itself. Thus, a people who seek to be truly and wholly transformative can only do so inasmuch as they participate with Christ in his work. Thus, Moltmann's seventh guideline: "What furthers life is, first and last, whatever makes Christ present, Christ who is the resurrection and the life in person; for in and with Christ the kingdom of eternal life is present, and this kingdom overcomes the destructive powers of death."[19] In *The Way of Jesus Christ*, we find Moltmann's most substantive Christology, focusing specifically on the identity of Christ and in this focus providing a substantive priority for the lives of all humanity.

Of all the theological emphases discussed so far, the topic of Jesus provides the most easily identifiable point of integration between Moltmann and the transformative churches. Indeed, the emphasis of Gibbs and Bolger is the very same emphasis of Moltmann's in *The Way of Jesus Christ*.[20] For both Moltmann and the transformative

19. Ibid.
20. This is certainly not just limited to Gibbs and Bolger. This discussion can and should be deepened in further studies, developing the themes of identifying with Jesus in more substantive

churches, then, the model of Jesus is not an idealistic hope but a transformative one, a messianic hope in which the call of the people of God in light of the work of Christ is to resonate this work in their particular contexts through the power of the Spirit. In seeing Jesus as a formative model as well as the substantive hope, the people of God become, in practice, oriented within the beloved community of Christ's orientation, looking at the future, and the present, and the past through the lens of expectation and fulfillment. In remembering the fulfillment and awaiting with expectation God's continued fulfillment, the people resonate with the transformative reality, rather than acceding to the determinative realities of a phenomenal history—realities that seek to dominate and establish identities in contrast to God's transcendent reality.

The Christ of history continues to engage the questions of history, through a Christology that is historically enacted in the person of Jesus and in the body that is the church. In identifying with Jesus, the people express this holistic Christology in a multiplicity of cultures, places, and contexts, living out the way of Jesus Christ as continuing representatives of the messianic mission. Who Jesus was and is becomes the guiding orientation for who we are to be as the people of God in wherever we are. The Christology of history, then, continues to be involved in history as a transformative reality leading to transformative renewal in every context. The key element of this is that such transformative renewals insist on understanding and engaging each particular context, interacting within them as representatives of Jesus, empowered by the Spirit so to be a

---

ways through looking at the many other resources transformative churches offer on this exact topic. Indeed, it is likely the case that of all the theological topics, this one offers the most relevant and focused discussions in transformative church writings. Worthy of particular note is Michael Frost and Alan Hirsch, *ReJesus: A Wild Messiah for a Missional Church* (Peabody, MA: Hendrickson, 2009). Hirsch's Jewish background adds significant insight into this transformative perspective on the Messiah.

transformative presence within them. Such an expression is always contextual—infinitely complex in expression as relating to the infinitely complex realities of a particular situational ecology. There are no vague or generalized expressions of a truly transformative way of Jesus. Such expressions are always particular and specific, even as Jesus was contextual and specific in his interactions. Thus, as it was with Jesus, it is out of the complexity—from below—that the model gains meaning, rather than being imposed from above.

With this in mind, the ideal of identifying with Jesus requires the imaginative posture emphasized by Huckins and his community in San Diego. We are to be like Jesus within the context that we are presently in, and this requires an awareness of our contexts and, more importantly, a persistent hope in God's continuing work. The messianic people are to live within the horizon of expectation for the context, seeing the possibilities that are contained within it, and being people who look to what may yet be in light of God's transformative work. It is, thus, important to shape such christocentric imagination by orienting it within the eschatological history of God, hoping with expectation rather than a hope shaped by fear and anxiety. The latter is a hope that looks to God to take us out of this world while the former is a hope that looks for God to transform this world.

This imaginative identifying with Jesus also, thus, insists on developing an embodied Christology in light of the relationship of Jesus to other people and in the context of his community with them. This exocentric practice emphasizes the call to real freedom, a message of new creation that enables people to let go of insufficient forms of identity that lead to division and alienation. This community with Jesus is a realistic community, drawn together through the realistic hope of present transformation exhibited throughout the Gospels and the continuing message of the New Testament.[21] This transformation includes the call for conversion and extends this call into an expression of discipleship—a community-oriented discipleship that enables people to live in new ways with and for each other in an open expression of transformative fellowship—creating space and providing contexts for each person to realize their possibilities within the context of the Spirit's continued work. Such exocentric fellowship reorients a holistic way of living, being proactively transformative rather than sectarian, seeking and including, not dividing and separated. Such transformative work involves the physicalized expressions of life in contrast to expressions of death and as such can, and should, include realized experiences of healing and being freed from forms of demonic control—as well as the no less important but more mundane experiences of finding social healing and relational renewal in the contexts of broken and defensive identities.

This involves living in light of God's eschatological reality and being an eschatological people in the midst of a specific context, looking for and participating in the possibilities that are oriented by seeing this world well beyond its temporary expressions. The promise of God embeds a real hope within a horizon of expectation. Only such eschatological people truly identify with Jesus and participate in a transformative reality. The eschatological Gospel is not the social gospel of the early twentieth century, which was a situational and limited expression of responding to present needs without offering real hope for a persistent transformation, and thus offered very little orienting hope in a transformed future. This was the idealist hope that likewise undermined the work of such leaders as Christoph Blumhardt, leading to despair and frustration. Eventually, this led to

21. See for instance Colossians 2, in which a cosmic Christology is oriented in the redemptive work of Jesus and leads to the call for the people to live their lives in light of this transformative and empowering transformation.

the turn by Barth away from Blumhardt and toward Schleiermacher, thus leading the Christology of history into a more existential priority.[22]

A messianic people, by definition, must see this Messiah as the orienting identity, and so the transformative practice of identifying with Jesus is the most vital of all the practices. Jesus, of course, was himself incarnated in a specific time and place, so identifying with Jesus in our present contexts involves the practice of imagination. This imagination provides a new way of seeing ourselves and seeing the world as Jesus sees it. As with the discussion of the church, this topic is among the most easily integrated with transformative church practices, indeed in many ways suggesting an identical emphasis. The most significant distinction is that Moltmann more fully embeds a pneumatology within his emphasis on the way of Jesus Christ, and in doing this provides a more thorough expression of God's holistic work. The messianic people are called to see the possibilities engendered by hope and empowered by the Spirit, participating in a way that awakens the life of Christ in each and every person, in and for every context.

Spirit

This Spirit-empowered imagination is, in essence, a way of participating with God himself, in which each person experiences the world in a more profound and substantive way, sharing an increasing resonance with life as a resonance with God himself is part of the transformative life. What furthers such a life is, as Moltmann's eighth guideline puts it, "the creative energies of the Spirit in which the uncreated and the created are bonded, and which renew the human

---

22. See Jürgen Moltmann, interview with the author, Tübingen, Germany, May 18, 2011, 6:05.

life from its foundations, making it immortal in the eternal fellowship of God."[23] In *The Spirit of Life*, we find such an emphasis on this work of the Spirit coming into focus, a holistic pneumatology that invests life into all that is, bringing all into a communion with God.

When coming to terms with God's mission in this world, two core questions radically affect our understanding of the church and its mission in this world. We ask where this mission is taking place and we ask how this mission is taking place. Where and with whom? If we begin with an anemic doctrine of the Spirit, our answers to these questions will take on the nature of such a theology. It can be argued, fairly convincingly in fact, that this is precisely the state of the church throughout much of Christian history—asserting a doctrine of the Spirit but developing a doctrine of the church built through "human wisdom." This utilizes a coherent theology that lacks integrity with a developed pneumatology, undermining the experience of God's transformative power. In light of the recent pneumatological turn in theological studies, however, we should pursue a doctrine of the church that is oriented in such a substantive doctrine of the Spirit. Indeed, this is precisely the distinctive that Moltmann offers in both his pneumatology and his developing ecclesiology.

Barth set up key boundaries in calling for a developed pneumatology, boundaries that likewise can and should be reflected in the subsequent ecclesiology. Such a doctrine of the Spirit can be neither an internalized pietism nor an overoptimistic anthropology. So too, a doctrine of the church can, thus, neither be a sectarian pietism nor an overrealized idealism of human society. The emphasis on the Spirit insists the emphasis should not be on human capability but rather must always be oriented toward God's efficacy in this world. This efficacy orients toward life, and the Spirit is always

23. Moltmann, *Experiences in Theology*, 150.

working in concert with all the persons of the Trinity in this same mission. This personhood of the Spirit for Moltmann is, as already mentioned, "the loving, self-communicating, out-fanning and out-pouring presence of the eternal divine life of the triune God."[24] Such a person has implications for our core question of how God works, where he works and in whom he works, implications that are likewise understood by transformative churches.

In light of a holistic pneumatology, we should say that the Spirit works broadly in all places and that the Spirit particularly invests the work of God in the people of God, furthering the messianic mission through those who resonate this mission in their contexts. This mission is neither isolating nor defensive, but transformative, as the awareness of God in, with, and beneath the experience of life makes Christ present and transforms the context, resonating deeply and broadly. The incarnation was God entering into this world, into the context of sinful humanity to be a transformative presence from within. The Spirit furthers this mission of the incarnation. God is the subject in this mission and God's Spirit orients this mission inwardly and outwardly, calling all contexts back toward a theocentric orientation, leading to a radical experience of renewal precisely in those places that seem the most Godforsaken. There is, then, a discovery of the transcendent in places we might otherwise label as secular—God enters into those places, outside the bounds of what many consider sacred, present among his people and all of creation.

In light of the Spirit, God's work is both participatory and responsive, investing the work of God in the people, transforming the people as they participate in this work. The Spirit, then, is the medium and space of such a transformative ecclesiology, not the object that should be handled with care but life experienced within

24. Jürgen Moltmann, *The Spirit of Life*, trans. Margaret Kohl (Minneapolis: Fortress Press, 1992), 209.

awakening possibilities. Community deepens in this experience, vitalizing transformative hope and stirring rapturous joy, renewing our outward life and outward reactions—forming us into a people who can then participate in such a life in all contexts where the Spirit is at work, which is all contexts.

In entrusting this mission to the people, the people of God experience transformation in the power of the Spirit. This transformation happens in their stages of life—filling in the gaps and pieces of a larger reality, solidifying a holistic identity—and in qualitative growth as the renewed life manifests in creative ways. This goes well beyond a set of ethical guidelines and reorients the people within life itself, providing a power and a way for this new life. Such participants live—are empowered to live—this life of exocentric freedom, expressing the everyday charismata of a transformed life in all their contexts and concerns. They are entrusted with the expression of this mission to and with others, and so their awareness of others is heightened and they seek participation together with others, experiencing the rebirth of self and context in the community of God's renewing power.

Such transformation forms a bond in those who might otherwise oppose each other in the quest to secure power or identity through alternative means. Instead of seeking domination or competition, the transformed people entrusted with God's work express this work in the wider contexts of this world, participating together within a shared mission of holistic life that is constantly orienting and reorienting itself toward the kingdom of God. This expression of church, then, can be seen as the wide space of the Spirit, working in all parts of this world, transforming the secular places into places that resonate the work and life of God, awakening a new passion for life and its possibilities, inviting others into this resonance, making space for others, entrusting them with their role in this mission. This is a life of love, a life of hope, a life in which faith in the triune God initiates transformative ways among a transforming people.

Engaging the Spirit's work as broad and as being entrusted to a wide context are important but not sufficient transformative practices, especially as such practices are often only implicitly connected to the work of the Spirit and thus lack a more mature discernment that would derive from a substantive pneumatology. These mentioned practices must include more thorough expression of the gifts and fruit of the Spirit, learning especially from Pentecostal and Eastern Orthodox communities and others who offer a deep well of thought on the movement of the Spirit in people's lives.[25]

Proposal for Future Work

This present work provides a programmatic structure for the development of transformative ecclesiology as it takes shape in the industrialized West, understanding the project in terms of a comprehensive liberation theology, one that would emphasize transformation in the lives of those who may be oppressors. It is not itself comprehensive but rather points to ways in which a comprehensive study could take shape. Each section in this present work could be its own substantive monograph, with each separate study providing better theological breadth, historical assessment, and practical examples, going well beyond the perspectives of our present interlocutors. Thus, the present work serves as a proposal of sorts, a way of first bringing together conversation partners that are not

---

25. Some of the difficulties with a more explicit applied pneumatology in transformative churches comes from the perceived abuse of such language, and practices, with a further implicit assumption that practices prioritizing the work of the Spirit are themselves the domain of Pentecostal and Charismatic churches, and are limited to the more "charismatic" gifts such as speaking in tongues. See Alan Hirsch, preface to *It's a Dance: Moving with the Holy Spirit*, by Patrick Oden (Newberg, OR: Barclay, 2007).

only separated by geography and occupation but by divisions in theological studies itself. These conversation partners serve as an important example to what a broader project could entail.

Indeed, these present conversation partners go well beyond simply offering an example of contributors from the separated realms of systematic and practical theology. They also share an important holistic methodology that, I argue, provides a substantive orientation for the development of the proposed future project. More specifically, they offer an implicit framework that could provide a substantively different approach to theology in general. Moltmann himself provided the substantive call for such a pursuit when he suggested that in addition to right beliefs, theology and the church must also pay attention to the standards of right feelings and right actions. Orthodoxy must be joined by orthopathy and orthopraxy, with these latter two elements insisting on a fully trinitarian theology that is informed by the fruit and gifts of the Spirit.

Developing each of the discussed topics in terms of orthodoxy, orthopraxy, and orthopathy would provide a triangulation of theological concerns in the context of expression and, thus, transformation. It is in the unity of these three elements that we can more fully discern the holistic expression of God, and in this discernment more fully and adequately propose a holistic framework of liberation that provides substantive transformation to the oppressor and the oppressed. Such triangulation requires participation from various approaches and diverse voices in order to be truly holistic. In bringing together participants from these oft-separated spheres, my goal is to continue a pattern of conversation that respects each participant within their own mode of expression, and, with this, helping the overall topic take comprehensive shape. A truly comprehensive liberation of the oppressor must be holistic and it must be engaging both thought and practice in a transformative way.

Coda

If theology is to be truly systematic, having coherence and integrity with God's identity and his work in this world, future theologians and church leaders must overcome divisions as they exist between the church and academic theology. It is only by listening to both aspects that theology can be, in fact, transformative. Indeed, I would argue that for theology to be truly Christian—reflecting the revelation of Christ—it *must* be transformative. I would also argue that for the church to be truly Christian—reflecting the work of the Spirit—it must be transformative. To be transformative, theology must take into account the whole of life and its expressions, the whole ecology of the cosmos in its varied forms of expression and encounters. To be transformative, the church must take into account who God is and how God works in, with, and for this world. A transformative theology requires a transformative church and a transformative church insists on a transformative theology—a holistic expression of a messianic movement initiated by God in history and expressed even in our day among those who are saved by Christ, a salvation that awakens life in, with, and for this whole world. It is in this experience of such a church that we become who we are called to be, who all are called to be, in and for this world, now and into eternity.

Do not be overcome by evil, but overcome evil with good.[26]

26. Romans 12:21. Cf. Jürgen Moltmann, "Sun of Righteousness Arise! The Freedom of a Christian—Then and Now—for the Perpetrators and for the Victims of Sin," *Theology Today* 69, no. 1 (2012): 16.

Bibliography

Althouse, Peter. *Spirit of the Last Days: Pentecostal Eschatology in Conversation with Jürgen Moltmann*. New York: T&T Clark, 2003.

Arpin-Ricci, Jamie. *The Cost of Community: Jesus, St. Francis and Life in the Kingdom*. Downers Grove, IL: IVP, 2011.

Banks, Robert J. *Paul's Idea of Community*. Rev. ed. Peabody, MA: Hendrickson, 1994.

Barth, Karl. *The Theology of Schleiermacher: Lectures at Göttingen, Winter Semester of 1923–24*. Translated by Geoffrey W. Bromiley. Edited by Dietrich Ritschl. Grand Rapids: Eerdmans, 1982.

Bauckham, Richard, ed. *God Will Be All in All: The Eschatology of Jürgen Moltmann*. Edinburgh: T&T Clark, 1999.

———. *Moltmann: Messianic Theology in the Making*. Basingstoke, Hants, UK: Pickering, 1987.

———. *The Theology of Jürgen Moltmann*. Edinburgh: T&T Clark, 1995.

Beaudoin, Tom. *Virtual Faith: The Irreverent Spiritual Quest of Generation X*. San Francisco: Jossey-Bass, 1998.

Begbie, Jeremy. "The Shape of Things to Come? Wright Amidst Emerging Ecclesiologies." In *Jesus, Paul and the people of God*, edited by Nicholas Perrin and Richard Hays, 183–208. Downers Grove, IL: IVP Academic, 2011.

Bessenecker, Scott. *How to Inherit the Earth: Submitting Ourselves to a Servant Savior.* Downers Grove, IL: IVP, 2009.

———. *Living Mission: The Vision and Voices of New Friars.* Downers Grove, IL: IVP, 2010.

———. *The New Friars: The Emerging Movement Serving the World's Poor.* Downers Grove, IL: IVP, 2006.

Blumhardt, Christoph. *Action in Waiting.* Farmington, PA: Plough, 1998.

———. *Christoph Blumhardt and His Message.* Edited by Robert Lejeune. 2nd ed. Rifton, NY: PloughHouse, 2006.

Boff, Leonardo. *Ecclesiogenesis: The Base Communities Reinvent the Church.* Maryknoll, NY: Orbis, 1986.

Bonhoeffer, Dietrich. *Ethics.* Translated by Reinhard Krauss, Charles West, and Douglas Stott. Vol. 6, Dietrich Bonhoeffer Works. Minneapolis: Fortress Press, 2005.

Brewin, Kester. *Signs of Emergence.* Grand Rapids: Baker, 2007.

Brink, Mary Louise. "The Ecclesiological Dimensions of Jürgen Moltmann's Theology: Vision of a Future Church?" PhD diss., Fordham University, 1990.

Bucher, Glenn R. "Toward a Liberation Theology for the 'Oppressor.'" *Journal of the American Academy of Religion* 44, no. 3 (1976): 517–34.

Claiborne, Shane. *The Irresistible Revolution: Living as an Ordinary Radical.* Grand Rapids: Zondervan, 2006.

Clawson, Julie. *Everyday Justice: The Global Impact of Our Daily Choices.* Downers Grove, IL: IVP, 2009.

Clayton, Philip. *Adventures in the Spirit: God, World, Divine Action.* Minneapolis: Fortress Press, 2008.

———. *Transforming Christian Theology: For Church and Society.* Minneapolis: Fortress Press, 2010.

Cole, Neil. *Organic Leadership: Leading Naturally Right Where You Are.* Grand Rapids: Baker, 2009.

Collins Winn, Christian T., and Peter Heltzel. "'Before Bloch There Was Blumhardt': A Thesis on the Origins of the Theology of Hope." *Scottish Journal of Theology* 62, no. 1 (2009): 26–39.

Comblin, José. *The Holy Spirit and Liberation*. Translated by Paul Burns. Maryknoll, NY: Orbis, 1989.

Conder, Tim, and Daniel Rhodes. *Free for All: Rediscovering the Bible in Community*. Grand Rapids: Baker, 2009.

Cox, Harvey. *Religion in the Secular City: Toward a Postmodern Theology*. New York: Simon and Schuster, 1984.

Cray, Graham, and Ian Mobsby. *Fresh Expressions and the Kingdom of God*. Norwich: Canterbury, 2012.

Croft, Steven J. L., and Ian Mobsby. *Fresh Expressions in the Sacramental Tradition: Ancient Faith, Future Mission*. Norwich: Canterbury, 2009.

Croft, Steven J. L., Ian Mobsby, and Stephanie Spellers. *Ancient Faith, Future Mission: Fresh Expressions in the Sacramental Traditions*. New York: Seabury, 2010.

Cunningham, David S. *These Three Are One: The Practice of Trinitarian Theology*. Malden, MA.: Blackwell, 1998.

Dabney, D. Lyle. "The Advent of the Spirit: The Turn to Pneumatology in the Theology of Jürgen Moltmann." *Asbury Theological Journal* 48, no. 1 (1993): 81–107.

Danto, Arthur C. *The Abuse of Beauty: Aesthetics and the Concept of Art*. Chicago: Open Court, 2003.

DeYoung, Kevin, and Ted Kluck. *Why We're Not Emergent: By Two Guys Who Should Be*. Chicago: Moody, 2008.

Fendall, Lon, Jan Wood, and Bruce Bishop. *Practicing Discernment Together: Finding God's Way Forward in Decision Making*. Newberg, OR: Barclay, 2007.

Fitch, David E. *The End of Evangelicalism? Discerning a New Faithfulness for Mission: Towards an Evangelical Political Theology.* Eugene, OR: Cascade, 2011.

———. *The Great Giveaway: Reclaiming the Mission of the Church from Big Business, Parachurch Organizations, Psychotherapy, Consumer Capitalism, and Other Modern Maladies.* Grand Rapids: Baker, 2005.

Fowler, James W. *Stages of Faith: The Psychology of Human Development and the Quest for Meaning.* San Francisco: Harper & Row, 1981.

Freire, Paulo. *Pedagogy of the Oppressed.* 30th anniversary ed. New York: Continuum, 2000.

Frost, Michael, and Alan Hirsch. *The Faith of Leap: Embracing a Theology of Risk, Adventure & Courage.* Grand Rapids: Baker, 2011.

———. *Rejesus: A Wild Messiah for a Missional Church.* Peabody, MA: Hendrickson, 2009.

———. *The Shaping of Things to Come: Innovation and Mission for the 21st-Century Church.* Peabody, MA: Hendrickson, 2003.

Gaddis, John Lewis. *The Landscape of History: How Historians Map the Past.* New York: Oxford University Press, 2002.

Gathje, Peter R. *Sharing the Bread of Life: Hospitality and Resistance at the Open Door Community.* Atlanta: Open Door Community, 2006.

Geiger, James W. *Christianity and the Outsider: A Lawyer Looks at Justice and Justification.* Eugene, OR Resource, 2012.

Gibbs, Eddie. *Churchnext: Quantum Changes in How We Do Ministry.* Downers Grove, IL: InterVarsity, 2000.

Gibbs, Eddie, and Ryan K. Bolger. *Emerging Churches: Creating Christian Community in Postmodern Cultures.* Grand Rapids: Baker Academic, 2005.

Grenz, Stanley J. *Theology for the Community of God.* Grand Rapids: Eerdmans, 2000.

Grenz, Stanley J., and John R. Franke. *Beyond Foundationalism: Shaping Theology in a Postmodern Context*. Louisville: Westminster John Knox, 2001.

Guder, Darrell L. *The Continuing Conversion of the Church*. Grand Rapids: Eerdmans, 2000.

———, ed. *Missional Church: A Vision for the Sending of the Church in North America*. Grand Rapids: Eerdmans, 1998.

Gutiérrez, Gustavo. *We Drink from Our Own Wells: The Spiritual Journey of a People*. Translated by Matthew J. O'Connell. 20th anniversary ed. Maryknoll, NY: Orbis, 2006.

Halter, Hugh, and Matt Smay. *The Tangible Kingdom: Creating Incarnational Community; The Posture and Practices of Ancient Church Now*. San Francisco: Jossey-Bass, 2008.

Hanson, R. P. C. *The Life and Writings of the Historical Saint Patrick*. New York: Seabury, 1983.

Hart, David Bentley. *The Beauty of the Infinite: The Aesthetics of Christian Truth*. Grand Rapids: Eerdmans, 2003.

Harvie, Timothy. "Living the Future: The Kingdom of God in the Theologies of Jürgen Moltmann and Wolfhart Pannenberg." *International Journal of Systematic Theology* 10, no. 2 (2008): 149–64.

Hatmaker, Brandon. *Barefoot Church: Serving the Least in a Consumer Culture*. Grand Rapids: Zondervan, 2011.

Hebblethwaite, Margaret. *Base Communities: An Introduction*. Mahwah, N.J: Paulist, 1994.

Hegel, Georg Wilhelm Friedrich. *Reason in History*. Translated by Robert S. Hartman. New York: Liberal Arts, 1953.

Helland, Roger, and Len Hjalmarson. *Missional Spirituality: Embodying God's Love from the Inside Out*. Downers Grove, IL: IVP, 2011.

Hirsch, Alan. *The Forgotten Ways: Reactivating the Missional Church*. Grand Rapids: Brazos, 2006.

Hirsch, Alan, Tim Catchim, and Mike Breen. *The Permanent Revolution: Apostolic Imagination and Practice for the 21st Century Church*. San Francisco: Jossey-Bass, 2012.

Hirsch, Alan, and Debra Hirsch. *Untamed: Reactivating a Missional Form of Discipleship*. Grand Rapids: Baker, 2010.

Holmes, Michael W., ed. *The Apostolic Fathers: Greek Texts and English Translations*. Updated ed. Grand Rapids: Baker Academic, 1999.

Huckins, Jon. *Thin Places: 6 Postures for Creating & Practicing Missional Community*. Kansas City: The House Studio, 2012.

Hunsberger, George R., and Craig Van Gelder, eds. *The Church between Gospel and Culture: The Emerging Mission in North America*. Grand Rapids: Eerdmans 1996.

Jones, Tony. *The Church Is Flat: The Relational Ecclesiology of the Emerging Church Movement*. Minneapolis: The JoPa Group, 2011.

———. *The New Christians: Dispatches from the Emergent Frontier*. San Francisco: Jossey-Bass, 2008.

Kärkkäinen, Veli-Matti. *Introduction to Ecclesiology: Ecumenical, Historical & Global Perspectives*. Downers Grove, IL: InterVarsity, 2002.

———. *The Trinity: Global Perspectives*. Louisville: Westminster John Knox, 2007.

Kärkkäinen, Veli-Matti, Kirsteen Kim, and Amos Yong, eds. *Interdisciplinary and Religio-Cultural Discourses on a Spirit-Filled World: Loosing the Spirits*. New York: Palgrave Macmillan, 2013.

Kimball, Dan. *Adventures in Churchland*. Grand Rapids: Zondervan, 2012.

———. *The Emerging Church: Vintage Christianity for New Generations*. Grand Rapids: Zondervan, 2003.

———. *Emerging Worship: Creating Worship Gatherings for New Generations*. El Cajon, CA; Grand Rapids: EmergentYS ; Zondervan, 2004.

———. *They Like Jesus but Not the Church: Insights from Emerging Generations*. Grand Rapids: Zondervan, 2007.

Lindbeck, George A. *The Nature of Doctrine: Religion and Theology in a Postliberal Age.* Philadelphia: Westminster, 1984.

Loder, James E. *The Logic of the Spirit: Human Development in Theological Perspective.* San Francisco: Jossey-Bass, 1998.

———. *The Transforming Moment.* 2nd ed. Colorado Springs: Helmers & Howard, 1989.

Loder, James E., and W. Jim Neidhardt. *The Knight's Move: The Relational Logic of the Spirit in Theology and Science.* Colorado Springs: Helmers & Howard, 1992.

Lonergan, Bernard J. F. *Method in Theology.* New York: Herder and Herder, 1972.

Loring, Eduard N. *The Cry of the Poor: Cracking White Male Supremacy—an Incendiary and Militant Proposal.* Atlanta: Open Door Community, 2010.

Lossky, Vladimir. *The Mystical Theology of the Eastern Church.* Crestwood, NY: St. Vladimir's Seminary Press, 1998.

Luhmann, Niklas. *Introduction to Systems Theory.* Translated by Peter Gilgen. Malden, MA: Polity, 2013.

———. *A Systems Theory of Religion.* Palo Alto: Stanford University Press, 2013.

Macchia, Frank D. *Spirituality and Social Liberation: The Message of the Blumharts in the Light of Wuerttemberg Pietism.* Metuchen, NJ: Scarecrow, 1993.

McDougall, Joy Ann. *Pilgrimage of Love: Moltmann on the Trinity and Christian Life.* New York: Oxford University Press, 2005.

McGonigal, Jane. *Reality Is Broken: Why Games Make Us Better and How They Can Change the World.* New York: Penguin, 2011.

McGovern, Arthur F. *Liberation Theology and Its Critics: Toward an Assessment.* Maryknoll, NY: Orbis, 1989.

McKnight, Scot. "Five Streams of the Emerging Church: Key Elements of the Most Controversial and Misunderstood Movement in the Church

Today." *Christianity Today*, http://www.christianitytoday.com/ct/2007/february/11.35.html.

McLaren, Brian D. *A New Kind of Christian: A Tale of Two Friends on a Spiritual Journey*. San Francisco: Jossey-Bass, 2001.

Mission and Public Affairs Council (Church of England), and Rowan Williams. *Mission-Shaped Church: Church Planting and Fresh Expressions of Church in a Changing Context*. London: Church House, 2004.

Moltmann, Jürgen. *A Broad Place: An Autobiography*. Minneapolis: Fortress Press, 2008.

———. *The Church in the Power of the Spirit*. Translated by Margaret Kohl. Minneapolis: Fortress Press, 1993.

———. *The Coming of God*. Translated by Margaret Kohl. Minneapolis: Fortress Press, 1996.

———. *The Crucified God*. Translated by R. A. Wilson and John Bowden. Minneapolis: Fortress Press, 1993.

———. *Ethics of Hope*. Translated by Margaret Kohl. Minneapolis: Fortress Press, 2012.

———. *Experiences in Theology*. Translated by Margaret Kohl. Minneapolis: Fortress Press, 2000.

———. *Experiences of God*. Translated by Margaret Kohl. Philadelphia: Fortress Press, 1980.

———. *The Future of Creation*. Translated by Margaret Kohl. Philadelphia: Fortress Press, 1979.

———. *God for a Secular Society: The Public Relevance of Theology*. Translated by Margaret Kohl. Minneapolis: Fortress Press, 1999.

———. *God in Creation*. Translated by Margaret Kohl. Minneapolis: Fortress Press, 1993.

———. *The Gospel of Liberation*. Translated by H. Wayne Pipkin. Waco: Word, 1973.

———. *History and the Triune God: Contributions to Trinitarian Theology.* Translated by John Bowden. New York: Crossroad, 1992.

———. "The Hope for the Kingdom of God and Signs of Hope in the World: The Relevance of Blumhardt's Theology Today." *Pneuma* 26, no. 1 (2004): 4–16.

———. *In the End—the Beginning: The Life of Hope.* Translated by Margaret Kohl. Minneapolis: Fortress Press, 2004.

———. *Jesus Christ for Today's World.* Translated by Margaret Kohl. Minneapolis: Fortress Press, 1994.

———. "Liberation of Oppressors." *Christianity and Crisis* 38, no. 20 (1978): 310–17.

———. "The Liberation of Oppressors." *Journal of the Interdenominational Theological Center* 6, no. 2 (1979): 69–82.

———. *Man: Christian Anthropology in the Conflicts of the Present.* Translated by John Sturdy. Philadelphia: Fortress Press, 1974.

———. *The Passion for Life: A Messianic Lifestyle.* Translated by M. Douglas Meeks. Philadelphia: Fortress Press, 1978.

———. *The Power of the Powerless.* Translated by Margaret Kohl. San Francisco: Harper & Row, 1983.

———. *Religion, Revolution, and the Future.* Translated by M. Douglas Meeks. New York: Scribner, 1969.

———. *The Source of Life.* Translated by Margaret Kohl. Minneapolis: Fortress Press, 1997.

———. *The Spirit of Life.* Translated by Margaret Kohl. Minneapolis: Fortress Press, 1992.

———. "Sun of Righteousness Arise! The Freedom of a Christian—Then and Now—for the Perpetrators and for the Victims of Sin." *Theology Today* 69, no. 1 (2012): 7–17.

———. *Sun of Righteousness, Arise! God's Future for Humanity and the Earth.* Translated by Margaret Kohl. Minneapolis: Fortress Press, 2010.

———. *Theology and Joy*. Translated by Reinhard Ulrich. London: SCM, 1973.

———. *Theology of Hope*. Translated by James W. Leitch. Minneapolis: Fortress Press, 1993.

———. "Theology of Mystical Experience." *Scottish Journal of Theology* 32, no. 6 (1979): 501–20.

———. *Theology Today: Two Contributions towards Making Theology Present*. Translated by Margaret Kohl. Philadelphia: Trinity Press International, 1989.

———. *The Trinity and the Kingdom*. Translated by Margaret Kohl. Minneapolis: Fortress Press, 1993.

———. *Two Studies in the Theology of Bonhoeffer*. Translated by Reginald H. Fuller and Ilse Fuller. New York: Scribner, 1967.

———. *The Way of Jesus Christ*. Translated by Margaret Kohl. Minneapolis: Fortress Press, 1993.

———. "Wrestling with God: A Personal Meditation." *Christian Century* 114, no. 23 (1997): 726–29.

Moltmann, Jürgen, and M. Douglas Meeks. *The Open Church: Invitation to a Messianic Lifestyle*. London: SCM, 1978.

Moltmann, Jürgen, M. Douglas Meeks, and Theodore Runyon. *Hope for the Church: Moltmann in Dialogue with Practical Theology*. Nashville: Abingdon, 1979.

Moltmann, Jürgen, and Elisabeth Moltmann-Wendel. *Passion for God: Theology in Two Voices*. Louisville: Westminster John Knox, 2003.

Moltmann, Jürgen, Robert E. Neale, Sam Keen, and David LeRoy Miller. *Theology of Play*. Translated by Reinhard Ulrich. New York: Harper & Row, 1972.

Moltmann, Jürgen, Nicholas Wolterstorff, and Ellen T. Charry. *A Passion for God's Reign*. Grand Rapids: Eerdmans, 1998.

Morey, Tim. *Embodying Our Faith: Becoming a Living, Sharing, Practicing Church*. Downers Grove, IL: IVP, 2009.

Morgan, Janine Paden. "Emerging Eucharist: Formative Ritualizing in British Emerging Churches." PhD diss., Fuller Theological Seminary, 2008.

Morse, Christopher. *The Logic of Promise in Moltmann's Theology*. Philadelphia: Fortress Press, 1979.

Müller-Fahrenholz, Geiko. *The Kingdom and the Power: The Theology of Jürgen Moltmann*. Translated by John Bowden. Minneapolis: Fortress Press, 2001.

Murphy, Nancey C. *Anglo-American Postmodernity: Philosophical Perspectives on Science, Religion, and Ethics*. Boulder, CO: Westview, 1997.

———. *Beyond Liberalism and Fundamentalism: How Modern and Postmodern Philosophy Set the Theological Agenda*. Valley Forge, PA: TrinityInternational, 1996.

Newbigin, Lesslie. *The Gospel in a Pluralist Society*. Grand Rapids: Eerdmans, 1989.

Niebuhr, H. Richard. *Christ and Culture*. New York: Harper, 1951.

Oden, Patrick. "An Emerging Pneumatology: Jürgen Moltmann and the Emerging Church in Conversation." *Journal of Pentecostal Theology* 18, no. 2 (2009): 263–84.

———. *How Long? The Trek through the Wilderness*. Newberg, OR: Barclay, 2011.

———. *It's a Dance: Moving with the Holy Spirit*. Newberg, OR: Barclay, 2007.

Outler, Albert Cook. "The Wesleyan Quadrilateral in John Wesley." *Wesleyan Theological Journal* 20, no. 1 (1985): 7–18.

Pagitt, Doug. *Church Re-Imagined: The Spiritual Formation of People in Communities of Faith*. Grand Rapids: Zondervan, 2005.

Pagitt, Doug, and Tony Jones, eds. *An Emergent Manifesto of Hope*. Grand Rapids: Baker, 2007.

Pannenberg, Wolfhart. *Anthropology in Theological Perspective.* Translated by Matthew J. O'Connell. Philadelphia: Westminster, 1985.

———. *Human Nature, Election, and History.* Philadelphia: Westminster, 1977.

———. *Systematic Theology.* Translated by Geoffrey W. Bromiley. 3 vols. Grand Rapids: Eerdmans, 1991–98.

Polkinghorne, J. C., and Michael Welker. *The End of the World and the Ends of God: Science and Theology on Eschatology.* Harrisburg, PA: Trinity International, 2000.

Prooijen, Ton van. *Limping but Blessed: Jürgen Moltmann's Search for a Liberating Anthropology.* New York: Rodopi, 2004.

Rasmusson, Arne. *The Church as Polis: From Political Theology to Theological Politics as Exemplified by Jürgen Moltmann and Stanley Hauerwas.* Notre Dame: University of Notre Dame Press, 1995.

Rollins, Peter. *How (Not) to Speak of God.* Brewster, MA: Paraclete, 2006.

Roxburgh, Alan J. "The Missional Church." *Theology Matters* 10, no. 4 (2004): 1–15.

Sargent, Brad. "*The Good News for* Marin, California," in *ViralHope: Good News from the Urbs to the Burbs (and Everything In Between),* edited by J. R. Woodward. Los Angeles: Ecclesia, 2010.

Shroyer, Danielle. *The Boundary-Breaking God: An Unfolding Story of Hope and Promise.* San Francisco: Jossey-Bass, 2009.

Shults, F. LeRon. *The Postfoundationalist Task of Theology: Wolfhart Pannenberg and the New Theological Rationality.* Grand Rapids: Eerdmans, 1999.

Sommers, Steven Craig. "Church as Subculture: Implications for the Pluriform Confession of Christ in Modern Pluralistic Contexts." PhD diss., Fuller Theological Seminary, 2001.

Studdert Kennedy, Geoffrey Anketell, and Kerry S. Walters. *After War, Is Faith Possible? The Life and Message of Geoffrey "Woodbine Willie" Studdert Kennedy.* Eugene, OR: Cascade, 2008.

Thomson, John B. *The Ecclesiology of Stanley Hauerwas: A Christian Theology of Liberation.* Burlington, VT: Ashgate, 2003.

Van Gelder, Craig, and Dwight J. Zscheile. *The Missional Church in Perspective: Mapping Trends and Shaping the Conversation.* Grand Rapids: Baker Academic, 2011.

Volf, Miroslav. *After Our Likeness: The Church as the Image of the Trinity.* Grand Rapids: Eerdmans, 1998.

———. *Exclusion and Embrace: A Theological Exploration of Identity, Otherness, and Reconciliation.* Nashville: Abingdon, 1996.

Volf, Miroslav, and William H. Katerberg, eds. *The Future of Hope: Christian Tradition amid Modernity and Postmodernity.* Grand Rapids: Eerdmans 2004.

Volf, Miroslav, Carmen Krieg, and Thomas Kucharz, eds. *The Future of Theology: Essays in Honor of Jürgen Moltmann.* Grand Rapids: Eerdmans, 1996.

Wakefield, James L. *Jürgen Moltmann: A Research Bibliography.* Lanham, MD: Scarecrow, 2002.

Webber, Robert, ed. *Listening to the Beliefs of Emerging Churches: Five Perspectives.* Grand Rapids: Zondervan, 2007.

Welker, Michael. *God the Spirit.* Translated by John Hoffmeyer. Minneapolis: Fortress Press, 1994.

———. *Theologie Und Funktionale Systemtheorie—Luhmanns Religionssoziologie in Theologischer Diskussion.* Frankfurt am Main: Suhrkamp, 1985.

Williams, Jane, ed. *The Holy Spirit in the World Today.* London: Alpha International, 2011.

Wood, Laurence W. *God and History: The Dialectical Tension of Faith and History in Modern Thought.* Lexington, KY: Emeth, 2005.

———. *Theology as History and Hermeneutics: A Post-Critical Conversation with Contemporary Theology.* Lexington, KY: Emeth, 2004.

Woodward, J. R. *Creating a Missional Culture: Equipping the Church for the Sake of the World*. Downers Grove, IL: Praxis-IVP, 2012.

Woodward, J.R., ed. *Viral Hope: Good News from the Urbs to the Burbs (and Everything in between)*. Los Angeles: Ecclesia Press, 2010.

Yoder, John Howard. *For the Nations: Essays Evangelical and Public*. Grand Rapids: Eerdmans, 1997.

Zizioulas, John. *Being as Communion: Studies in Personhood and the Church*. Crestwood, NY: St. Vladimir's Seminary Press, 1985.

Index

exploration, theological, 41, 51,
176

faith, 44, 67, 80, 91, 99, 110, 112,
116, 119, 125–26, 130–31, 136,
152, 154, 160, 165, 173–74,
255
faithfulness, 125–26, 128, 173,
225, 283
Father, 10, 67, 96, 103, 117, 119,
138, 143, 147–50, 168, 193–95,
207, 229, 235–36, 257, 271,
281, 286–87
fellowship, 48, 76, 87–89, 91, 100,
111, 141, 144–45, 148, 160,
168–69, 172, 177–78, 209,
287–88; of Christ, 83, 88, 165
formation, spiritual, 1, 194
forsakenness, 87, 95, 116–17,
119–20, 129, 215, 220–21,
280–82
foundationalism, 31–34
framework, theological, 12–13,
27–30, 59–60, 65, 69, 166, 262,
266–67
freedom, 52, 78–79, 86, 89, 91,
106, 127, 140–41, 144, 148–52,
177, 206, 236, 239, 244,
262–63, 287; experience of, 10,
14, 50, 151, 158, 175–77, 200,

250, 277; of God, 101, 119,
149–51; of love, 140, 144
Fresh Expressions, 3, 16–17,
22–25, 266
friction, 35, 37–38, 75, 130–31
fruits, 112, 115, 128, 285, 297–98
fulfillment, 10, 112, 116, 126–27,
129–31, 133, 141, 144, 150–51,
153, 164–65, 197, 217, 229,
268, 270, 283, 290; of Christ,
165

Gaddis, John Lewis, 8
generosity, 12, 217, 219, 221–23,
283, 285
gifts, xi, 14, 97–98, 199–200, 208,
217, 231–33, 236–38, 240,
297–98; spiritual, 200, 240
glory, 69–70, 103, 106, 115,
149–51, 163–64, 215; kingdom
of, 76, 149–50
God, experience, 68, 131, 139,
169–70, 174
gospel, 42, 147, 158–59, 175, 177,
194–95, 217, 221–23, 226, 230,
233, 242, 246, 256, 291
grace, 10, 105, 119, 146, 150, 217,
221–22, 244
guilt, 54, 85–86, 110, 133, 139–40,
218

CPSIA information can be obtained at www.ICGtesting.com
Printed in the USA
LVOW04s1135051214

417351LV00004B/6/P

9 781451 474701